CONTRARY MUSIC

Old St. Paul's Cathedral: the Choir facing East
From an engraving by Wenceslaus Hollar

Contrary Music

THE PROSE STYLE OF JOHN DONNE

Joan Webber

The University of Wisconsin Press • *Madison, 1963*

Published by

THE UNIVERSITY OF WISCONSIN PRESS
430 Sterling Court, Madison 6, Wisconsin

Copyright © 1963 by the
Regents of the University of Wisconsin

Printed in the United States of America by
George Banta Company, Inc., Menasha, Wisconsin

Library of Congress Catalog Card Number 63-8557

for my Mother and Father

Preface

A first task of every man is to find an idiom in which to sing or stammer himself, by which to allow others to define him as well as they can, through which to achieve expression, engage in conflict, and seek for common ground. Without linguistic traditions that represent some shared certainties about man and the world, he is nearly powerless. Without the ability to vary or transmute these traditions, he is also powerless, for then, become lifeless, they will rule him inhumanely. To assign this high importance to language does of course require the assumption that style *means* something. The critic-rhetorician takes it for granted that the writer's only unique power is his ability to forge an idiom whose esthetic and moral accuracy is superior to that of others. By these commonplaces, the business of literary stylistics must be ruled.

To come more directly to the case in point. Every student of seventeenth-century prose owes much to the hard pioneer work that has been done by critics like Morris Croll, George Williamson, R. F. Jones, and W. Fraser Mitchell. We are now very familiar with such descriptive words as *Ciceronian* and *Senecan, witty, pointed, ornate,* and *plain,* and we know something about the political, philosophical, and religious climates that brought forth works that can be so described. But when we turn our attention to any particular writer, we inevitably find that such words do not fully define him. To call Milton a Ciceronian and Donne a Senecan, without any qualification, is to open the way to a complete misunderstanding of their individualized styles of thought.

What I have done here, then, is to read Donne's prose in the light of the traditions he knew, and to show how and why he made of them what he did. I have tried to write humanly about rhetoric, in a way that will be understandable to people who are not specialists without boring those who are. No man in Donne's own tradition would for a moment have accepted a rhetorical study which severed form from meaning; while we can be more objective than he about his accomplishment, we must not lose sight of the fact that style can only be great by virtue of the life it has which reaches out to ours.

Some of the critics whose work has helped me to construct my own method in stylistics are Morris Croll, Ruth Wallerstein, W. K. Wimsatt, R. W. Chambers, Jonas Barish, Madeleine Doran, Walter J. Ong, and Leo Spitzer. Although they are all very different from one another, and perhaps would not even like to be grouped together, they all combine historical knowledge with critical independence; they know both the age and the text. Leo Spitzer's explanation of method is probably closest to what I have discovered is my own: knowing the traditions and the writer's contemporaries, one looks for the distinctive techniques in a given text, until a pattern begins to emerge. Finding what patterns run through all his work and comparing them with those of his traditions and his contemporaries, one can begin to make some conclusions about the meaning and value of the writer's style.

A grant from the American Association of University Women gave me the freedom necessary for research and for the preliminary organization of this book. The editors of *Anglia* have kindly granted me permission to reprint in expanded form, as my seventh chapter, an article entitled "The Prose Style of John Donne's *Devotions Upon Emergent Occasions*," which appeared in *Anglia,* LXXIX (1962), 138–52. For library facilities, and particularly for the use of rare books, I am indebted to Cambridge University, the University of Rome, the New York Public Library, and Union Theological Seminary. To Dr. Sonne and his staff at General Theological Seminary, I owe special thanks for generous assistance and long-term loans of books.

Some personal debts must be mentioned. William Gilman taught me much of what I know about prose style. William Haller and

Kathrine Koller have been a source of inspiration and encouragement for many years. Ruth Wallerstein's advice and enthusiasm led me to expand a short study of the *Devotions Upon Emergent Occasions* into this full-length analysis of Donne's prose. Madeleine Doran and Helen C. White read and criticized the first draft of the manuscript and saved me from many errors and much depression. I am indebted to Marilyn Hochfield and Julian Markels for extensive and expert assistance in proofreading. For their interest and their suggestions, I must also thank Ruth Hughey, J. P. Hieronimus, Claude Simpson, Harold J. Wilson, Edwin W. Robbins, and Paul Wiley.

Finally, I thank Margaret, Katherine, and Michael Webber for the tolerance, sympathy, and sense of humor that seem to be needed for life with someone who is writing a book. They too have warded off depression and dullness; they have my best love, and my gratitude.

J. W.

Columbus, Ohio
January, 1962

NOTE ON DOCUMENTATION

References to Donne's sermons in text and notes are to the ten-volume *The Sermons of John Donne,* ed. George R. Potter and Evelyn Simpson, Berkeley, 1953–1961. Quotations are identified by volume, sermon, and line. References to statements made in the introductions to this edition, since the editors worked jointly, will for the sake of convenience be ascribed to Mrs. Simpson, who continued the work alone after the death of George Potter in 1954.

References to Donne's minor prose are to the following editions:
Biathanatos. New York, 1930.
Devotions upon Emergent Occasions, ed. John Sparrow. Cambridge, 1923.
Essays in Divinity, ed. Evelyn Simpson. Oxford, 1952.
Iuvenilia, New York, 1936.
Pseudo-Martyr. London, 1610.

Contents

CONTRARY MUSIC

AND TRULY, in our spirituall raising of the dead, to raise a sinner putrified in his owne earth, resolv'd in his owne dung, especially that hath passed many transformations, from shape to shape, from sin to sin, (he hath beene a Salamander and lived in the fire, in the fire successively, in the fire of lust in his youth, and in his age in the fire of Ambition; and then he hath beene a Serpent, a Fish, and lived in the waters, in the water successively, in the troubled water of sedition in his youth, and in his age in the cold waters of indevotion) how shall we raise this Salamander and this Serpent, when this Serpent and this Salamander is all one person, and must have contrary musique to charme him, contrary physick to cure him?

Sermons, IV, No. 13, ll. 102–12

The Making of a Prose Style

Shakespeare expected to be remembered by his lyric verse, and Donne by his prose; both were mistaken. Posterity has been kinder to Shakespeare the poet than to Donne the preacher; not until the mid-twentieth century have the sermons been readily available in their original form, and few even of the scholars of the period have undertaken to read them through. But a journey through Donne's prose, from beginning to end, though admittedly it has its dull hours, is an exciting experience —and much easier than it used to be, now that Simpson and Potter's chronological edition of the sermons is complete. It teaches us more (and teases us more) about Donne as man and artist, and sheds new light on seventeenth-century prose style. For despite the many parallels which have been drawn between his poems and selected bits of his prose, the form and texture of his sermons are quite different. I think it is fair to say that in the pulpit Donne achieved his fullest artistic expression, and came even closer than in his poetry to reflecting the spirit of his age.

Donne took naturally to the art of poetry. Born when the Renaissance was at its height, when the chief concern of most literary men was to make English verse beautiful and responsible, Donne rejected their aims both in spirit and in technique. Others, in the role of poet-teacher, might drink clear water from beechen cups[1] and assume the priestly mantle. Donne was mellifluous when he chose, craggy and obscure when he chose, courting his readers no more than they courted him.[2] He got away with it because he was good, despite Ben Jonson's grumbling.

He was of much the same mind when he began his prose career, but here his talent is less obvious. The *Iuvenilia* consist of a number of conventional paradoxes and problems. There is a mock-logical sequence of thought, but the paragraphs move hoppingly, not smoothly; individual sentences, pointed by antithesis and wordplay masked as logic, are set off from one another, preserving their evanescent thoughts like a series of aphorisms:

Gold that lyeth still, rusteth; Water, corrupteth; Aire that moveth not, poysoneth; then why should that which is the perfection of other things, be imputed to Women as greatest imperfection? Because thereby they deceive men. Are not your wits pleased with those jests, which coozen your expectation? You can call it Pleasure to be beguild in troubles, and in the most excellent toy in the world, you call it Treacherie: I would you had your *Mistresses* so constant, that they would never change, no not so much as their *smocks*, then should you see what sluttish vertue, Constancy were (*Iuvenilia*, Paradox I).

The poems react against conventional Petrarchan sonnets; and to some extent, I suppose, these paradoxes and problems stand in the same relation to Euphuistic prose. Jonas A. Barish has described the dualism in Lyly's writing, the Ramian "either-or" categorization of reality which results in the logical balancing of words, clauses, and situations against one another.[3] Donne's prose, Euphuistic in inspiration, spills over its boundaries and hurries the reader onward to an illogical conclusion.[4] But despite this significant innovation, the prose is not really very original; as W. Frazer Mitchell remarks, it could have been managed by "any ordinary young man of his day."[5] Compared with his early poems, it looks flat.

Donne was no natural-born prose writer, and confronted only with this early evidence of his work, we might justifiably relegate the *Iuvenilia* to the scrap heap. But in the light of his later writing, we can make some serious suggestions even about this piece of youthful levity. Donne disliked logic, and he disliked confinement. In the *Iuvenilia* and in the poetry, these predispositions are no problem. He has a good time with logic when he is not forced to depend on it. In the paradoxes, of course, he mocks it, and because he is not writing soberly, he has no need to respect grammatical boundaries.

In the poetry, logic is made into a kind of affective superstructure,[6] and confinement, which in prose is an aspect of logical writing, is in poetic meter and rhyme a flexible emotional device.

If Donne had not been an essentially public, dramatic personality and if he had not needed, as Shakespeare did, to exercise his genius in large as well as in small things, he might have continued in prose as he did in poetry, and perhaps eventually he would have learned to write original paradoxes or little essays.[7] But he needed, and finally got, a stage; and in retrospect, all his early prose seems to be a casting around for a way to use that stage when it was given him. He required space; never again in prose did he write anything so short as the pieces in the *Iuvenilia*. Lengthy writing requires complex organization—one problem, among many, which his poems had not encountered. And I think that in beginning to recognize the extensive labor and careful organization that a long work involves, he became audience-conscious as he had not been before. He talked to the reader directly in the preface of *Biathanatos;* and yet when he had written it, he was uncertain about whether it should be made public.[8] He thought he might have been too subtle, and he was quite right. Like the *Iuvenilia*, *Biathanatos* is uninteresting as literature, but it is most important to an understanding of his prose style, because it represents a second stage in his progress and because it is a rejection of formal logic as a primary means of organization and communication in prose.

The style of *Biathanatos* is quite different from that of the shorter paradoxes. Its sentences are long, sometimes periodic, sometimes formed by haphazard piling of clause on clause, and there is none of that glittering superficial wit of which the *Iuvenilia* are made. For years it was read as a serious defense of suicide, and learned men took pains to point out the defects in its logic.[9] What it actually appears to be is a somewhat half-hearted, somewhat unsuccessful satire on scholastic and casuistical reasoning.[10] In the *Iuvenilia*, Donne turned logic upside down; in *Biathanatos* he demolishes it by presenting a problem to which there is no solution. And this problem is a result of the same attempt to make words conform to logic which diverted a younger Donne and his friends. Once martyrdom and suicide have been placed in the same category to be considered with the same rational tools, there is no logical way of separating one from the other. And Donne certainly does not attempt to find one.

The tone of the whole book is foreshadowed in an incredibly complex analogy in the preface: "And as the eyes of *Eve* were opened by the taste of the Apple, though it bee said before that shee saw the beauty of the tree, So the digesting of this may, though not present faire objects, yet bring them to see the nakednesse and deformitie of their owne reasons, founded upon a rigorous suspition" (*Biathanatos,* p. 22). Putting himself in the position of the serpent, Donne invites the reader to run the risk of seeing in his convictions about suicide the kind of nakedness and deformity that Eve saw in herself after she had eaten the apple. But Eve's condition in her state of innocence could not have been described as naked and deformed; it was the acquisition of forbidden knowledge that gave meaning to these words. And in the same way, Donne implies, the knowledge contained in *Biathanatos* is not conducive to right thinking. But, to double the paradox, the reader, being a descendant of Eve, may be assumed already to reason only deformedly, and to be unable, as Eve was not, to see beauty truly. Either way the reader loses.

The style of *Biathanatos* is formed by the use of external, arbitrary, logical devices; its shape is imposed from the outside, and the meaning is presented to the reader in a series of formal and ostensibly separate compartments—the division and subdivision of topics into parts, distinctions, and sections, the excessive use of which is a satiric device, employed, like his many quotations, "because scholastic and artificiall men use this way of instructing" (p. 23). The emptiness of the technique is emphasized by the fact that the distinctions and sections are not named and that very often his train of thought crosses their boundaries, so that the divisions hinder rather than assist the reader's process of thought, and do not even possess their supposed merit of logic.

Within this framework are contained several different kinds of attacks on the sort of formal reasoning employed by Catholic logicians and casuists. From them come the great majority of his quotations and the syllogistic organization of his paragraphs and sentences. For while he had an obvious admiration for Aquinas and such casuists as Azor and Soto, Donne was uneasy about indiscriminate use of some of their techniques. In *Pseudo-Martyr,* for example, he says, "But as *Erasmus* said of that Church in his time, *Syllogismi nunc sustinent Ecclesiam,* wee may justlie say, that this Doctrine of temporall jurisdiction is sustained but by Syllogismes, and those weake, and impotent, and deceivable" (*Pseudo-Martyr,* Preface, sec. 27).

Most of the paragraphs and sentences in *Biathanatos* are little more than logical formulae (syllogisms and hypothetical arguments) and their grammatical structure is so arranged as to give these formulae force and continuity. Sentences almost always begin with connectives—*and, but, which, or, if therefore, since, so that, upon which* —that show their "logical" relationship to what has gone before. But to advance through the often tangled syntax of Donne's qualifying phrases and clauses is rather like climbing over boulders, boulders sometimes designedly high enough to obscure the view. In his later writing Donne builds sentences whose clauses, even when periodic, move associatively rather than logically, to give the reader a sense of sharing in the author's experience. Here he commits himself with a vengeance to externalized writing; his continual references to sources and his excessive use of various typographical devices are purposely employed, together with the unwieldy and inadequate syntax, to mock the kind of writing that *Biathanatos* imitates. I copy the following illustration exactly as it appears in the text, because even the footnote letters contribute to the effect:

Yea the parent of all sinne, which is hereditary originall sin, which (i) Aquinas calls, [a languor and faintnesse in our nature, and an indisposition, proceeding from the dissolution of the harmony of originall Justice] is by him said to be in us, [(k) *quasi naturale*] And is, as he saith in another place, so (1) naturall, [that though it is propagated with our nature, in generation, though it be not caused by the principles of nature.] So (m) as if God would now miraculously frame a man, as he did the first woman, of another's flesh and bone, and not by way of generation, into that creature, all infirmities of our flesh would be derived but not originall Sinne. So that originall sinne is traduced by nature onely, and all actuall sinne issuing from thence, all sinne is naturall (pp. 37–38).

The laborious integration of Aquinas into Donne's sentence, the brackets and parentheses, and the failure of Donne's period syntactically to survive the burden emphasize the glibness of the *ergo* that concludes the double syllogism:

All things transmitted by nature are natural.
Original sin is transmitted by nature.
Therefore, original sin is natural.

Original sin is natural.
All sin issues from original sin.
Therefore, all sin is natural.

The first syllogism depends upon a shift in the use of the word "nature"; the second depends upon its faulty first premiss, as well as upon a continued confusion of biology with theology.

Much more frequent than syllogism in Donne's sentence structure is the hypothetical argument: if one proposition is true, another, based on it, is also true; for example, if the king rules by divine right, good Christians must obey the king. Such sentences are introduced by the words "if therefore," or simply "if," and while they do not necessarily express doubt, their constant repetition tends to imply it, and thus to permit a reinforcement of the ambiguity that underlies so many of his statements. The following sentence is an example:

If therefore after a Christian protestation of an innocent purpose herein, And after a submission of all which is said, not only to every Christian Church, but to every Christian man, and after an entreaty, that the Reader will follow this advice of *Tabaeus, Qui litigant, sint ambo in conspectu tuo mali & rei,* and trust neither me, nor the adverse part, but the Reasons, there be any scandall in this enterprise of mine, it is Taken not Given (p. 19).

It will be noticed that again Donne has built up slowly to a fast conclusion, a psychologically useful device frequent in *Biathanatos*. Here the reader is without warning left with all the responsibility, and at the same time given no assurance about whether he should accept it, since the argument *is* hypothetical, and he can have no way of knowing whether its conditions are true.

An ironic piling up of examples in these subordinate clauses may be followed by a brief *ergo* which leaves the reader no out whatsoever; it is damaging to both sides. A good example of this is the argument beginning, "Since the Church is so indulgent, and liberall to her children, that at the point of death shee will afford her treasure of baptism to one which hath been mad from his birth," and continuing through a long series of examples introduced by "if" clauses to "If lastly she absolve some whether they will or no, why should we abhorre our mothers example, and being brethren, be severer than the Parent?" (p. 31). The savagely ironic picture of the church forcing baptism on all men is opposed to the uncharitable alternative in such a way that neither choice is appealing; this is a variation of what Thomas Wilson called the "dilemma" or "horned argument."[11] It is frequent in *Biathanatos;* the previous passage quoted is another example of it, where Donne evidently offers the reader a choice between creating scandal and accepting an apparently dangerous hypothesis. He found the trick not only in rhetoric books, but also in the casuists' treatment of cases which seemed to them to necessitate a choice between one sin and another;[12] and in *Biathanatos* he adapts it in more than one way to his own satirical purposes.

Finally—and this is an example of almost complete departure from meaning—Donne employs the long sentence in such a way as to obscure the issue by substituting irrelevant for relevant information; the syllogism is implied rather than explicit, although the same psychological effect is obtained by his following the slow introductory clauses with an abrupt conclusion. The first sentence of the preface is a masterpiece of this kind:

BEZA, A man as eminent and illustrious, in the full glory and Noone of Learning, as others were in the dawning, and Morning, when any, the least sparkle, was notorious, confesseth of himself, that only for the anguish of a Scurffe, which over-ranne his head, he had once drown'd himselfe from the Millers bridge in *Paris,* if his Uncle by chance had not then come that way; I have often such a sickely inclination (p. 17).

The conspicuously triumphant rhetoric momentarily overshadows the obvious confusion of intellectual with moral character here in Donne's attempt to conceal the real issue by expatiating upon Beza's learning and to insert his own morbid *persona* into this illustrious company. Still, this much can be seen. But only a reader who took the trouble to look up the marginal references—as Charles Moore did in 1790—could know that, without ever predicating an untruth, Donne has conveyed an altogether false impression of the situation described. What Beza actually wrote was that as a very young child, regularly enduring frightful pain, he had been tempted by a companion to jump from the bridge.[13] Technically, Donne's arrangement of language is a concealed example of the fallacy *secundum quid,* confusion of absolute and qualified statement, for the reader inevitably takes Beza's adulthood and fame to be sufficiently absolute as to include his suicidal impulse. Language is here completely severed from truth.

One slightly different type of sentence structure used in *Biathanatos* should be mentioned. The analogy, which can also be read as syllogism, is classified as "example" by the logic books. Both the grammar and the intrinsic interest of the comparison half-convince the reader that he is being given a logical argument:

For as in Cramps which are contortions of the Sinewes, or in Tetars, which are rigors and stiffnesses in the Muscles, wee may procure to our selfe a fever to thaw them, or we may procure them in a burning feaver, to condense and attemper our bloud againe, so in all rebellions and disobediences of our flesh, wee may minister to our selves such corrections and remedies, as the Magistrate might, if the fact were evident (p. 171).

If Donne's other arguments carried more conviction, the analogies would not be forced to bear so much weight, but in his purposeful denigration of all varieties of reasoning, a syllogism means no more than a metaphor.

Other techniques of satire and ambiguity are the juxtaposition of numerous examples of martyr-suicides, some absurd and some serious, to show the impossibility of basing judgment upon external circumstances (pp. 139–40); the casuistical balancing of one sin against another in an atypical framework to draw such conclusions as that lying is worse than suicide (pp. 36–37); and the shifting use of certain key words, like "nature" and "self-preservation." From all these devices, even though the book itself is a trick, we can learn much.

Clumsy as Donne's sentences are, he is moving away from the pointed wit of the *Iuvenilia* to a more discursive kind of writing. The long periods are shaped very much like the long sentences of the sermons—slow build-up, fast conclusion—but their pseudo-logical form makes their conclusions painful to the reader rather than esthetically gratifying. In the sermons, scholastic apparatus is minimized, and sentence structure becomes dependent upon emotional rather than strictly logical progress. There the periods can discard syntactical unity, not because Donne cannot achieve it, but because it is no longer important. Sound and rhythm and symbol take its place.

Recent scholarship tends to take *Biathanatos* seriously as a plea for right reason,[14] but I think it can only be considered such in a very negative sense. The book is a paradox; its argument is perforce unresolved. And the strain of voluntarism running through it[15] would indicate, if anything, a rejection of human reason and an intention on Donne's part to look elsewhere for truth. Sister Thomas Marion's definition of it as a cross between a problem and a casuistical case seems to fit it very well, but I am not sure that Donne himself quite knew what he wanted to do.[16] Too satirical to be seriously convincing and too clumsily written to be convincing satire, *Biathanatos* may actually be its author's way of protecting himself against his own fascination with the subject of suicide.

A good satirist must be able to imitate seriously the style he wants to ridicule. Donne knew by the time he had finished writing *Biathanatos,* if he had not known it before, that he himself was not well suited to learn or to be convinced by formal logic and casuistry. And he makes it quite clear in his prose, as in his poetry, that his vocation was not to teach or to prove anything. He would take responsibility for what he preached, but not in this way. In the sermons, reason and faith are both upheld as primary guides to Christian knowledge, but for Donne faith came first, and his own faith, so far as it is reflected in the style of his sermons, is based on an intuitional and literary rather than on a rational and logical mode of apprehension.

Donne, as a writer, was only good at one thing, though that one thing is very intense and valuable. He was good at communicating his own experience, and he could only do this by showing what the experience was made of. In the poems he could say, "It was like this and this and this," and all the while he was building up these analogies, he was also communicating the feeling of the experience in his own tough music. He seems not to have known for a long time that prose could be used for such a purpose. Certainly he had no English models to show him that it could. What we know of his education and of his library suggests that he had been almost exclusively exposed to logic, casuistry, and polemics. He would have known meditational writings, of course, and they eventually helped him. But the greatest influence upon his later style was undoubtedly an increasing familiarity with the church Fathers, from Augustine to Bernard of Clairvaux.

The severance of language and truth which he effects in *Biathanatos* is diametrically opposed to the kind of expression on which his later career depended, the celebration of a faith wholly reliant upon the written word of Scripture. And although in *Pseudo-Martyr* he attempted a seriously argumentative essay, the result is a dull piece of controversy almost as casuistical as *Biathanatos*. In order to make his writing accurately reflect his feelings and ideas, he needed to be able to rest more meaning and confidence upon the words themselves, and this he could only do when freed from the necessity of either obeying or mocking a non-verbal scheme. His own experience was intensely verbal, literary, and symbolic. But when forced into a syllogism, words can be made to perform functions independent of their traditional assigned meanings; he needed therefore to develop a style which would put the word and the experience itself at the center of his organization.

The *Essays in Divinity* were probably written less than eight years after *Biathanatos,* and in them, while his thoughts are announced in a positive rather than in a negative way, his style changes to keep pace with his ideas. Near the beginning, he sets the tone, speaking of St. Augustine's desire to understand the creation:

Thus did he whom thou hadst filled with faith, desire reason and understanding; as man blest with great fortunes desire numbers of servants, and other Complements of honour. But another instrument and engine of thine, whom thou hadst so enabled, that nothing was too minerall nor centrick for the search and reach of his wit, hath remembred me; *That it is an Article of our Belief, that the world began.* And therefore for this point, we are not under the insinuations and mollifyings of perswasion, and conveniency; nor under the reach and violence of Argument, or Demonstration, or Necessity; but under the Spirituall, and peaceable Tyranny, and easie yoke of sudden and present Faith (*Essays in Divinity,* p. 16).[17]

It is interesting that at this point he is able to appeal to Aquinas himself, the "other instrument," for justification in setting logic aside. Reason is a servant, and an unruly one at that. Grateful reliance upon faith is a keynote of the *Essays.* Christian doctrines are examined and clarified, but never questioned.

Gosse, not without reason, described the *Essays* as lecture notes.[18] Donne must have been engaged in omnivorous reading at the time. He quotes lavishly, and the pronoun "I," which is a signal aspect of his usual style, is relatively rare. To a reader coming straight to them from *Biathanatos* and *Pseudo-Martyr,* the *Essays* probably would look rather fragmentary. But they are by no means dry notes; their appearance indicates another and very significant change in style. Calmer perhaps than any of his other writing, the *Essays* are organized like sermons, foreshadowing those which he was to preach, while internally, from sentence to sentence, they follow almost naturally the flow of his thought. He never prepared them for publication; they cannot equal the sermons and the *Devotions,* but they provide us with a valuable insight into a second stage in his thought, standing as they do at a turning point, mid-journey between *Biathanatos* and the sermons.

The sentence continuity obtained in *Biathanatos* by use of connective words as openings occurs here and is increased by the employment of many fragmentary sentences, which depend for meaning upon what goes before and after. But because Donne is depending less upon logic and grammar and more upon the conformation of his words to the movement of his mind, and because his own attitude is no longer obviously ambiguous, there is much less of the kind of tangled obscurity that in *Biathanatos* results from the attempt to fit a long unwieldy period into syllogistic form or to buttress it with undigested bits from other writers.

There are really two kinds of sentence style in the *Essays*. In the first, there is still little use of formal sentence devices to organize the prose and simplify the reader's task. The tone is meditative and the progression associative, but the emphasis is still intellectual, and it is difficult to follow the thought:

Since the intention of God, through *Moses,* in this, was, that it might be to the Jews a *Book of the generation of Adam;* since in it is purposely propounded, That all this Universe, *Plants,* the chiefest contemplation of Naturall Philosophie and Physick, and no small part of the Wisdom of *Solomon,* [*who spake of plants, from Cedar to Hyssop:*] And *Beasts,* who have often the honour to be our reproach, accited for examples of vertue and wisdome in the scriptures, and some of them seposed for the particular passive service of God in Sacrifices (which hee gave to no man but his Son, and withheld from *Isaac:*) And *Man,* who (like his own eye) sees all but himself, in his opinion, but so dimly, that there are marked an hundred differences in mens Writings concerning an *Ant:* And *Spirits,* of whom we understand no more, then a horse of us: and the receptacles and theaters of all these, *Earth, Sea, Air, Heaven,* and all things were once nothing: That Man chusing his own destruction, did what he could to annihilate himself again, and yet received a promise of a Redeemer: That Gods mercy may not be distrusted, nor his Justice tempted, since the generall Deluge, and *Joseph's* preservation are here related, filling an History of more than 2300 yeers, with such examples as might mollify the Jews in their wandering. I say, since this was directly and onely purposed by *Moses;* to put him in a wine-presse, and squeeze out Philosophy and particular Christianitie, is a degree of that injustice, which all laws forbid, to torture a man, *sine indiciis aut sine probationibus* (p. 14).

The difficult content and the absence of guiding rhetorical devices force the reader's attention to concern itself largely with untangling the thought. But if the sentence were somewhat less associative and if some repetition and parallelism had been employed, it would be practically identical with one of his typical sermon patterns. The progress of the thought is slower, easier, and more charged with meaning at each stage than in *Biathanatos*. The structure is periodic, but he frees himself of syntactical obedience and loosens the framework by such devices as very wide separation of subject from verb; parentheses and digressive clauses; and natural, rather than conventional, punctuation. The period after "mollify the Jews in their wandering" signals a pause at the height of the piled subordinate clauses; the "I say" supplies the "sentence" with a hinge and a turning point. He is learning the same kind of broken music, created by unexpected variations upon an understood framework, that he practiced in his poetry.

The *Essays* also contain very imaginative sections, which pick up all the real musical devices and guidelines that we have missed in his writing so far:

A prince is Pilot of a great ship, a Kingdome; we of a pinnace, a family, or a less skiff, our selves; and howsoever we be tossed, we cannot perish; for our haven (if we will) is even in the midst of the Sea; and where we dy, our home meets us. If he be a lion and live by prey, and wast among Cedars and pines, and I a mole, and scratch out my bed in the ground, happy in this, that I cannot see him: If he be a butterfly, the son of a Silkworm, and I a *Scarab,* the seed of durt; If he go to execution in a Chariot, and I in a Cart or by foot, where is the glorious advantage? If I can have (or if I can want) those things which the *Son of Sirach* calls Principall, water, fire, and iron, salt and meal, wheat and hony, milk, and the blood of grapes, oyle, and clothing; If I can *prandere Olus* and so need not Kings; Or can use Kings, and so need not *prandere Olus:* In one word, if I do not *frui* (which is, set my delight, and affection only due to God) but *Uti* the Creatures of this world, this world is mine; and to me belong those words, *Subdue the Earth, and rule over all creatures;* and as God is proprietary, I am *usufructuarius* of this Heaven and Earth which God created in the beginning. And here, because *Nemo silens placuit, multi brevitate,* shall be the end (p. 36).

In these passages, the figures of speech, rather than the progress of the logic take the reader's attention. The "if" clauses are no longer intended to confuse the reader, as they were in *Biathanatos*. Emotional clarity is gained by repetition of the same words at the beginnings of successive clauses, by parallel construction, and by repetition of the same idea in several different ways, through metaphor. There is no longer proof through argument, but persuasion through word and sound.

The variation in the *Essays* between intellectual endeavor and a kind of thanksgiving for ideas emotionally apprehended is reminiscent of some parts of Augustine's *Confessions,* for example, the sections on time and memory or on the creation, where he moves back and forth between discursive writing and prayer, between the eager pursuit of answers and rejoicing in intuitive understanding. These passages were clearly in Donne's mind at the time.[19] The chief differences are that Augustine develops original ideas, while Donne pulls together, with selective sensitivity but not always with logic, the thoughts of others; and that in his imaginative passages Donne relies to a far greater extent upon imagery. Augustine can make an idea exciting through sheer intellectual vigor, while Donne prefers to concentrate on its concrete, palpable application to his human situation.

Externally, the *Essays* are organized according to an accepted method of homiletic structure; they are, in effect, two closet-sermons, and he himself calls them sermons, citing the authority of Gerson, *"Scriptor manu praedicat"* (*Essays,* p. 41). Each begins with a preamble much longer than would be customary in a spoken sermon; the texts are the first verse of Genesis and the first of Exodus. The concern which he expresses for the way in which Biblical texts are taken out of context, their meaning mutilated, is met here by a method which we will often find him using in his sermons. He chooses a text which he can think of as a summary of a whole book of the Bible, and is thus freed from considering it as "shapeless and unsignificant rags of a word or two" (*Essays,* p. 39).

He speaks of the first verse of Genesis as a threshold and proceeds to divide the sermon in traditional fashion:

Before we consider each stone of this threshold, which are 1. The *time,* In the begin[n]ing: 2. The *person, God:* 3. The *Action, He created:* And 4.

The *Work, Heaven and Earth;* we will speak of two or three other things, so many words. Of the *Whole Book;* Of the *Author* of those first 5 Books; And of this *first book.* For earthly princes look for so many pauses and reverences, in our accesses to their table, though they be not there (p. 6).

The matter of these divisions includes a wide range of subjects reflecting Donne's reading at the time and anticipating many of his primary concerns in the sermons. The manner of treatment is either straightforward discussion, associative progress of thought, or a symbolic method of moral application that later becomes a major organizing device in the sermons. The first needs no comment. For associative movement, we may consider a passage from a section beginning with the meaning of the word *creation,* eventually concerned with whether the world was created out of nothing, and imaginatively occupied with the meaning of nothingness, especially to man.

After introducing various philosophical conclusions about the problem of creation, he continues as follows:

But because all which can be said hereof is cloudy, and therefore apt to be mis-imagined, and ill interpreted, for, *obscurum loquitur quisque suo periculo,* I will turn to certain and evident things; And tell thee, O man, which art said to be the Epilogue, and *compendium* of all this world, and the *Hymen* and Matrimoniall knot of Eternal and Mortall things, whom one says to be *all Creatures,* because the Gospel, of which onely man is capable, is sent to be *preached to all Creatures* . . . know ye by how few descents ye are derived from Nothing? (pp. 29–30)

He continues to speak of man's nothingness, his derivation from lust and excrement, the transience of life, the recent non-existence of each separate soul. Honor and pleasure, the most "spirituall and delicate parts" of man, pass quickly from nothing to nothing; "which even at the last great fire, shall not befall the most wretched worme, nor most abject grain of dust. . . . For to be Nothing, is so deep a curse . . . that Hell and the prisoners there . . . cannot wish so great a loss to themselves." This leads him into discussion of the unimaginable enormity of the pains of hell, which he considers for some eighteen lines before returning again to his point: "In Hell, I say . . . none is ever said to have wished himself Nothing." An analogy in the next sentence, far from being used for any semblance of proof, as it would have been in *Biathanatos,* gives him the opportunity to draw in still another tangential thought:

Indeed, as reposedly, and at home within himself no man is an Atheist, however he pretend it, and serve the company with his braveries (as Saint *Augustine* sayes of himself, that though he knew nothing was blameable but vice, yet he seemed vicious, lest he should be blameable; and fain'd false vices when he had not true, lest he should be despised for his innocency;) so it is impossible that any man should wish himself Nothing (p. 31).

Even in the *Essays,* however, another technique helps to counteract the disorganizing effect of associative thinking, and in the sermons it becomes predominant. The analogies by which Donne later chooses to explain the relationship between Word and word illuminate his concept of the function of the sermon. The Word of God is to the sermon as is the honey to the honeycomb (*Sermons,* VIII, No. 12, ll. 40–44), the candle to the candlestick (*Sermons,* V, No. 14, ll. 785–88), the soul to the body:

Our errand hither . . . is to heare, and to heare all the words of the Preacher, but, to heare in those words, the Word, that Word which is the soule of all that is said, and is the true Physick of all their soules that heare. *The Word was made flesh;* that is, assumed flesh; but yet the Godhead was not that flesh. The Word of God is made a Sermon, that is, a Text is dilated, diffused into a Sermon; but that whole Sermon is not the word of God. But yet all the Sermon is the Ordinance of God (*Sermons,* V, No. 1, ll. 760–68).

Samuel Hieron, a near contemporary of Donne's, spoke of preaching as the unfolding of a garment (the text) which cannot be seen to best advantage folded up in Scripture;[20] it is this concept which underlies Donne's sermon method. The unfolding of the text is for Donne the diffusion or dilation of the text, ordinarily by extension of a symbol inherent in it. In the *Essays,* for example, having considered at length the exodus from Egypt in its literal historical sense, he continues as follows:

Only to paraphrase the History of this Delivery, without amplifying, were furniture and food enough for a meditation of the best perserverance, and appetite, and digestion; yea, the least word in the History would serve a long rumination. If this be in the bark, what is in the tree? If in the superficiall grass, the letter; what treasure is there in the hearty and inward Mine, the Mistick and retired sense? Dig a little deeper, O my poor lazy soul, and thou shalt see that thou, and all mankind are delivered from an Egypt; and more miraculously than these (p. 74).

He then goes on to consider, first, the Egypts encountered in this life, and then the Egypt that is the world, from which the soul is delivered by entrance into the "heavenly Hierusalem" (pp. 75–76). The proper method of Biblical exegesis is one of the important subjects of the *Essays* and is central to the style of any sermon of the time. Allegorical interpretation, by which Donne means an over-elaborate figurative and perhaps fanciful rendition of a passage (p. 40), is something which he flatly rejects; the literal sense only is acceptable, but the literal sense is the principal intention of the Holy Ghost in that place. That is to say, the literal sense is not necessarily the superficial meaning of the words; it is, rather, a literary sense, which allows for use of metaphors (*Sermons,* VI, No. 2, ll. 1–19). Donne's insistence on the literal sense is in his practice qualified by two considerations. First, the common reference to the Holy Ghost as author of the words,[21] and the further reference to Moses and other reputed authors as secretaries of the Holy Ghost, implies that the principal intention may have been a broader one than the historical literal meaning includes. Second, the standard homiletic practice of applying the text to the congregation enables Donne to extend the sense of the words farther into symbolism than perhaps he would have been willing to go in exposition alone; for application of the words to immediate situations was something that he considered legitimate and salutary when the literal sense was not thereby perverted.

In the sermons we will find a shift in the proportionate amount of space given to each part of the three-fold interpretation employed in this Egypt passage. Here, in the *Essays,* the major emphasis is on the historical sense; the moral and anagogical senses (this last always for Donne involves consideration of man's entrance into eternal life) are much more briefly considered. In the sermons, with their

different purposes, the moral sense becomes all-important, the anagogical sense second, and the historical sense is explained only
enough to provide a clear basis for the rest. The sermons will be
organized according to the development of a symbol (like the Egypt
symbol used here) through the three senses, ending with the highest.
By this means the human words of the preacher should blend most
imperceptibly with the sacred Word of the text, and the whole
should become a single thing. Donne thought of the words of the
Bible much in the same way he thought of sacraments, as "outward
and visible signs of inward and spiritual grace"; and while the
preacher's words are not the same thing, the intrinsic connection of
Word and sermon infuses into the sermon something like sacramental power.

I have said that Donne could write only of his own experience.
In making these symbols from the words of the text, he gives them
an immediate and personal meaning, making himself and his congregation, for instance, inhabitants of an Egypt. He discusses the
verses of the Bible not as history or as dogma, but as real and present
emotional, physical, and spiritual human conditions. The symbols—
the words of the text—give the sermons, and to some extent the
Essays, a central unity, around which the associative pattern of his
thought can flow. Unlike the syllogism, they make no demands upon
sentence structure, and they give much more freedom to language.
Stylistically, as well as ecclesiastically, they present Donne with a
very congenial basis for a coherent prose.

What we have seen Donne learning here is a workable method
and theory for the development of a prose style in which he could
believe. And of course he acquired these together with a subject
matter in which he also believed and to which they could be applied.
His next stage of development is the sermons, and they are very different, again, from the *Essays,* much more rich, complex, and varied,
indeed, than anything that he had done previously could have led
anyone to suspect. To be treated justly, they must be broken down
into their component parts in the succeeding chapters. But here I

want to provide a kind of preview by making some generalizations about them in order to show how Donne fits into the traditions of his age and what relevance some familiar critical terms have to his writing. These generalizations, then, will be based less on what we have seen so far than on what is to come. The reader, I hope, will be able to use them as guidelines, and I hope he will also want to check their accuracy.

Donne's preaching begins, of course, with the Bible. Dennis Quinn, in his article, "Donne's Christian Eloquence,"[22] has shown how different Donne's theory was from that of the typical preacher of his day. Increasingly, during the Renaissance, the Bible had come to be considered a book of history and dogma; more and more often, the Puritans called their sermons lectures.[23] The homily became an argument, a doctrinal exposition, bristling with proof-texts. Donne stood in the older Augustinian tradition in which the preacher applied the words of the Bible to the congregation, forcing them to recognize these words as physical evidence of spiritual reality. The Bible is a work of love; it has sacramental power to restore and waken the sleeping conscience. As Quinn explains it, "it is not a book containing certain facts and truths which one may extract for use—not like a painting from which we may draw facts and morals, but like the paint and the brush out of which the painting is made, an infinitely adaptable spiritual tool."[24] Hence Donne's use of words as symbols, his extraordinary and witty concentration on language, and his many and repeated quotations from Scripture.

With this direct reliance on the theory of the Fathers, which stems from the explanation of Christian eloquence in Book IV of Augustine's *Christian Doctrine*, Donne's style needs almost no explanation in terms of the ecclesiastical rhetorics of the Renaissance (which were written mainly by Puritans). The Senecan-Ciceronian controversy ought to be mentioned, but Donne's use of these methods too must be understood largely in relation to his own commitments.

Of the two main classic styles, Attic and Asiatic (called in the Renaissance, Senecan and Ciceronian), the one is theoretically concerned with the working out of ideas and feelings and the other with a beautiful rendition of them; the one is perhaps primarily concerned to record the movement of thought and emotion and the other to express thoughts fully formed, or even, especially when influenced by Platonism, to symbolize the eternal Ideas.[25] The Renaissance Senecans abandoned the highly wrought, logical, periodic Ciceronian sentence—the vehicle of one who knows what he is going to say before he begins—and adopted the loose and curt styles in which persuasion was less important than meditation. They abandoned decorative figures of speech, which they considered useless, and adopted the thought figure.[26]

In many respects, the Attic, or Senecan, style lends itself to Donne's theory. His purpose is to get at the memory, not at the intellect, to remind rather than to teach.[27] The image of God, according to the Fathers, is inherent in man, and gives him his instinctive knowledge of religion, which, says Augustine, is stored up in the memory, "the stomach of the soul."[28] Impressions received through the senses, according to Augustine, are re-formed in the memory to shape knowledge not directly experienced. And as Donne points out himself, his congregations, born and brought up in the Anglican church, can be exposed to no new doctrines; they are simply to be made fully aware of what they already know.[29] Donne has no need for the persuasive logic of the Ciceronian period. He shapes his prose in such a way as to appeal directly to the memory, by use of the long loose "Senecan" sentence that Morris Croll calls meditative,[30] and that seems to advance with the progress of thought and emotion, a sentence shaped for exploration and recollection of known truths, rather than for exposition and persuasion.

The Senecan thought figure also has its place in this scheme of things. Donne is deeply and personally aware of the disunity of men's minds, their inability to see anything whole. The analogy helps to bring together the scattered experiences and images dormant in the memory. But analogy is not enough; and we find, during the course of his sermons, a tendency to transmute analogy into symbol, to carry the Senecan process one stage farther. For only in symbolism is there a real coherence of human vision.

Donne's use of Ciceronian traditions also springs directly from his rhetorical theory. He is as fierce as Ascham in his defense of "outward things," of formal language, for with his Christian-Platonic view of words, denigration of their value seemed to him a sacrilege.[31] Augustine had questioned the secular worth of Biblical eloquence. That, says Donne, was because Augustine had read the Bible only in translations, "which could not maintaine the Majesty, nor preserve the elegancies of the Originall." Now perfect knowledge of languages shows us that the Bible surpasses all other writing in rhetorical excellence, "and they mistake it much, that thinke, that the Holy Ghost had rather chosen a low, and barbarous, and homely style, then an eloquent, and powerfull manner of expressing himselfe" (*Sermons*, VI, No. 1, ll. 611–12, 642–45). Donne neglects to mention that his own opinion is based chiefly on Vulgate Latin and King James English, rather than on the Holy Ghost's Hebrew (a language of which he had, at best, a working knowledge),[32] but certainly these translations gave him a central advantage over Augustine in the defense of rhetoric. Again and again, he exclaims over the superior eloquence of the books of the Bible, the powerful and harmonious accents of the Holy Ghost, and in the Bible he finds a unity of thought and expression that is essential to his whole theory and practice of style. For if in human rhetoric there is always an uncertainty about the validity of eloquent expression, there can be none in the Bible, which is truth itself.

Now if we define Ciceronianism as its Renaissance opponents did, as a style which prohibits thought and proliferates frivolous adornment, then Donne is not in the least Ciceronian. In his sermons he constantly attacks fanciful and mindless eloquence. But he disliked extemporaneous speeches; he considered that texts contrived by the Holy Ghost deserved the best of human skill. In his own theory, he added to the admission of the ecclesiastical rhetoricians that eloquence is a tool for forceful application of Christian truth,[33] the Christianized classical ideal of rhetoric as a symbolic expression of order in God's world, his own sense that ceremony is part of the moral law written in the heart of man,[34] and the medieval belief that the concinnities are one kind of affirmation of Christian joy.[35] Eloquence in Donne is not just an extension of the words of the Holy Ghost—it is all these things as well. It is a more functional and more apparently spontaneous rhetoric than that of Cicero or Hooker, but it is much too lavish and musical to be acceptable to an ardent Senecan.

Finally, Donne has a great appreciation of the thunderous force that a Ciceronian period could achieve. We have already seen his great interest in periodic constructions, as well as his distrust of their logical basis. In his sermons, he uses figures of speech and coherence of tone to hold such periods together without benefit of syntactical continuity. In an age when rhetorical battlelines seemed to be sharply drawn, any good writer (witness Milton as well as Donne) could get the best of both worlds.

If Donne's prose style were entirely dictated by the Augustinian tradition, with some assistance from contemporary rhetoric, this discussion could end here. But we cannot say, as Dumontier does of St. Bernard, that Donne "speaks Bible";[36] his eloquence is not fully explainable in terms of Scripture. If anything, when he incorporates Scripture into his prose, he makes it speak Donne. And so I must add to this mainly ecclesiastical approach a somewhat more secular one. A passage in Jonas Barish's book on Ben Jonson's prose is worth quoting in full, because it summarizes this different perspective:

> If we assume that the restlessness of baroque style expresses some restlessness within the writer, some inner conflict or war with the world at large, we can see that it lends itself admirably to the needs of authors like Donne . . . . Donne's tensions are not merely obvious: they form the subject matter of his art. In sermon and poem alike, he dramatizes his own paradoxes of feeling, his struggles between carnal love and religious devotion, his craving to unite matter and spirit. There are the obvious doubts, and the obvious suffering.[37]

This is the old approach to Donne, and one which those who work with him as a preacher in a preaching tradition would like to discredit, just as those who embraced him as a fellow-rebel in the earlier part of this century preferred to ignore his orthodox characteristics. But in order to be fair and precise, we must acknowledge that these two aspects of Donne are inseparable—that he embraced tradition because he honestly believed in it and desperately needed it, and that with the help of the tradition, he became more himself, more of an individual than he had ever been before.

The word "baroque" has been very much abused. It is so evocative that it is almost unmanageable; and yet, just because it is evocative, it is irreplaceable. Enough respectable scholarship has now been completed in this field to make it possible to talk about a literary baroque without constant reference to the other arts—and this in itself can save a great deal of confusion. I take the word to refer to some specific artistic techniques and attitudes when they occur in significant abundance in a work of art produced in the late sixteenth or the first half of the seventeenth century. My remarks in the following paragraphs are substantially indebted to the work of Morris Croll on English baroque prose, and to that of Marcel Raymond and Jean Rousset on French baroque poetry. Odette de Mourgue's *Metaphysical, Baroque and Precieux Poetry* is also useful.[38]

Perhaps the main problem to be settled for English literature is that of the relationship between "metaphysical" and "baroque." Scholars working separately with these concepts very often describe the same characteristics being used to somewhat different ends. The most important of these are analogy and conceit (with all that they imply both in respect to confusion of genre, bridging of gaps, and verbal play); transformation and illusion, especially in metaphor; the dramatic, the theatrical, and the rhetorical; contrast and surprise. But whereas the use of all these characteristics in metaphysical poetry is controlled by intellectual motivation and intellectual restraint, the baroque motivation is emotional and sensuous. Metaphysical poetry is more private and difficult, compact to the point of being esoteric; baroque poetry is aggressively public and copious. Oddly, it sometimes weakens its own purpose, through overemphasis, ambiguity, or undercutting. It is a restless style. The contrast, in poetry, is between the metaphysical Herbert and Vaughan on the one hand; the baroque Crashaw and Giles Fletcher on the other. Donne's poetry stands somewhere between the two.[39]

In attempting to define a prose baroque, we can begin with Morris Croll's description of the long, loose, meditative anti-Ciceronian sentence and of the curt style, with its equally meditative turning around a single metaphor or thought. Join with this (I think now of Donne in particular) a restless and uncertain balance, openness, expansiveness, constant multiplication of words and images, prolific and sensuous rhythms, translation and transmutation of metaphor and language, and neglect of boundaries. Compare this then with the highly compressed, knotty, rational, and calm style of Lancelot Andrewes, and you have at least a tentative impression of the difference between a baroque and a metaphysical prose. Andrewes is no more difficult to read than Donne, for poetic obscurity in a sermon is of course undesirable. And certainly the two preachers overlap at many points: they can both be called Senecan; their exegetical methods are very similar; but given the characteristics which I have described, anyone could easily identify a passage taken out of context.

Donne's prose is seldom sheerly descriptive in the way that Crashaw's poetry is. His basic sermon technique, like that of Andrewes, is verbal, not pictorial. The music of his prose and its passionate texture are what is sensuous about it. We can also consider here, from another viewpoint, that fascination with words which he was finally able to utilize in an Augustinian homiletic technique. Father Walter Ong has noticed that a fundamental Christian problem of trying to make language adequate to the expression of religious concepts manifests itself in witty writing.[40] And Leo Spitzer suggests that a chief baroque concern was very similar: the baroque writer recognized that words are not enough—and this recognition accounts for various sorts of frantic reactions like cultism, preciosity, wittiness.[41] It might also account for the violent energy that Donne expends in justifying and practicing the belief that Biblical words are truth.

There is a tendency among scholars to talk about the "baroque personality," and it is probably justifiable, because the beauty (and the treachery) of the word "baroque" is that it must be used to indicate the whole texture of a prose, which certainly includes the tone created by the sensibility and the beliefs of its author. A unique aspect of baroque art is that it so often forces us to think about the artist. It may be a stylistic defect caused by the artist's inability or refusal to satisfy his audience. It may be the result of his inability to come to terms with his own subject. It is because of this basic ambiguity that scholars have worried so much about which of Donne's poems are serious and which are not; it is because of this that his *Biathanatos* has seemed so enigmatic. In one of his sermons, he translates a straightforward quotation from Ambrose, *"Mens in sermonibus nostris habitat, & gubernat verba,"* to read, "The soul of a man is incorporate in his words; As he speaks, *we think* he thinks" (VIII, No. 15, ll. 220–22). The last italics are mine, and they speak for themselves. It is possible for a writer to put himself into his prose without making the reader wonder what he was *really* like, but Donne was unable to do that because he so constantly questioned his own sincerity, and in his art, implicitly at least, expressed and criticized his own conflicting feelings.

The baroque personality seems to doubt and suffer, to see every question from all sides, to engage in skepticism, relativism, our kind of modernity. And it is intensely self-conscious. But in its religious manifestations, at least, and in some of its secular aspects as well,[42] it seeks and finds a way to demonstrate that human doubts have human limitations, and to indicate a wholeness that its vision and art can only partly comprehend. Donne's sentence structure, his metaphor, his tone of voice all depict a way of thought familiar to our time. But they lie within and indeed help to shape a structure that is less familiar and presents to us a surprisingly stable Christian world-view that is quite unaffected in Donne's mind and only qualified in his art by his personal doubts and fears.

The baroque personality seems to be far less certain of itself than of its world. It attempts to define the self by flaunting the self, by appearing on stage in pose after pose. Witness the number of different attitudes Donne worked through in his poetry, and the different styles he tried in his prose. Witness his attempts to model himself on Augustine and Paul (who had no need to model themselves on anyone). Witness his thorough identification of himself with his congregations, and his choice of pride, despair, and self-fragmentation as his main preaching themes. Other preachers extinguished themselves in their subjects. Donne *is* his own subject, becomes his own prose; he is the hot youth and the cold old man to whom he would apply his contrary music.

Consider for a moment that stock-in-trade of baroque art, the optical illusion. Does not this concept explain the whole confused history of Donne and his critics? In his poetry, when was he John and when was he Jack, when serious and when a mocker? Is *Biathanatos* a work of impiety or of devotion, a defense or a rejection of reason? What are we to think when he says wittily that he regrets having committed the sin of wit? In his sermons, was he a medievalist or a modern, an orthodox preacher or a consummate actor? When he posed in his graveclothes on his deathbed, was he surrendering himself to God's will or creating a last theatrical and egocentric tableau? The truth is that opposites combine in Donne. The essence of the optical illusion is that it can say two or more things at the same time. Anyone who tries to make it hold still is missing the point. Donne was both a "spirit in conflict" and "an angel preaching from a cloud."

He needed tradition. His sermons are decisively influenced by the Bible, by the Fathers, by all the stable forms and beliefs of his church. But his prose is as much like that of Augustine or Bernard as Bernini's columns are like those of the early Roman basilicas; the concepts are old, but their seventeenth-century realization belongs to the seventeenth century, and to all the conflicting forces that created these artists at this time.

II

The Baroque Reflection

Now for the next five chapters, I am going to talk exclusively about Donne's sermons, because they constitute the greatest and most important part of his prose writings. Sentence structure makes a good beginning, for even the most casual reader of selections from Donne's sermons cannot help noticing the peculiarly restless and nervous rhythm of his periods. To place a paragraph of Hooker's prose, for example, beside one of Donne's is to realize vividly in literature Jean Rousset's contention that a baroque façade is a Renaissance façade reflected in shimmering water.[1] The long and gracious periods of the Ciceronian Hooker are replaced by even longer ones, whose broken lines, creating a kind of musical stammer, overlap one another; there is as much climax, even as much suspension of thought in Donne as in Hooker, but we are always much more aware in the later writer of smaller units combining in a seemingly tenuous way to make up the whole. The means by which Donne makes this broken, meditative, apparently uncertain movement form an orderly and harmonious sentence enable him to reconcile the Attic ideal of tracing the progress of the reflective mind with the Asiatic aim of persuasive grace, and to legitimatize his own needs and tensions.

Thirty years ago Morris Croll described the two aspects of seventeenth-century baroque prose as the curt style, or *stile coupé,* and the loose period. These he categorized in general as the "two sides of the seventeenth-century mind: its contentiousness, its penetrating wit, its Stoic intensity on the one hand, and its dislike of formalism, its roving and self-exploring curiosity, in brief, its skeptical tendency, on the other."[2] George Williamson, in a book which is almost en-

tirely devoted to discussion of the curt style, has more recently
emphasized its many varieties and has called attention to the fact
that this style could become as schematic as Lyly's,[3] thus presenting
a formalism no less rigid than the Ciceronianism against which all
manifestations of the Senecan style had been supposed to be a reaction. The brief, hopping sentences of Owen Felltham's *Resolves*[4]
illustrate yet another kind of rigidity, that of the pointed sentence,
whose diamond hardness enforces such attention to the individual
period or aphorism that a more encompassing rhythm cannot pos-
sibly be heard. Between these two extremes—the clear surfaces of
the pointed or schematic period and the flowing roundness of the
Ciceronian—range the more pliant varieties of the curt and loose
styles. And because Donne's sentences are more often loose than
curt, we may begin with Croll's definition of the anti-Ciceronian
"long sentence," a definition which need not be challenged, but
which can be both qualified and extended in its specific application
to Donne's sermons.

For Croll, the chief marks of the loose period are coordinating
conjunctions, including subordinating conjunctions and relative pro-
nouns used loosely, the absolute participle, the parenthesis, and, of
course, length. The figure of a circle, which describes the Ciceronian
period because all members point back or forward to a central
climax, or because the sentence ends where it began, cannot be used
to describe the loose style, which "requires rather the metaphor of
a chain, whose links join end to end."[5] Conjunctions frequently bind
their clauses, not to the whole clause or sentence preceding, but
only to its final word: "The period . . . moves straight onward
everywhere from the point it has reached."[6] And it does not reach
its height in the middle and then end composedly like a Ciceronian
sentence; rather it opens outward to conclude at its fullest imaginative or intellectual expansion.

We will certainly find in this rejection of grammatical discipline
much that Donne approves and adopts. But he is not quite so fond
of asymmetry as the Senecan is supposed to be.[7] Nor do his periods
really conform to Croll's chain analogy; Donne is not Ciceronian

in syntax, but in affective intent he is. His sentences, when they do not circle around a single word, are apt to build to a climax before they end; and they are apt to end where they began. The ways in which his sentences are broken up are repetitive and musical as well as thoughtful.

When we look at one of Donne's sentences, it can be rather difficult to determine where it actually begins and ends. As Jonas Barish has said of Ben Jonson's prose, "there is no sense of clearly defined spatial limits."[8] Seventeenth-century punctuation is of course partly responsible; Donne makes no consistent grammatical distinction between semicolon and comma, or among colon, semicolon, and period. But beyond this, he does not even seem to think in terms of sentences; his units of organization are sermon division and paragraph. Croll's distinction between the sentence, which is defined by punctuation and syntax, and the rhetorical period, which is defined by completion of thought or satisfaction of emotion,[9] must therefore be kept in mind during the course of this analysis, for when a choice must be made, it is the period, not the sentence, to which attention ought to be given; only in this way can we see the rhythm and architecture of Donne's style as he conceived it. Paragraph and period are apt to coincide even when several sentences occur within the paragraph; therefore, a single sentence may seem incomplete or disproportioned, when it is really part of a larger harmony.

All the separate devices that Donne uses contribute to what Croll calls the "hovering imaginative order"[10] of the period, lessening its grammatical coherence, increasing its associative or conceptual unity; the period does not progress with grammatical or logical smoothness, but imitates the action of the memory, recovering or recognizing truths quickly or slowly, by means of the meditational process which Croll identifies with the loose style, and which Donne identified with the sermon.[11] But as we shall see especially in analysis of whole periods, there is a comprehensive order to the sentence; its inward and apparently spontaneous development meets an outer and confirming frame.

It is best to begin with minor devices, for one has the feeling that Donne too began here, and by juggling and expanding them, eventually arrived at a sentence. Two most important general characteristics are open form and shifting balance or stress. By open form in sentence structure, I mean that the sentence is not wholly controlled in movement or defined in space by grammar and logic. Rarely contained within itself, it requires, sometimes even for the sake of intelligibility, a context either of other sentences or of thoughts and feelings present in the reader's mind. In its own movement it is uncommitted, and can at almost any point veer off from one kind of progression into another. Tension becomes part of this style when its development obviously stands against normal or expected grammatical order. But free as the form is, it always seeks out its own order and music, and the harmony of these meditative periods is a major source of our delight. By shifting balance or stress, I mean that the sentence does not always appear to have a central point of focus, but that its balance shifts as the reader progresses or as the speaker continues. This is why, if we can speak of a sentence in terms of lines, the lines seem to be broken; the sentence does not unfold in one steady and predictable movement, but is made up of a series of lesser units which in turn receive the center of attention and the emotional stress. These two categories cannot always be clearly differentiated, but for purposes of analysis I shall begin with those devices which seem most important to open form.

The whole period often seems to be pulled out of a brief and disconnected opening—perhaps a Latin or English phrase, or a reference to another writer—which, while it is the basis of all that follows, is absolved from grammatical responsibility to the rest of the sentence by its own elliptical or otherwise isolated form: "And first *videbunt & non contremiscent;* This is a Blessednesse" (VII, No. 13, l. 587); "First then, here are *sorrows;* A passion which we cannot expresse" (IX, No. 18, l. 27); "S. *Augustine* observing aright, That at this time, of which this Text is spoken, The waters enwrapped all the whole substance" (IX, No. 3, ll. 271–72). Here is often the whole meditation in little, the center around which all the subsequent discussion revolves; Donne does not seek to prove, but to elaborate and describe. The fact given may be briefly expressed and simple: "Here are sorrows." The period may then proceed to look at this fact in many different ways and under different aspects, free of any logical responsibility to its theme.

Later, in examination of some whole rhetorical periods, we will see how Donne's famous "that" clauses are marshalled into paragraphs, sometimes with no main clause at all, sometimes with one as brief and grammatically detached as possible. But whether with the help of "that" clauses, or unpatterned sentence fragments, an imaginative elaboration of an idea may spring from almost anything, a word or phrase buried in one sentence serving as pivot for a string of grammatically disconnected thoughts, as here:

As the world is the whole frame of the world, God hath put into it a reproofe, a rebuke, lest it should seem eternall, which is, a sensible decay and age in the whole frame of the world, and every piece thereof. The seasons of the yeare irregular and distempered; the Sun fainter, and languishing; men lesse in stature, and shorter-lived. No addition, but only every yeare, new sorts, new species of wormes, and flies, and sicknesses, which argue more and more putrefaction of which they are engendred. And the Angels of heaven, which did so familiarly converse with men in the beginning of the world, though they may not be doubted to perform to us still their ministeriall assistances, yet they seem so far to have deserted this world, as that they do not appear to us, as they did to those our Fathers (VI, No. 16, ll. 452–63).

"Decay" is the antecedent for the clauses and phrases following the first sentence, but as antecedent it is not only far removed from those clauses, but cut off from them as well by a full stop and by complete lack of grammatical connection. The clauses swing freely from this pivot, accepting, while the reader's eye is on them, the whole weight of the attention, and pulling it outward in a widening imaginative sweep. The absolute participles, aiding the movement by the "becomingness" of their construction, are a device that Croll considered characteristic of the loose period, since they free the writer from previous and from subsequent obligation to the form of his sentence. The finished conclusion of the period is typical of Donne. Shaping his periods into circles of a totally different kind from those associated with Ciceronianism, he likes to begin and end on the same note—the same word, thought, or, as here, the grammatical form of the independent sentence. The period opens imaginatively at the same time that its pattern reaches completion; the closing is a concession to the reader's need for a sense of esthetic fulfillment, but it does not nail the thought down with the finality of a closed period. In content, this period answers Croll's description of the curt style—we will often see how the characteristics of curt and loose periods are shared. The thought here does not progress intellectually—the idea of decay is sufficiently explained in the first sentence; the following members are an imaginative development.

Sometimes Donne creates purposeful syntactic disunity among the parts of sentences by omission of transitional words or by a definite shift in construction; the reader is never allowed to feel that a single line can carry him through the sentence; he is continually confronted by gaps and shifts that force him to recognize that the over-all concept, not the grammatical structure, is the important thing:

So also let us blesse him for that holy tendernesse, to be apt to feele his hand in every accident, and to discerne his presence in every thing that befals us (VI, No. 10, ll. 521–24).

From which example, I humbly offer to you these two general considerations; first, that every man is bound to do something before he dye; and then to that man who hath done those things which the duties of his calling bind him to, death is but a sleep (VIII, No. 7, ll. 32–35).

The thought is perfectly clear in each case; only the grammar does not conform to the expected pattern. But here, as always in Donne, it is apparent that irregularity has its limitations: the unexpected infinitive is immediately joined by another, parallel to it; key words in the second "consideration" echo those in the first. The members create their own music, rather than being forced into it by the requirements of the sentence.

When Donne employs conversation as illustration, he often does it abruptly, without the usual "he said" formula, and this too gives an impression of disruption, of an element forcibly interpolated into the sentence:

> . . . hee shall desire that *day of the Lord,* as that day signifies *affliction* here, with *David, Bonum est mihi quòd humiliasti me,* I am mended by my sicknesse (II, No. 18, ll. 527–29).

> And when hee is thus come to that consideration, Lord! how have I mistaken my selfe, Am I, that thought my selfe, and passed with others, for a sociable, a pleasurable man, and good company; am I a leprous Adulterer, is that my name? . . . he will also say, may that blessing of thine enlarge it selfe farther, that as I am come . . . to know that I mistooke my selfe all this while, so I may proceed to . . . a perfit sifting of my conscience (IX, No. 13, ll. 142–55).

Of course the rapid shift in point of view also contributes to the disjunction of parts and exemplifies an aspect of Donne's style (consideration of a subject from different viewpoints) that we will meet with often. It is also noteworthy that in the second example, the sentence is not so much broken as it is braced apart by the quotation.

Two related techniques may be considered here: the wedging apart of a sentence by interpolation of words independent of it and an unexpected arrangement of words that separates such closely related pairs as coordinate subjects, noun and modifier, pronoun and antecedent. What Barish says of the second technique can often stand for both: "One might, then, tentatively add to Croll's types of baroque effect the kind of tension that arises when the syntax is doing one thing grammatically and another rhythmically."[12] Typical of his illustrations from Jonson is "Men are decay'd, and studies," where the rearrangement endows the clause with force and cadence. Examples in Donne are always less violent and more musical; the difference is a matter of degree and indicative to some extent of final purpose.

Donne particularly likes to keep a word or phrase out of context to use as a refrain at the end of a sentence, a refrain doubly effective because the grammatical suspension makes the reader feel the need for some resolution:

And then, the glorious *qualities,* which shall be imprinted on them, who are saved: first, that salvation is a more extensive thing, and more communicable, then sullen cloystrall, that have walled salvation in a monastery, or in an ermitage, take it to be; or then the over-valuers of their own *purity,* and righteousnesse, which have determined salvation in themselves, take it to be (VI, No. 7, ll. 39–43).

The order of arrangement is not unusual; but the length of the subordinate material and the brevity of the refrain create the effect of something stretched to its limit and then suddenly snapped back into place, the tension of disruption unexpectedly giving way to order.

When Donne dislocates words, the dislocation, as in the grammatical shifts previously mentioned, often introduces a fresh musical pattern:

No liquor comes so clearly, so absolutely from the vessel, not oyle, not milk, not wine, not hony (IX, No. 13, ll. 677–78).

There are words in the text, that will reach to all the Story of S. *Pauls* Conversion, embrace all, involve and enwrap all (VI, No. 10, ll. 23–24).

It is indeed difficult to see what else he might have done with these lists, which shoot off from the sentence into their own harmony. Donne's rhythms, which are for the most part created by repetition of words, are a good deal less subtle than Jonson's; but the rhythms are not necessarily coordinate with grammatical structure; as in Jonson, they come into being by way of a flouting of normal grammar and adoption of patterns that do not hold a steady external course, but imitate the more associative movement of the mind. In each of these examples, the thought, with the syntactic pattern completed, is still preoccupied with one aspect of that pattern, and moves back freely to it again.

A most important device in Donne for achievement of sentence freedom, rhythm, and depth is the parenthesis, also mentioned by Croll as characteristic of baroque style.[13] Croll does not discuss its use, but in the rhetorical pattern which he describes, the parenthesis would be another means to free the writer from strict logical progression, to allow him to qualify or explore an argument, or simply to digress. The parenthesis is often used in this way in *Biathanatos* and in the *Essays,* and not always skillfully. Evelyn Simpson's comment on its excessive use in the *Essays*[14] is really a reflection on Donne's lack of art, for the parenthesis is as frequent in the sermons as it had ever been. But here it serves not as distracting digression or qualification, but as harmonic counterpoint.

Donne uses the parenthesis in his sermons to emphasize or elaborate a point, to illustrate, to explain metaphors, to quote, and to produce an effect similar to that of refrain. In most cases, the interpolation is an independent clause or thought, so that the device almost always seems to increase the freedom of the sentence, to give it an appearance of spontaneity, and to create a slight sense of tension from the forcible incorporation into the period of elements that have no grammatical connection with it. Often, too, the parenthesis gives the sentence an added dimension in its demonstration of one thought lying directly behind another, as reality lies behind symbol, or inspiration behind elaboration. It is another way of releasing the period from strict syntactical confinement.

The use of parenthesis to emphasize or elaborate a point is interestingly shown in the following example, since the period that includes the parenthesis is as suspended as anything in Hooker, and yet remains clearly Donne's:

And truly, howsoever *the love of money be the roote of all evill,* (He cannot mistake that told us so) Howsoever *they that will be rich* (that resolve to be rich by any meanes) *shall fall into many tentations,* Howsoever a hasty desire of being suddenly and prematurely rich, be a dangerous and an obnoxious thing, a pestilent and contagious disease, (for what a perverse and inordinate anticipation and prevention of God and nature is it, to looke for our harvest in May, or to looke for all grains at once? and such a perversenesse is the hasty desire of being suddenly and prematurely rich) yet, to go on industriously in an honest calling, and giving God his leasure, and giving God his portion all the way, in Tithes, and in Almes, and then, still to lay up something for posterity, is that, which God does not onely permit and accept from us, but command to us, and reward in us (II, No. 14, ll. 175–87).

The two "howsoever" clauses, with their parentheses, that open the series, set up an expectation in the reader that prepares him for the longer pair; this order in interruption is something that he had not achieved in *Biathanatos* or in the *Essays*. The parentheses themselves are three asides;[15] it is as if Donne were giving a guided tour of his own sentence; and thus an added dimension is provided, Donne pointing from outside into his prose, and behind it to Scripture. This long and strongly buttressed opening supports a main thought which, with some overlapping, moves straight forward until it spreads briefly again at the close. The first movements of Donne's sentences are characteristically much more massive than their conclusions, even when the conclusion bears the weight of the thought.

One particular sort of parenthetical emphasis that he sometimes employs is exclamation: "If his eye be upon me, and mine upon him, (O blessed reflexion! O happy reciprocation! O powerfull correspondence! *Ipse evellet, He will plucke my feet out of the net,* though I be almost ensnared, almost entangled, he will snatch me out of the fire, deliver me from the tentation" (IX, No. 16, ll. 674–79). Here the interpolation gives the effect of a man reading his own words for the first time; he makes himself both preacher and congregation. And it is generally characteristic of Donne, both in imagery and sentence structure, to leave nothing unsaid. If his writing is thought to be unevocative, it is partly because the image or the thought cannot be taken farther than he does take it along the lines which he establishes for its movement. And these lines are as much psychological or emotional as they are pictorial or descriptive. In his sermons he constantly acknowledges the reaction of the reader to the thing read. The meditation that he presents to the congregation is his own meditation, as he is the actor in his own drama. And although this technique is unexceptionable in its manifestation here, unexceptionable esthetically anywhere, we may sometimes have reason to question its spiritual validity in the art of preaching, to ask whether the lack of distinction between subject and object here is not a blending of Donne with his sermon, rather than an involvement of the congregation with the thing preached.

The parenthesis is frequently used to illustrate a point, often very vividly: "wilt thou rely upon the Prophet, he can teach thee; or upon thy Brother, he does love thee; or upon thy Son, he should love thee; or the Wife of thy bosome, she will say she loves thee; or upon thy Friend, he is as thine owne soule?" (III, No. 12, ll. 193–96). These are examples of unmarked parantheses, sentences interpolated as illustrations without the expected punctuation. Of course in a spoken sermon, the two methods are not distinguishable; when the sermon is read in printed form, absence of parenthesis makes the juxtaposition more striking.

This quotation is also an illustration of the added dimension. Donne alternates his questions with what he takes to be the unspoken reactions of the reader, achieving an expression of double consciousness, and the repetitions of "thee" create a running refrain that makes the second consciousness seem almost continuous with the first. It is also, of course, another example of incorporation into the work of art of the supposed feelings of the person experiencing it.

He uses parenthesis to give a running explanation of metaphor, again bringing his meaning together from two different directions, doing the reader's work as well as his own. The following period shows clearly how arbitrary the punctuation marks often are: Donne moves freely from metaphor to translation of metaphor, and the sentence pockets that are the explanations are like glosses incorporated into the text:

Of Silver (of the virtue of thankfulness) there are whole Mines, books written by Philosophers, and a man may grow rich in that mettle, in that virtue, by digging in that Mine, in the Precepts of moral men; of this Gold (this virtue of Repentance) there is no Mine in the Earth; in the books of Philosophers, no doctrine of Repentance; this Gold is for the most part in the washes; this Repentance in matters of tribulation (II, No. 11, ll. 4–10).

This kind of weaving back and forth between word sign and symbol has of course a directly didactic purpose. But despite its conventional and practical intention, it does help to illuminate another facet of Donne's mind—a kind of indifference about the relative value of sign or symbol. Dennis Quinn has pointed out that when the text fails to supply him with a ready figure, he simply works with words as if they were images;[16] and he works with images as if they were things. There is not always a clear distinction for Donne among images, signs of things, and things; all can seem to him equally real, and at the same time equally removed from true reality. So the parentheses in this passage fall away; the two readings acquire equal and independent value.

Donne's concept of the sermon as meditation upon a Biblical text also leads him to the parenthesis as a way of reminding the listener of the Scripture from which the sermon is drawn. Here the interpolations provide an echo for Donne's discussion, but are also reminders of the original inspiration for the sermon itself:

> I know no figurative speech so often iterated in the Scriptures, as the name of a *House;* Heaven and Earth are called by that name, and wee, who being upon earth, have our conversation in heaven, are called so too, (*Christ hath a House, which House wee are*) And as God builds his House, (*The Lord builds up Ierusalem,* saith *David*) so hee furnishes it, he plants Vineyards, Gardens, and Orchards about it, He layes out a way to it, (*Christ is the way*) He opens a gate into it, (*Christ is the gate*) (VII, No. 12, ll. 85–92).

These quotation parentheses occasionally so heavily interlard the text of the sermon that a macaronic effect is produced, Donne's words alternating with those of the Bible (II, No. 14, ll. 69–82). The characteristic independence of the parenthesis from the structure of the sentences gives the impression that two voices are speaking alternately—that of Donne and that of the person whom Donne would call the Holy Ghost. Donne seems to have left spaces in his prose through which the Scriptures are to be heard, and thus again another dimension, or another aspect, is added to the period.

The parenthesis gains rhythm only in its interaction with the rest of the sentence; its incorporation into the period gives it the depth, and the sense of refrain and double consciousness that counterpoint the main theme. By free development of separate clauses, by construction of periods from themes briefly and independently stated at the outset, by the creation of syntactic disunity among the parts of the sentence, by separation of words ordinarily joined together, and by frequent use of parentheses, Donne liberates the sentence from any inevitable grammatical constraint. Grammar appears to give thought formal status independent of writer or hearer, making it into something that exists "out there," an object apparently separated from its subject. The more grammar is disregarded, the more aware one becomes that the sentence is spoken by one person, and heard by another; the clauses, which must have something to relate to, seem to conform themselves to the movement of the perceiving mind, or to the movement of the mind producing them. Thus this style is shaped to emphasize interior rather than exterior meaning, and blurs the esthetic threshold. At the same time, another boundary disappears—the outline of the sentence itself. A period not shaped chiefly by grammar has no fixed beginning and end, and the mind easily moves beyond and behind it. The sentence becomes not so much an arrangement of signs standing for something else, as the visible portion of something else into which its edges and open spaces recede. These are the meanings of open form in Donne's writing.

The next group of devices, those that involve shifting balance or stress, all contribute to the sense that the speaker's thought unfolds with the progress of the period. The sentences of Milton and Hooker are based upon the main clause, or the climax, toward which all the subordinate members point. Donne often rests his periods momentarily upon a single word or phrase or clause not grammatically central. Thus, his emphases are more distributed, and the reader has a sense of wavering balances, of accents shifting from one center to another as the sentence progresses. Because it is not so grammatically stable as a Ciceronian period, it is able to foster this characteristic impression of constant movement and elusiveness. The Ciceronian sentence is there to be accepted. The more delicate balance of Donne's is calculated to respond to the action of the reader's mind.

We can see this happening very clearly in a device which (at the risk of having it become confused with the cursus, the word for the classical prose rhythms used to point up conclusions of period or clause) I should like to call the run. Elizabethan and Jacobean rhetorics gave the name "heaping" to the practice of piling up synonymous words or phrases in a sentence,[17] but, as the name suggests, this was often a disorderly and purposeless business, justifiable only as an expression of an exuberant and hyperbolical spirit. The word "run," with its connotations of rhythm and harmony, more aptly describes Donne's technique.

In writing his sentences, Donne often begins with the word, and lets doubling and piling up, first of words, then of phrases, very largely determine the final structure of the period. Sometimes this is the textbook kind of thing—using two words where one will do, or heaping up adjectives or nouns. But more often the runs represent the making of a thought, the associative progress of a mind's movement, as one word reminds it of a better one, and the better one, again, of a best. Even his doublets illustrate this movement in little. Very infrequently he formally disavows his first choice (epanorthosis): "of the Distillation, nay Inundation, of the largenesse, nay the infinitenesse of the blessings, and benefits of Almighty God" (VII, No. 14, ll. 4–6). He purposely leaves the rejected words in the sentence in order to emphasize the deliberateness of the hyperbole—to make it seem, even, less hyperbole than literal truth. His usual manner of doubling looks more spontaneous: "the lightnesse, the hollownesse of a spunge" (IV, No. 13, l. 559); "but ceremoniall, but hypocriticall complements" (II, No. 6, ll. 524–25). Out of so simple a device, used more than once in almost every sentence, Donne brings several results. First, a sense of groping excitement and urgency is felt in the preacher's tone, both because of the brachylogiac[18] rapidity of the device and because of its indication that a man is speaking while he thinks. There is also, as in the example of epanorthosis, contrast value: the word "infinitenesse" seems stronger when it is substituted for "largenesse" before one's eyes. What is conveyed is not so much the fact itself as the realization of a fact, for example, that ceremonial compliments are often hypocritical or that a sponge is light because it is hollow. Donne is leading his congregation through a meditation, and the process of thought involved in meditation has really as much to do with the style of his sermons as do any conclusions from which they begin and to which they return again.

Although little of the material in the books of ecclesiastical rhetoric can much illuminate Donne's sentence structure, I would like to mention here one figure from these books which seems relevant to the runs that I am about to discuss. Keckermann and Erasmus, and all the subsequent authors of handbooks inspired and influenced by them, are not teachers of rhetoric in the sense that Thomas Wilson and George Puttenham are. They handle the figures as illustrations of devices by which the preacher can arouse the emotions of his audience, and they purposely limit the number of schemes or tropes mentioned in order to remind Ecclesiastes (Erasmus' name for the preacher) that he is not a rhetorician, but the instrument of the Holy Ghost, that only those figures may be used which come most naturally to mind and prove most practical. Therefore, the fact that most of these books list *incrementum* and *congeries,* which are, respectively, types of climax and heaping, is probably significant. It is explained that by *incrementum* particularly, the affections of the hearers can be aroused, and useful contrasts can be made between the lesser and the greater, as each word in succession becomes more intense.[19]

Specific kinds of runs are represented in the secular rhetoric books (for example, a run in which a noun precedes several verbs is called "diazeugma"),[20] but because the parts of speech involved are really less important than the different effects achieved, it is more helpful to make the distinctions on bases other than theirs. The first kind of run, then, is no more than an expanded doubling, but its expansion adds climax to the previously discussed qualities: "There is a considerable, a remarkable, indeed a singular manner of expressing it, (perchance you finde not the like in all the Bible)" (II, No. 14, ll. 223–25); "for the losse, or for the absence, or for the unkindnes, or imagination of an unkindness of a friend" (II, No. 1, ll. 601–2). Sometimes he dwells upon a single word, staying very close to its original meaning, but pulling that meaning out into expanded versions or more vivid renderings. The word comes to life and grows before the reader's eyes, and the effect, again, is of a meditation in little. Often a Latin word is the basis for this: *"lux vestra,* your light, the light of good works" (X, No. 3, ll. 265–66); "a valediction, a parting, a taking leave, (shall I say so?) a shaking hands with God" (IX, No. 9, ll. 149–50). A third kind of run indicates temporal progression: "there is nothing so little in his hand, as cannot discomfort thee, discomfit thee, dissolve and powr out, attenuate and annihilate the very marrow of thy soul" (II, No. 2, ll. 522–24). Finally, the effect of climax may be achieved by increasing emotional intensity, expressed by increased vividness of expression: "his extortions, his oppressions, his grindinge of the poore by color of an office" (II, No. 6, ll. 229–31); or by increased intensity in meaning or action: "to the shame, to the scorne, to the paine, to the death of the Crosse for us" (IX, No. 17, ll. 184–85).

One example of this last kind of run can here illustrate briefly the manner in which the run can come to dominate the sentence: "But when this *Discipline* prevaild not upon them, *God sold* them away, *gave* them away, *cast* them away, in the tempest, in the whirl-winde, in the inundation of his indignation, and scatterd them as so much dust in a windy day, as so many broken strawes upon a wrought Sea" (VII, No. 2, ll. 245–49). The subordinate clause leads into the center of the thought "God sold," from which the members of the run move outward in a widening imaginative sweep. From the word "sold" as Donne meditates upon it come those more extreme examples of God's displeasure, until the repeated "away" combines with "cast" to imply the never expressed idea of a cast-away, which makes him think of a storm and opens the sentence into the second run; then by the same process "storm" grows to "whirlwind" and "inundation" and these two words move together into the simultaneous images of the dusty storm and the stormy sea.

What should be particularly stressed here, as something which has perhaps not received sufficient attention until now, is the way in which Donne shapes the period to join the two theoretically opposed effects of order and spontaneity. We have seen how it grows out of his meditation upon the single word. But we can see too that he first balances three verbs against three nouns and then, still keeping the same subject, widens the period to its close with two parallel analogies. The first run moves with a heavy bouncing beat on the three verbs; in the second run, the repeated words precede the stressed words, the nouns, which are longer and lighter; the final pair is very much longer and wider in scope. The period is so constructed that each succeeding rhythm accepts the whole force and direction of the sentence. The changing rhythms play a part somewhat analogous to that of the separate clauses of a curt period, imparting a sense of separateness of tone to each section of the sentence.

Many of the runs have a noticeable prose rhythm that binds them together. Sometimes, with the same word repeated at beginning and end of a run, the intervening beat is doubled in speed. The key word is emphasized at the beginning, while a regular, relatively slow rhythm is established; then, with the expected word suspended and the words of the run laid down in rapid succession, the speed of the rhythm is quickened both in anticipation of the return of the key word and in adjustment to the more staccato quantity of the run. These are some examples: "thy soule, thy weake soule, thy sicke, and foule, and sinfull soule" (VI, No. 7, ll. 287–88); "may not see him scourged again, wounded, torn and mangled again" (III, No. 9, ll. 449–50); "the stones shall not brain us, overwhelm and smother, and bury us" (II, No. 3, ll. 629–30); "The person must actuate it self, dilate, extend and propagate it self" (VIII, No. 7, ll. 145–46).

It is important in analyzing these rhythms to recognize that one particular run never controls a sentence. We have seen that even when the whole period is dominated by the growth of one run out of another, the rhythms change and, far from becoming hypnotic, break against one another. Most of Donne's sentences are very long, most of his runs are very short, and so this rhythmic device often takes a minor and momentary part in shaping by variation the larger and more comprehensive structure of the period. For example, one of the runs quoted is taken from a sentence made up, for the most part, of a number of long "that" clauses, and, in context, it looks like this:

That those Angels which see Christ Jesus now, sate down in glory at the right hand of his Father; all sweat wip'd from his Browes, and all teares from his Eyes; all his Stripes heal'd, all his Blood stanch'd, all his Wounds shut up, and all his Beauty returned there; when they look down hither, to see the same Christ in thee, may not see him scourged again, wounded, torn and mangled again, in thy blasphemings, nor crucified again in thy irreligious conversation (III, No. 9, ll. 444–51).

What the run does here is to speed up the rhythm for a brief intensification of emotion that sharply contrasts this series with the one preceding it.

A more traditional way of binding the run together is by like word-endings, or homoeoteleuton: "the right use of the true and naturall, the native and genuine, the direct, and literall, and uncontrovertible sense of the words" (VII, No. 4, ll. 67–69). Notice here the movement from two pairs of adjectives to the run of three that concludes the series, as well as the skill with which the homoeoteleuton of the "l" ending is sounded once in the first pair, and then returned to again in the final words of the run, employed just enough to hold the run together and to emphasize the importance of the last words—it emphasizes without gaining ascendance over the meaning.

Almost all the runs employ repetition of short words—articles, conjunctions, or adverbs—to bind the series, to maintain order in variety, to ensure emphasis on individual words, and to shape the rhythm. Unmitigated brachylogia very seldom occurs, for the effects of speed and sharpness that it creates are generally accompanied by a stripped spareness that is foreign to Donne, whose style is both copious and musical. As George Williamson remarks in another context, "scriptural style for Donne would not have entitled the Holy Ghost to membership in the Royal Society";[21] nor would the same Holy Ghost, as inspirer of sermons, have enabled Donne himself to apply.

Although the run may depend on context for completion of its meaning and rhythm, the end of the series is often set off from the previous words, its close marked either, as previously illustrated, by return of the key word or by shift in rhythm: "and receive a soveraigne tincture, and a lively verdure, and a new life into my dead teares" (II, No. 14, ll. 483-84); "That brightnesse, that clearnesse, that peace, and tranquillity, that calme and serenity, that acquiescence, and security of the Conscience" (IX, No. 11, ll. 466–68). The alternating homoeoteleuton of this run (every other word, after the first pair, ends in "ity") makes the run with its conclusion into something like a poetic stanza, an effect that we will later see achieved again in different ways in larger units. Rhyme, less frequently employed, and always with enjambement, produces similar results: "Dost thou love learning, as it is contracted, brought to a quintessence, wrought to a spirit, by *Philosophers?* the eldest of all them in that whole book, *Quod Deus latens, simul & patens est,* testifies all that, and nothing but that, that as there is nothing so dark, so there is nothing so cleare, nothing so remote, nothing so neare us, as God" (IV, No. 6, ll. 127–32). I have included some of the context here in order to re-emphasize the fact that these devices do not dominate the period. Rhyme begins to be felt in the paired verbs of the question, is picked up again in the homoeoteleuton of the quotation from Trismegistus, and comes out strongly in the closing paradoxes. But the chimes differ and are used differently each time. They serve to heighten the paragraph at its close and to point antitheses; they do not override the thought. The chiming Latin prose which here inspires Donne's is often, through the Middle Ages, far more mannered than his; and although he justifies his use of music by frequent references to the harmonies of his predecessors, his sentences are never as sweetly cadenced as those, for example, of Hugh of St. Victor, or even of the mellifluous St. Bernard, whom Donne loved and to whom Lipsius, a pioneer in the Senecan style, gave his approval.[22]

I have been concerned to make this clear because many of these rhythmic devices are so close to revivalist preaching techniques that this section might otherwise be considered further proof of T. S. Eliot's claim that Donne is a spellbinder who belongs in the same category with Billy Sunday.[23] There is some truth in the remark; he does play upon the emotions of his audience (the figure of the congregation as a stringed instrument played upon by the preacher is at least as old as Gregory's *Pastoral Care*) ;[24] the insistent chimes and repetitions of his runs are one of his major techniques for doing so. But Donne thinks of himself rather than the congregation as his instrument. The broken, nervous rhythms express his own sensibility, which is a good deal more complex, more self-conscious, and —I must say—more baroque than that of the revivalist. And the runs are justifiable in terms of meditational purpose, for Donne's baroque is not that extreme and mindless variety that one meets in the degeneration of the style. The rhythms illustrate and change with his thought, breaking, re-forming, and widening within the scope of paragraph or period, and very often these lesser rhythms serve to emphasize or set apart one meaning that deserves particular attention, to direct the memory as well as the emotion. When the run itself, or the word that inspires the run, is the period's center, the rhythms underline the outward opening of the thought, as it moves, not smoothly, but with a series of pronounced rhythmic and emotional changes. The fact that the runs are not simply heaps of words, but maps of a mind thinking and feeling, provides them simultaneously with meaning and with music.

When the run is part of a long sentence that has its own order, it can often achieve an importance greater than its grammatical place in the sentence would indicate, because, ignoring the grammar in order to fulfill its own development, it creates its separate musical order, its own beginning and end, and its separate emphasis and meaning. Even though these merge with the larger meaning, they are in a sense set apart, and to some extent their "apartness" breaks against the orderly progression of the period. The run itself shifts its emphases as it proceeds when each succeeding word modifies or cancels the preceding one. And the completeness of the run in any case takes the reader's attention while it is in progress, no matter what incomplete grammatical constructions it may have left behind. At its close the period rocks back again to the main thought.

The run may be combined with a sentence device by which part or all of a period is made to pivot on a word or phrase not grammatically prominent, which makes the word seem a freely and spontaneously chosen center for associative, though orderly development. "Not" and "never" are the words most frequently so used, and the very fact that negatives are singled out for this repetition is important because they create a minor pull against whatever positive point he may be making: "they never, never went about to pull them out; never resisted a tentation, never lamented a transgression, never repented a recidivation" (II, No. 1, ll. 609–10). Contrast with a textbook example of its rhetorical equivalent, diazeugma, shows how differently Donne has used this figure, defined as one in which one noun serves many verbs: "The people of Rome destroyed Numance, overthrew Carthage, cast down Corinth, and raced Fregels."[25] The repetitions of "never" in the Donne illustration make that word more important than the pronoun, so that the sentence is shaped out of its emotional rather than its grammatical subject: "they were the sins of some that shall never thank thee, never know that thou borest their sins, never know that they had any such sins to bee born" (II, No. 1, ll. 799, 801). The building up of the series upon this grammatically off-center pivot gives it both a freedom from grammatical constraint, and an ability seemingly to rock the sentence to one side, until whatever follows shifts the emphasis again.

Another kind of technique, which illustrates in little a characteristic form of Donne's periods, creates a disproportion in sentence weight, by massing most of the period in what seems to be the wrong place, at a point which does not coincide with the main import of the statement. The following is an example of the heavily weighted subject:

The voyce of God whom he hath contemned, and wounded, The voyce of the Preacher whom he hath derided and impoverished, The voyce of the poore, of the Widow, of the Orphans, of the prisoner, whom he hath oppressed, knocke at his doore, and would enter, but there is no roome for them, he is so full (III, No. 10, ll. 425–29).

Donne's disregard for grammar is immediately apparent in the grammatical ascription of the knocking to the agency of the voices—the emotional impact carries the sense. The shift in tone and perspective is important and makes the sentence successful; the copious description, from their viewpoint, of the crowd of victims outside, shifts to a quiet and ironic description of the man within, supposedly from his viewpoint. Yet there is some strain; the word "knocke," when it appears, seems at once too thin to be the predicate of such a heap of subject matter and too detached from any specific subject; what should be the major portion of the sentence rises like a narrow spire from its heavy base. The clearly controlled ironic conclusion forces the massive subject to be part of a sentence, to cohere, and the change in texture, while it seems to weaken the structure of the sentence, increases its emotional force.

Disproportion is often created with other parts of speech, for this weighting of a thought is only an expansion of a run and can occur wherever a run occurs. The effect can also be achieved with a disrupted or oddly made sentence. Here long prepositional phrases, caught between two different constructions, give the appearance of disproportion:

And, though he that is rich with a good conscience may, in a good measure, do so too, (sleepe in peace) yet not so out of the spheare and latitude of envy, and free from the machinations, and supplantations, and underminings of malicious men, that feed upon the confiscations, and build upon the ruines of others, as the poore man is (II, No. 14, ll. 203–8).

Since the poor man does not appear until the end of the sentence and since the phrases describing his freedom are couched in terms of the things he is free from and because the verb is arbitrarily changed at the end from "do" to "is," most of the sentence attaches itself to the rich man, the most available subject. The disproportion is thus achieved by a dislocation that leaves "as the poore man is" to stand briefly for the simplicity of the poor man's existence, as the clause is really shoved out of the mass of complications that do not concern him.

Another balance-shifting device is a kind of repetition which can best be described as overlapping. It is akin to the rhetorical climax, which marks progressive stages of intensity by repetition, in each phrase, of the final word immediately preceding it. Donne uses real climax often, as in the following illustration: "But *Vincenti &* *credenti*, to him that beleeves aright, and overcomes all tentations to a wrong beliefe, God shall give the accomplishment of fulnesse, and fulnesse of joy, and joy rooted in glory, and glory established in eternity, and this eternity is God" (V, No. 13, ll. 834–37). The word *gradatio* is even better suited to description of this figure, which proceeds to its conclusion by a series of overlapping steps.

Another related device, which should first be mentioned briefly, is immediate repetition for emphasis (epizeuxis): "though he kill me, kill me, kill me . . . yet I will trust in him" (IV, No. 1, ll. 497–98); "which of us ever, ever sayes over that short Prayer, with a deliberate understanding" (VII, No. 10, ll. 259–60). This is one way of holding the beat, or focus of attention on a word or phrase, forcibly increasing the weight of a single element in a sentence.

What I have called overlapping has some relation to both these figures, and even more to anadiplosis, a scheme in which the final word of a member is repeated at the beginning of the following member. The more interesting instances of overlapping in Donne, however, interrupt the normal flow of a thought, rather than serving as a kind of intensified punctuation. The following are examples: "You must depart, depart by death, before yee come to that rest" (II, No. 14, ll. 736–37); "the body shall rest, rest in the sense of that glory" (V, No. 10, ll. 572–73); "And when he hath confest all, all that he remembers" (V, No. 16, ll. 93–94). The various ways in which he employs this frequently occurring figure constitute one reason why one can say that, while Hooker builds his sentences in one continuous line, Donne makes his with many short, overlapping lines. We are reminded again of the broken outlines of the building reflected in water. It is no doubt a convenient way to pause for breath; but the continuity is broken, and the words that follow the comma seem to depend only on the one word before and after it, rather than on all to which they might logically be related. And there is a sense of spontaneity, of the second part springing out of the momentary inspiration signalized by the repetition.

The balance of the sentence also shifts in the process of this transition; there is an apparent finality in the first phrases that appears to center the weight of the meaning within their scope; when the overlapping is followed by an extension of the thought, the balance shifts to accommodate the enlarged intention. The repeated word, which had been only the end of a clause, becomes a fulcrum.

The overlapping can be much more complicated, and somewhat less obvious:

But yet, come thou so farre: Come, or be content to be brought, to be brought by example, to be brought by a statute, to be brought by curiosity, come any way to touch the hem of his garment, yea the hem of his servant, of *Aarons* garment, and thou shalt participate of the sweet ointment, which flowes from the head to the hem of the garment (V, No. 17, ll. 198–203).

The word "come," being repeated, suggests an alternative that develops into a run of prepositional phrases bound by the repeated infinitive; the next line begins again with "come" and progresses so far as to explain the immediate purpose of coming; then another brief overlapping amplifies on the garment to be touched; and finally the sentence proceeds to its real point and conclusion. These units do have a forward movement; their meaning is clearly only completed when the sentence ends. But they do not move smoothly; there is no one line that carries us surely to the climax, but rather a series of restless, constantly re-forming movements.

In connection with overlapping, I must mention Donne's habit of following Latin quotations with an English translation. It would in fact be difficult to overestimate the pervasive importance of Donne's

use of Latin in his sermons. Quotation was of course so characteristic of Anglican preaching that it came to be considered a metaphysical vice;[26] but the fact that Donne shares this habit with his
contemporaries makes it no less relevant to our understanding of
his writing, particularly when his individual uses of it coincide with
a major stylistic landmark.

A Latin phrase may be used to shift the construction in such a
way that what follows the Latin depends upon it and not upon
what has gone before; during the pause for overlapping of Latin
with English, the direction of the sentence changes:

> S. *Augustine* cites, and approves that saying of the morall Philosopher,
> *Omnes odit, qui malos odit,* he that hates ill men, hates all men, for if a
> man will love none but honest men, where shall he finde any exercise, any
> object of his love? (III, No. 18, ll. 106–9)

More often, the overlapping is as simple as when both phrases are
in English, and identical: "and him I shall see *In carne, in the flesh,*
which is another degree of Exaltation in mine Exinanition" (III,
No. 3, ll. 769–70). Wherever introduced, the Latin imparts a depth
and shift in tone to the sentence and a momentary pause that jogs
the period from smooth progression. And the act of translation itself
is a kind of transformation of material analogous to all the metaphorical and literary kinds of change which Donne effects in his
writing and which are a major character of his style.

We have already noticed, in discussion of parentheses, Donne's
habit of translating his metaphors. Such translations often form, not
only parentheses, but also another kind of overlapping, as in the
following illustrations:

> Though thou have a West, a darke and a sad condition, that thou art but
> earth, a man of infirmities, and ill counsailed in thy selfe: yet thou hast herein
> a North, that scatters and dispells these clouds, that God proposes to thee
> (IX, No. 2, ll. 289–92).

> But as Physitians are forced to doe sometimes, to turne upon the present cure
> of some vehement symptome, and accident, and leave the consideration of
> the maine disease for a time, so Christ leaves the doctrine of the kingdome for
> the present, and does not rectifie them in that *yet,* but for this pestilent symp-

tome, this malignant accident of precedency, and ambition of place, he corrects that first (III, No. 6, ll. 43–48).

Parenthesis, run, and multiple subject, although they have their own uses, contribute as well to the general effect of overlapping. His constant use of repetition, too, calls attention to this device and increases the force of the intense and nervous style.

One final set of figures must be briefly mentioned. Donne, like his colleague Lancelot Andrewes, habitually used some of those flashier schemes which are generally linked with the metaphysical or witty style. Neither man seems to hunt them out; they are part of a natural mode of expression. In Donne, they act as another kind of emphasis, another way to create a center around which the thought swirls briefly before continuing. There is no need to subject the reader to a display of rhetorical terms, and I shall illustrate with only two: antimetabole and paronomasia. Antimetabole is a reversal of order of the words of a phrase already written: "For these men that died in their sins, that sinned in their dying" (VI, No. 18, l. 394); "he . . . *delivers* us over, to *punishments* for *sinne,* and to *sin* for *punishment*" (VII, No. 2, ll. 235–36). This figure momentarily boxes in the thought, and holds the attention, by its boldness; then the sentence breaks free again, leaving the scheme behind like a knot on a string.

Paronomasia is a play on words that sound almost alike, although their meaning is different: "But thou must have teares first: first thou must come to this weeping, or else God cannot come to this wiping" (VIII, No. 8, l. 346); "sin hath not onely a place, but a Palace" (II, No. 3, ll. 175–76). Again, the figure is momentarily arresting as it unites or distinguishes between two different ideas; it makes its contribution, creates a pause, but does not dominate.

We have now explored in relative isolation a number of devices formative to Donne's periods. Those that release him from dependence upon strict logical progression are the free development of separate clauses; the elaboration of ideas out of a nucleus independently laid down at the beginning of a sentence; the use of words grammatically subordinate as pivots upon which can turn a number of words, phrases, or clauses; interpolation into the period of quotation and parenthesis; and grammatical dislocation. There is no absolute freedom. The reader is certainly aware of logical structure, and this awareness of a framework that sometimes bends, breaks, or vanishes creates a tension that is fostered by real conflict between grammatical and rhetorical development. Yet if this tension implies rebellion against constraint, it also represents an attempt to find a flexible musical pattern that can change with the meditative progress of the sentence.

By means of his relative freedom, Donne is enabled to build sentences whose emphases shift as they are read; the weight of the period is distributed variously and may rest briefly upon something not even grammatically connected with it, like the parenthesis, or upon something momentarily singled out from its place in the period for disproportionate emphasis, like the run, the multiple subject, or the flashy figure. Overlapping increases the apparent tenuousness of the forward movement, constantly creating shifts or pauses that help to make unclear the exact outline of the sentence. Parentheses, quotations, and Latin phrases add dimensions or depths that a normal period could not possess, by presenting a background, a double consciousness, or double point of view. To the metaphorical extent that clauses printed on a page can become multidimensional and unstable, Donne has made them so.

It is time now to look at some whole sentences. No period or paragraph in Donne is altogether complete, but by analyzing some long passages, some rhetorical periods, we can certainly arrive at a fuller understanding of the pattern of his style than has been possible so far.

Morris Croll has said that it would be merely pedantic to attempt classification of all the varieties of the loose period,[27] and even when our inquiry is confined to a single author, his stricture holds. The most accurate and final statement on Donne's sermon style could at best indicate some typical ways in which his sentences are made. Analyses of single sermons or courses of sermons will always reveal new patterns, suited to the expression of particular meanings. But the sentences which I am about to describe are fairly representative; and even in others that take different shapes, the general tone and technique remain the same.

Because I have so much stressed the prevalence of the loose period in Donne, I had best first make clear that any page of his sermons will reveal examples of what Croll calls the *stile coupé;* some critics have in fact believed that Donne's usual unit is the short sentence, and I shall have to explain, after giving some illustrations to support their view, why I have chosen to put my emphasis elsewhere.

There are, first of all, many examples of a short sentence similar to that which Thomas Browne employs. The characteristics that Croll gives to the curt style are studied brevity of members; hovering, imaginative order; asymmetry; and omission of the ordinary syntactic ligatures.[28] The following are examples of this mode in Donne:

Here we are but *Viatores,* Passengers, way-faring men; This life is but the high-way, and thou canst not build thy hopes here; Nay, to be buried in the high way is no good marke; and therefore bury not thy selfe, thy labours, thy affections upon this world (III, No. 13, ll. 499–502).

The Honours of this world, are farre from being *weights,* or *fraights,* or *ballast* to carry us steady; they are but light *froths,* but leaven, but fermentation, that puffes and swells us up. And they are as farre from being *eternall;* for, in every family, we know, in which father, or grandfather the Honour began, and wee know not how soon, or how ignominiously it may end; but such ends of worldly Honours, we see every day (IX, No. 4, ll. 233–39).

Analysis of these periods need not detain us long, for their characteristics are fairly obvious. The members are brief, and move rather by imaginative than by logical development; each examines various aspects of a metaphor. Subject and construction shift from member to member, with repetition of construction only once in the second quotation, and the length of the members also varies. Semicolons rather than conjunctions are used to connect the clauses. But it is important to notice that the constant use of various kinds of repetitions, runs and doublets, together with rhyme in the second quotation, distinguishes these periods from those of others.

There are times when Donne's curt periods assume the manner of Thomas Browne, whose short sentences are for the most part more clipped and pointed, more aphoristic, and more stable. Here, for comparison, are two very similar passages, the first from a sermon of Donne's, the second from the *Religio Medici:*

Adam sinnd, and *I* suffer; I *forfeited* before I had any *Possession,* or could claime any *Interest;* I had a *Punishment,* before I had a *being,* And *God* was displeased with *me* before *I* was *I;* I was built up scarce 50. years ago, in my Mothers womb, and I was cast down, almost 6000. years agoe, in *Adams* loynes; I was *borne* in the last *Age* of the world, and *dyed* in the first (VII, No. 2, ll. 174–80).

Before Abraham was, I am, is the saying of Christ; yet is it true in some sense, if I say it of my self; for I was not onely before my self, but Adam, that is, in the Idea of God, and in the decree of that Synod held from all Eternity. And in this sense, I say, the World was before the Creation, and at an end before it had a beginning; and thus was I dead before I was alive: though my grave be England, my dying place was Paradise: and Eve miscarried of me before she conceived of Cain.[29]

The extreme emphasis on the "I," the lack of variation in the clauses, and the tone of voice (Donne's "murmuring") in this period still distinguish it from Browne's. Otherwise, the method is the same. Each single member is entirely distinct, arresting the attention by use of paradox, aphorism, or antithesis; what imaginative growth there is seems to occur from clause to clause, while in the first type of Donne's short sentence growth happens everywhere, chiefly because of repetitions and runs. And if Donne ordinarily prefers the first manner to the second, and a long sentence to either one, developing his thoughts openly, urgently, amply, and obviously, the reasons are not far to seek, in the different personalities of the two men and in the different requirements of their vehicles of expression.

The curt period is more characteristic of Donne's early, than of his later sermon style. As the wit becomes less obvious, the paradoxes less pronounced, as he grows older and his faith grows stronger, so the harmonies of period and paragraph more and more override the brevities of the curt style, which remain as contrast and variation with the loose period. Certainly his method changes according to the demands of his text.[30] And it changes according to the character of his congregation: he is an orator at St. Paul's, a wit at Lincoln's Inn, a scholar at Whitehall, and a parson at St. Dunstan's.[31] In general, however, the brief period is not as good a key to an understanding of his writing as the loose period is. Except in the earlier sermons, we do not often find any number of curt sentences, of the kind we have been looking at, placed one after another. When short sentences do occur, they generally have the characteristics of his earliest prose; they are linked to what goes before and after, and are not given sufficient point, sufficient individual and self-contained structure to be considered apart from their context. Donne's medium is the paragraph, and even when it is partly composed of short sentences, the paragraph is what ought to receive most of our attention.

Donne's "that" clauses are justly famous, and it is worth pointing out that one of the best known of his passages is not a sentence at all, but a collection of thoughts held together only because they are, for most of the period, all "that" clauses and because they constitute a meditation upon the meaning of falling out of the hands of God. The period of which they are the greater part comes to a rich conclusion in a restatement of theme that completes the circular sweep so characteristic of his paragraphs. And here I must commence quoting at length:

. . . but to fall out of the hands of the living God, is a horror beyond our expression, beyond our imagination.

That God should let my soule fall out of his hand, into a bottomlesse pit, and roll an unremovable stone upon it, and leave it to that which it finds there, (and it shall finde that there, which it never imagined,   5 till it came thither) and never thinke more of that soule, never have more to doe with it. That of that providence of God, that studies the life and preservation of every weed, and worme, and ant, and spider, and toad, and viper, there should never, never any beame flow out upon me; that that God who looked upon me, when I was nothing, and   10 called me when I was not, as though I had been, out of the womb and depth of darknesse, will not looke upon me now, when, though a miserable, and a banished, and a damned creature, yet I am his creature still, and contribute something to his glory, even in my damnation; that that God, who hath often looked upon me in my foulest uncleannesse,   15 and when I had shut out the eye of the day, the Sunne, and the eye of

the night, the Taper, and the eyes of all the world, with curtaines and windowes and doores, did yet see me, and see me in mercy, by making me see that he saw me, and sometimes brought me to a present remorse, and (for that time) to a forbearing of that sinne, should so turn him- 2 0
selfe from me, to his glorious Saints and Angels, as that no Saint nor Angel, nor Christ Jesus himselfe, should ever pray him to looke towards me, never remember him, that such a soule there is; that that God, who hath so often said to my soule, *Quare morieris?* Why with thou die? and so often sworne to my soule, *Vivit Dominus,* As the Lord liveth, I would 2 5
not have thee dye, but live, will neither let me dye, nor let me live, but dye an everlasting life, and live an everlasting death; that that God, who, when he could not get into me, by standing, and knocking, by his ordinary means of entring, by his Word, his mercies, hath applied his judgements, and hath shaked the house, this body, with agues and 3 0
palsies, and set this house on fire, with fevers and calentures, and frighted the Master of the house, my soule, with horrors, and heavy apprehensions, and so made an entrance into me; That that God should loose and frustrate all his owne purposes and practises upon me, and leave me, and cast me away, as though I had cost him nothing, that 3 5
this God at last, should let this soule goe away, as a smoake, as a vapour, as a bubble, and that then this soule cannot be a smoake, nor a vapour, nor a bubble, but must lie in darknesse, as long as the Lord of light is light it selfe, and never a sparke of that light reach to my soule; What Tophet is not Paradise, what Brimstone is not Amber, what gnashing is 4 0
not a comfort, what gnawing of the worme is not a tickling, what tor-ment is not a marriage bed to this damnation, to be secluded eternally, eternally, eternally from the sight of God? (V, No. 13, ll. 779–823)

A summary of this in grammatical form would perhaps read thus: The damnation of seclusion from God is so unimaginably ter-rible that all other torture is bliss in comparison to this damnation. (The summary is not quite just, since it ignores the suspension of the "that" clauses; the point is that this suspension is emotional rather than logical.) I have incorporated into the thought the end of the preceding paragraph, for the idea expressed there is what he begins to build upon. Paragraphs, like periods, are not always dis-tinct in Donne. Taking this fact into account, then, we see that the rhetorical period completes a circle; it ends with its beginning. The imaginative progress made during its course enables it to meet its beginning again with a far richer and more forceful emphasis than that with which the point was at first suggested. And although the period is, in this sense, circular, it does not move with flowing roundness from beginning to end. The same disproportion that has been observed in shorter units is present here; the "that" clauses are piled up to four times as much length as the turn is given; the clipped series of hyperboles at the end is intended to contrast sharply with what has gone before, gaining its impact by concentration and surprise rather than by sheer bulk. A long, slow-paced development is followed by a rapid fall into the thin line that spirals out toward the next sentence—which is not another sentence at all, but a continuation of this one, beginning "Especially for us . . . ."

Numerous devices momentarily divert the flow of the sentence, free it from constriction or accept the weight of the thought. The parenthesis in lines 5 and 6 overlaps with what precedes it, shifts the point of view, and causes a corresponding shift of thought toward the unimaginable nature of hell. In line 6, "never" is briefly made the emotional pivot of the sentence, changing the emphasis from God and his action, to the finality of the soul's imprisonment. The "ever . . . never" of lines 22 and 23 performs a similar function. There is repetition for emphasis in line 9 and in line 43, and overlapping of Latin with English in lines 24–25; between lines 28 and 33 metaphor and translation overlap several times. Sufficient to create some strain is the wide separation of subject from verb between lines 10 and 12 ("God . . . will not look"), lines 15 and 20 ("God . . . should so turne"), and lines 23 and 26 ("God . . . will neither let"); in each case, and particularly in the last, the intervening clauses seem to have wedged the sentence apart. Among several minor grammatical shifts and ellipses are "and never a sparke of that light reach to my soule," in line 39, which is not syntactically connected with what precedes it, and the characteristic freedom of the infinitive in line 42. The heavily weighted contrast that concludes the period balances four startling paradoxes against one very short phrase, "to this damnation," after which Donne tips the emphasis back where it ought to be in the concluding phrase by means of the triple repetition of "eternally." The polysyndetic heaping of lines 8 and 9 slows the rhythm; runs throughout the passage vary the rhythms and emphases in their respective places. Repetition of all sorts holds together word heaps and runs, points up parallelism, adds tension, nervousness, and a sense of growth to the developing meditation.

Finally, let me stress once more the complete freedom of the period. The series of "that" clauses is the equivalent of the subordinate member; the clipped hyperboles at the end take the place of a main clause. Nothing holds it all together. Each "that" clause has its own independent development; the hyperboles shoot out without acknowledging what has preceded them; yet nothing could be farther from disunity. The sentence moves like a series of waves, rising higher and higher in a long cumulative surge that breaks sharply at the end. Relief comes from the complete shift in tone and rhythm rather than from completion of grammatical suspension.

The following circular sentence does have grammatical coherence:

> And when you shall find that hand that had signed to one of you a *Patent* for *Title,* to another for *Pension,* to another for *Pardon,* to another for *Dispensation, Dead:* That hand that settled Possessions by his *Seale,* in the *Keeper,* and rectified *Honours* by the *sword,* in his *Marshall,* and distributed relief to the *Poore,* in his *Almoner,* and *Health* to the *Diseased,* by his *immediate Touch,* Dead: That Hand that ballanced his *own three Kingdomes* so equally, as that none of them complained of one another, nor of him, and carried the *Keyes* of all the Christian world, and locked up, and let out *Armies* in their due season, Dead; how poore, how faint, how pale, how momentany, how transitory, how empty, how frivolous, how Dead things, must you necessarily thinke *Titles,* and *Possessions,* and *Favours,* and all, when you see that Hand, which was the *hand of Destinie,* of *Christian Destinie,* of the *Almighty God,* lie dead? (VI, No. 14, ll. 354–67)

The period can be summarized as follows: When you see that hand dead that did so many good things for you, how empty must you think worldly things, when you see that hand dead. The circle of this sentence then is different from that of the preceding one, for here the conclusion or climax is reached with the "how poore, how faint" run of words and the clauses connected with it, toward which both beginning and end of the sentence point. This pattern seems to coincide almost exactly with that "circuit" which we ordinarily think of as Ciceronian, but the signature of Donne is written large.

Separation of normally united parts of speech here creates a powerful rhythm. "Dead" is a predicate adjective belonging to the understood complementary infinitive "to be" and its subject "hand," but in each case the noun and its modifier are separated by a lengthy clause and forced to set up a rhythm which is at odds with the grammar, in the repetitions of "hand" at the beginning and "dead" at the end of each member. With each repetition, the two words are pried a little farther apart, the subject and verb upon which they and all their clauses depend left a little farther behind, so that when the main thought pours in with its mass of adjectives, the reader scarcely has time to think back to the specific construction that has supposedly led up to it, before he reaches the same construction again at the period's close. The first part of the sentence is slow-moving and heavy-rhythmed; the climax, fast-moving and light-rhythmed, is followed again by a slow-paced and impressive conclusion. And this is very much like what we saw in the first passage. In both cases, I think, the conclusion seems longer than it is because of the contrast. Climax and conclusion together, even in this period, are only half as long as the opening, and the same fast curve precedes the final heavy syllables.

Very often, to look at a short sentence immediately preceding a long one is to realize that when the circularity is not built into the grammatical period it is provided for in the rhetorical period, the whole thought span; and the larger the unit considered, the more frequently will this pattern appear. We saw this in the first passage cited, as we do here:

Tu absconsio, Thou art my hiding place, sayes the Primitive Church, and so may the Reformed Church say too. For when the Roman Church made this *Latibulum,* this hiding place, this refuge from Persecution, Ermitages and Monasteries, to be the most conspicuous, the most glorious, the most eminent, the richest and most abundant places of the World; when they had drawne these, at first remote corners in the Wildernesse, first into the skirts, and suburbs, then into the body and heart of every great City; when for revenew and possession, they will confesse, that some one Monastery of the Benedictines had ten thousand of our pounds of yearely rent; when they were come for their huge opulency to that height, that they were formidable to those States that harboured them, and for their numbers, (other Orders holding proportion with that one) to reckon out of one Order, fifty two Popes, two hundred Cardinals, seven thousand Archbishops and Bishops, and almost three hundred Emperours and Kings, and their children, and fifty thousand declared and approved Saints; when they were come to that over-valuation of their Religious Orders, as to say, That a Monke, a Fryer merited more in his very sleep, or meales, then any secular man, (though a Church-man too) did in his best works, That to enter into any Order of Religion was a second Baptisme, and wrought as much as the first; Their revenew, their number, their dignity being come to this, And then their viciousnesse, their sensuality, their bestiality, to as great a height and exaltation, as that; yet in the midst of all these, *Tu absconsio mea,* may the Reformed Church say, The Lord was their hiding place, that mourned for this, when they could not helpe, and at all times, and by all meanes that God afforded them, endeavored to advance a Reformation. And though God exposed them as a wood to be felled, to a slaughter of twenty, of forty, of sixty thousand in a day, yet *Ille absconsio,* He hath beene our hiding place, He hath kept the roote alive all the way; And though it hath beene with a cloud, yet he hath covered us (IX, No. 15, ll. 108–39).

After the point of departure and return is established with the Latin quotation, a long series of adverbial "when" clauses is piled up, until finally with the first "yet" the sentence turns, and the Latin *absconsio* appears twice in the eight concluding lines. The rise and fall of this period are hinged with an absolute participle construction ("Their revenew, their number, their dignity being come to this") which mediates between the two parts. Croll suggests that baroque stylists used the absolute participle to help them escape from suspended clauses that could not easily be resolved.[32] Donne also uses it here to provide a momentary suspension of thought between subordinate and independent members, as one means to keep the weight of the adverbial clause series from overwhelming that which follows. The absolute construction poises the period for a moment at the farthest reach of its outward movement and, looking backward in content and forward in syntax, prepares the mind for the downward sweep. In the other two periods examined, the change of pace has been sufficient to keep the two movements separate; in the meditation upon the soul's falling out of the hands of God, for example, the whole construction is so free, and the shift from the long "that" clause so striking, that no such hinge is required for the maintenance of equilibrium. But where the construction is more grammatically unified and where the style does not change, the absolute participle, or a device capable of producing a similar effect, is often used. Thus, after a page-long series of "if" clauses on the use of natural reason, a parenthesis recapitulates and acts as brake and hinge; I quote only the relevant part of the period:

... if after all this, thou canst turne this little light inward, and canst thereby discerne where thy diseases, and thy wounds, and thy corruptions are, and canst apply those teares, and blood and balme to them, (all this is, That if thou attend the light of naturall reason, and cherish that, and exalt that, so that that bring thee to a *love of the Scriptures,* and that *love to a beleefe* of the truth thereof, and that *historicall faith* to a *faith of application, of appropriation,* that as all those things were certainly done, so they were certainly done *for thee*) thou shalt never envy the lustre and glory of the great lights of worldly men (III, No. 17, ll. 489–97).

The sentence with a slow upward movement and rapid answering descent is one major pattern in Donne's prose. I have called it circular because it begins and ends on the same note, but a circle does not really describe its effect, which can better be diagrammed as that of a diagonal line moving from lower left to upper right, met by a vertical line that carries the eye downward again to lower right, where a shorter diagonal takes it into the next sentence. There is asymmetry within the greater symmetry of the whole.

Another pattern is a series of paired clauses, often moving toward resolution. These clauses are seldom sharply antithetical. The paradoxical antithesis, so typical of traditional Catholic use of the curt period, may be illustrated by this passage from Augustine:

He is great as the Day of the angels, small in the day of men; the Word God before all time, the Word made flesh at a suitable time. Maker of the sun, He is made under the sun. Disposer of all ages in the bosom of the Father, He consecrates this day in the womb of His mother; in Him He remains, from her He goes forth. Creator of heaven and earth, He was born on earth under heaven. Unspeakably wise, He is wisely speechless; filling the world, He lies in a manger; Ruler of the stars, He nurses at his mother's bosom.[33]

Donne, translating Bernard, confirms the source and continuity of the tradition, as well as his appreciation of it:

He is the ancient of daies, and yet in minority; he is the Word it selfe, and yet speechlesse; he that is All, that all the Prophets spoke of, cannot speake: . . . He is *Puer sapiens,* but a child, and yet wiser then the elders, wiser in the Cradle, then they in the Chaire: Hee is more, *Deus lactens,* God, at whose breasts all creatures suck, sucking at his Mothers breast, and such a Mother, as is a maid (VI, No. 8, ll. 583–89).[34]

But although Donne does perpetuate this tradition and is with some justice called a preacher of paradox, ordinarily sheer length tends to engulf an antithesis in larger movements; the changing emphases of his sentences are likely to rest their weight on oppositions only momentarily, and the urge is almost always toward reconciliation. Even the following brief period can illustrate the difference between the method of the foregoing passage and that which he more frequently employs:

And into that gate they shall enter, and in that house they shall dwell, where there shall be no Cloud nor Sun, no darkenesse nor dazling, but one equall light, no noyse nor silence, but one equall musick, no fears nor hopes, but one equall possession, no foes nor friends, but one equall communion and Identity, no ends nor beginnings, but one equall eternity (VIII, No. 7, ll. 645–50).

The expected antitheses, cloud and sun, darkness and dazzling, fears and hopes, are in each case doubled together on one side, and from them come not oppositions but resolutions. The rhythmic clauses that open the period prepare the mind for the reconciliations that follow.

Donne does often write sentences whose whole basis is antithetical, but the opposing members are generally composed and arranged in such a way that their quality is something quite other than the sharp and vivid point of the Augustine passage:

And can these persons meet? in such a distance, and in such a disparagement can these persons meet? the Son of God and the son of man? When I consider Christ to be *Germen Jehovæ,* the bud and blossome, the fruit and off-spring of Jehovah, Jehovah himself, and my self before he took me in hand, to be, not a Potters vessell of earth, but that earth of which the Potter might make a vessel if he would, and break it if he would when he had made it: When I consider Christ to have been from before all beginnings, and to be still the Image of the Father, the same stamp upon the same metall, and my self a peece of rusty copper, in which those lines of the Image of God which were imprinted in me in my Creation are defaced and worn, and

washed and burnt, and ground away, by my many, and many, and many sins:
When I consider Christ in his Circle, in glory with his Father, before he
came into this world, establishing a glorious Church when he was in this
world, and glorifying that Church with that glory which himself had before,
when he went out of this world; and then consider my self in my circle, I
came into this world washed in mine own tears, and either out of com-
punction for my self or compassion for others, I passe through this world as
through a valley of tears, where tears settle and swell, and when I passe
out of this world I leave their eyes whose hands close mine, full of tears too,
can these persons, this Image of God, this God himself, this glorious God,
and this vessell of earth, this earth it self, this inglorious worm of the earth,
meet without disparagement? (III, No. 11, ll. 333–57).

The sentence after all is only another version of those which we
have already seen. The antitheses are not so much opposed to one
another as listed in a single series which piles up until the turning
comes. The length of each separate member and its individual development cause the movement to seem to proceed from member to
member rather than from pair to pair, and the problem is only
brought into sharp relief at the end, in the precipitate and pointed
conclusion so typical of Donne. In two of the images, man is made
to seem not the opposite of Christ but a damaged replica; the defaced coin and the giddy circle are recurrent figures in Donne to
describe a condition that can be repaired, so that one has the sense
here too that the opposition is not absolute.

The circle of the period is formed thus: Can these persons meet,
when I consider these things, can these persons meet? The period is
grammatically disconnected; the subordinate adverbial clauses cannot logically depend on "can these persons meet." And the section
beginning "I came into this world" is completely separated from the
word preceding it.

Very often the two sides of a pair represent not opposites at all,
but two intricately related possibilities like cause and effect, or action
and sequel, as in the following example:

God doth not raise his children to honour, and great estates, and then
leave them, and expose them to be subjects, and exercises of the malice
of others, nor he doth not make them mightie, and then leave them, *ut
glorietur in malo qui potens est,* that he should thinke it a glory to be

able to do harm. He doth not impoverish and dishonour his children, 5
and then leave them; leave them unsensible of that Doctrine, that
patience is as great a blessing as aboundance: God giveth not his children
health, and then leaveth them to a boldnesse in surfetting; nor beauty,
and leave them to a confidence and opening themselves to all sollicita-
tions; nor valour, and then leaveth them to a spirit of quarrelsomenesse: 10
God maketh no patterns of his works, no modells of his houses, he
maketh whole pieces, he maketh perfect houses, he putteth his children
into good wayes, and he directeth and protecteth them in those wayes:
For this is the constancy and the perseverance of the love of Christ
Jesus, as he is called in this Text a stone (II, No. 8, ll. 121–35). 15

The second halves of the pairs act as a refrain because of the repetitions of "and then leaveth them," so that the rising movement of the
first part of the sentence is continually held back by the plateaus of
the echoes. This is not at all what we ordinarily think of as balance;
the whole series is on the same side, but the forward movement is
broken by the refrains, as well as by the overlapping of Latin and
English in lines 3 and 4, and of "leave them" in line 6. As the period
progresses, the pairs become briefer, elliptical in construction, signal-
ing the imminence of the resolution, which is composed of the characteristic brief antithesis, and a return to the words of the sermon
text.

Another example of this construction works upon repetition of
"as though":

Let no man therefore think to present his complexion to God for an
excuse, and say, My Choler with which my constitution abounded, and
which I could not remedy, enclined me to wrath, and so to bloud; My
Melancholy enclined me to sadnesse, and so to Desperation, as though thy
sins were medicinall sins, sins to vent humors. Let no man say, I am continent
enough all the yeare, but the spring works upon me, and inflames my concupiscencies, as though thy sins were seasonable and anniversary sins. Make
not thy Calling the occasion of thy sin, as though thy sin were a Mysterie,
and an Occupation; Nor thy place, thy station, thy office the occasion of thy
sin, as though thy sin were an Heir-loome, or furniture, or fixed to the free-
hold of that place: for this one proposition, *God is no accepter of persons,*
is so often repeated, that all circumstances of Dispositions, and Callings, and
time, and place might be involved in it (III, No. 13, ll. 434–47).

I do not wish to imply, by calling the repetitive clauses a refrain, that they are not integral parts of the period, for clearly the thought would not make sense without them. Here these clauses perform the function of an ironic undercutting of the quotations that represent the sinner's point of view. And again in this passage, as in the one previously cited, the length of the illustrations grows shorter, closing in toward the conclusion that is to resolve all.

Finally, there is a period pattern which in Donne shapes not only periods, but paragraphs and sermons as well—the repetition of a single word. In his non-sermon prose, such repetition is often completely unpatterned; the sentences revolve about this central word or thought, which returns again and again like a persistent beat to underline the concentration of his mind as it strives to know the meaning of the idea that the word signifies. This is a habit which he shares with Augustine; both men are fascinated and infuriated by language; and unpatterned repetition is a fine illustration of Augustine's rhetorical theory—word figures occur, not by careful planning, but spontaneously.[35] In Donne the habit also signalizes an instinctively associative and imaginative way of thought:

> He that stands in a place and does not the duty of that place, is but a statue in that place; and but a statue without an inscription; Posterity shall not know him, nor read who he was. In nature the body frames and forms the place; for the place of the natural body is that *proxima aëris superficies,* that inward superficies of the air, that invests and clothes, and apparals that body, and obeys, and follows, and succeeds to the dimensions thereof. In nature the body makes the place, but in grace the place makes the body: The person must actuate it self, dilate, extend and propagate it self according to the dimensions of the place, by filling it in the execution of the duties of it (VIII, No. 7, ll. 138-47).

In this passage, the word "place" is not just a sign of a thing or concept. The strong insistence upon the word, the way in which it is made the physical center of the period, causes it to seem to be something real itself, or perhaps, as has been suggested earlier, the physical shadow of reality. The relationship that the word "place" has to the period is like the relationship that the place of honor has to the things and people around it. Donne tries to make words become more than just print on paper or sounds in air.

In the following passage, two short clauses, used always together,

recur as the word "place" did, to form at irregular intervals a refrain central to the thought. This is the same kind of repetition
shown in the previous example, but in its extension and more predictable recurrence, it has been more fully adapted to the needs of
pulpit oratory. It will also be noticed that, while on one level, Donne
is hammering out a symbol by intensive insistence upon it, on another
level, he is making the clauses themselves become the symbol, because their movement is like the movement of the sea:

The world is a Sea in many respects and assimilations. It is a Sea, as it is
subject to stormes, and tempests; Every man (and every man is a world)
feels that. And then, it is never the shallower for the calmnesse, The Sea is
as deepe, there is as much water in the Sea, in a calme, as in a storme; we
may be drowned in a calme and flattering fortune, in prosperity, as irrecov-
erably, as in a wrought Sea, in adversity; So the world is a Sea. It is a Sea,
as it is bottomlesse to any line, which we can sound it with, and endlesse to
any discovery that we can make of it. The purposes of the world, the wayes
of the world, exceed our consideration; But yet we are sure the Sea hath a
bottome, and sure that it hath limits, that it cannot overpasse; The power of
the greatest in the world, the life of the happiest in the world, cannot exceed
those bounds, which God hath placed for them; So the world is a Sea. It is
a Sea, as it hath ebbs and floods, and no man knowes the true reason of those
floods and those ebbs. All men have changes and vicissitudes in their bodies,
(they fall sick) And in their estates, (they grow poore) And in their minds,
(they become sad) at which changes, (sicknesse, poverty, sadnesse) themselves wonder, and the cause is wrapped up in the purpose and judgement of
God onely, and hid even from them that have them; and so the world is a
Sea. It is a Sea, as the Sea affords water enough for all the world to drinke,
but such water as will not quench the thirst. The world affords conveniences
enow to satisfie Nature, but these increase our thirst with drinking, and our
desire growes and enlarges it self with our abundance, and though we sayle
in a full Sea, yet we lacke water; So the world is a Sea. It is a Sea, if we
consider the Inhabitants. In the Sea, the greater fish devoure the lesse; and
so doe the men of this world too. And as fish, when they mud themselves,
have no hands to make themselves cleane, but the current of the waters must
worke that; So have the men of this world no means to cleanse themselves
from those sinnes which they have contracted in the world, of themselves, till
a new flood, waters of repentance, drawne up, and sanctified by the Holy
Ghost, worke that blessed effect in them.
All these ways the world is a Sea (II, No. 14, ll. 690–723).

These periods, unlike the others that we have looked at, have no
predictable form. They are made up of short sentences, but these

sentences have little individual clarity, because the ultimate stress is on the repeated word, phrase, or clause around which they revolve. Thus, again, grammar becomes less important as a structural device than the natural relations of the parts of the symbol itself, the words and their imitation of reality.

With these four sentence patterns—curt period, and the variant antithetical or paradoxical periods; diagonal period concluded by a quick fall; clause-paired and refrain periods, whose pairs often close in toward the end; and period centered around a single word or image—I conclude this chapter. There are other patterns, but these are the most impressive and the most recurrent. And other periods, whose form is different, always partly overlap in development or technique with those which I have described. In each case the period has considerable freedom of movement. It is not held firmly to a logical structure, but seeks, in various ways, release from the requirements of grammar in order to seem to reach closer to the actual movement of thought and imagination. Contrast of tone and rhythm, the apparently spontaneous ebb and flow of thought around a central word, the affective rather than logical resolution of a suspended period—these things appear to create the structure of the sentence. To end as I began, with a reference to the baroque, I might recall for comparison, how consistently the baroque architects, by use of columns or doorways or play of light, concealed the walls of their buildings, so that the rhythms of these devices attained independent and free movement, while the invisibility of the walls gave an effect of infinitely receding space behind them. It is this same effect of voluntary grace attesting to infinite meaning that we find in the periods of Donne. Yet, as we have seen, this is grace in process of becoming, made to seem nervous and even wavering. The road to infinity is in the meditational process, in the memory. To open the memory, the premeditated certainty of the grammatically stable sentence is put aside. The game is dangerous. Concealing walls may seem to bring infinity closer, but it also raises doubts about the solidity of the building. The restless disquiet of Donne's sentences may find a stronger response in his readers than his often thunderous music can subdue.

III

The Manacled Abstraction

Critics characterizing Donne's metaphor have variously called it original and traditional, abstract and concrete, intellectual and sensuous and realistic, bizarre and ingenious and homely. Most of these claims can be reconciled, for Donne blends qualities that would seem to be opposed to one another. In this first chapter on his imagery, I mean to concentrate on occasional figures, on metaphors that, for the most part, are not carried through long sections of his sermons. They are, however, highly contributive to the tone of the sermons; they are intended to arouse the emotions, and they all demonstrate his intention to explain spiritual processes in physical terms.

If English preaching metaphor, taken from Anglo-Saxon days straight through to Donne, can be said to have one ancestor among the Latin Fathers, that ancestor is certainly Gregory the Great. He is the only one who always thinks concretely, illustrating his sermons with direct, vivid, homely figures, the only one whose style is more characterized by its imagery than by any other single technique. For an understanding of the brief, immediate metaphor in Donne, we may well begin with his use of this source, which will illuminate for us the way in which he borrows (for he almost always borrows his figures from someone) and the extent of his originality.

A chief authority for consideration of bodily resurrection was the fifteenth chapter of St. Paul's First Epistle to the Corinthians, where he writes, "But some man will say, How are the dead raised up? and with what body do they come? Thou fool, that which thou sowest is not quickened, except it die: And that which thou sowest, thou sowest not that body that shall be, but bare grain, it may chance of wheat, or of some other grain." Gregory enlarged upon this as follows:

Sunt vero nonnulli qui, considerantes quod spiritus a carne solvitur, quod caro in putridinem vertitur, quod putredo in pulverem redigitur, quod pulvis ita in elementa solvitur, ut nequaquam ab humanis oculis videatur, resurrectionem fieri posse desperant; et dum arida ossa inspiciunt, haec vestiri carnibus rursumque ad vitam viridescere posse difidunt. Qui si resurrectionis fidem ex obedientia non tenent, certe hanc tenere ex ratione debuerant. Quid enim quotidie nisi resurrectionem nostram in elementis suis mundus imitatur? Per quotidiana quippe momenta lux ipsa temporalis quasi moritur, dum, supervenientibus noctis tenebris, ea quae aspiciebatur subtrahitur, et quasi quotidie resurgit, dum lux ablata oculis, suppressa iterum nocte reparatur. Per momenta quoque temporum cernimus arbusta viriditatem foliorum amittere, a fructuum prolatione cessare; et ecce subito quasi ex arescenti ligno velut quadam resurrectione veniente videmus folia erumpere, fructus grandescere, et totam arborem redivivo decore vestiri. . . . Consideremus ergo parvum cujuslibet arboris semen, quod in terram jacitur, ut arbor ex illo producatur, et comprehendamus, si possumus, ubi in illa tanta brevitate seminis tam immensa arbor latuit, quae ex illo processit. . . . Quid ergo mirum, si tenuissimum pulverem, nostris oculis in elements redactum, cum vult, in hominem reformat, qui ex tenuissimis seminibus immensa arbusta redintegrat.[1]

This theme is constant in Christian literature, and is picked up again in the seventeenth century, by Lancelot Andrewes, in a sermon which Donne may well have known:

For, *first fruits* imply *fruits:* And so we, as the *fruits* of the earth, falling, as doe the graines or kernels into the ground, and there lying, to all mens seeming, putrified, and past hope, yet on a sudden, against the great Feast of *first fruits,* shooting forth of the ground againe. The other . . . the *Apostle* letteth goe, and fastens on this of *fruits,* and followeth it hard, thorow the rest of the *Chapter:* shewing, that the *rising againe* of the *fruits* sowen, would be no lesse incredible, than the *Resurrection,* but that, we see it so, every yeare.[2]

Paul does perhaps show this, but he does not say it. Gregory and Andrewes both overshoot Paul in this respect. And Andrewes is moving in a direction which Donne carries to an extreme in the following paragraph:

And yet as *Solomon* sends us to creatures, and to creatures of a low rank and station, to Ants and Spiders, for instruction, so Saint *Gregory* sends us to creatures, to learne the Resurrection. *Lux quotidie moritur, & quotidie resurgit;* That glorious creature, that first creature, the light, dyes every day, and every day hath a resurrection. *In arbustis folia resurrectione erumpunt;* from the Cedar of *Libanus,* to the Hyssop upon the wall, every leafe dyes every yeare, and every yeare hath a Resurrection. *Vbi in brevitate seminis, tam immensa arbor latuit?* (as he pursues that meditation.) If thou hadst seen the bodies of men rise out of the grave, at Christs Resurrection, could that be a stranger thing to thee, then, (if thou hadst never seen, nor hard, nor imagined it before) to see an Oake that spreads so farre, rise out of an Akorne? Or if Churchyards did vent themselves every spring, and that there were such a Resurrection of bodies every yeare, when thou hadst seen as many Resurrections as years, the Resurrection would be no stranger to thee, then the spring is (III, No. 3, ll. 230–46).

Now if we were to believe Donne, we would have to take this to be a simple résumé of Gregory, with an opening reference to Solomon. Some research shows that there is at least a possibility that he did not even mention all that influenced him—witness the Andrewes passage. In one sense, certainly, Donne is entirely reliant upon tradition. But it is quite easy to see that the figure, in his version, becomes something different from what it was in Gregory's or Andrewes'. Gregory emphasizes the rhythm of all things, the natural process of death and resurrection that obtains in the world, and the facility with which a God who brings a tree from a seed can bring resurrected man from dust. Donne seems to be doing the same thing, but he actually manages to emphasize the inadequacy of the analogy. Under what circumstances would bodily resurrection not be remarkable? It would not be remarkable if it happened every year (Andrewes' suggestion is reversed). An easily acceptable resurrection, that is to say, would not be merely vaguely analogous to the spring, but *identical* with it. Donne tries to use the analogy as a kind of trap to bring spiritual concepts into the framework of the natural world. And this attempt to manacle the concept makes it not less surprising, but more so. The oddity, the tension, and the intensity of the resultant figure are the violent collision and somewhat surrealistic fusion of two levels of thought.

This occasional imagery in Donne is remarkably specific, concrete, and even, at times, topical. Notice how Gregory's *arbusta* become cedar and hyssop; his *arbor* and *semen* become oak and acorn. And Gregory himself is an unusually concrete writer. However, Donne is in general concerned not with the sensuous properties of things but with the degree to which they can successfully embody and explain beliefs and abstractions. Adjectives are relatively infrequent in his prose,[3] and sensuous adjectives hardly occur at all; the lack of adjectival shading contributes to the clarity and hardness of his metaphor. At the same time, his very specific imagination inspires his use of visual nouns; we respond emotionally to Donne's imagery both because it is accompanied by the sound patterns discussed in the previous chapter, and because we see it. But it is not evocative in the ordinary sense, nor descriptive; it is dramatic imagery made more forceful by presentation of a minimal number of props.

In his essay on wit in medieval hymnology, Father Walter Ong points out that when an image is a last resort, when it seems to be the only possible way of catching in perceptible form a metaphysical abstraction, one inevitably has the sense that he is seeing only part of the whole, that much of the abstraction remains outside the body provided for it.[4] This condition creates a kind of tension that is almost intrinsic to Christian literature. But there are different ways of dealing with it, as we have just seen. The whole movement of baroque seems to me in one sense to be a declaration of war upon the intangible, the abstract, the remote—an attempt to force them to accept an incarnate and so immediately effective power. Donne's figures are precise. His images try to pin down abstractions much more rigorously than is apparently possible, and their sharp outlines seem to leave insufficient room for the abstractions to move in and out of their vehicles. Though apparently manacled, they fight back; there is always a visible conflict, of which the wild distortion of the natural world in the Gregory-inspired passage is one example.

Let me illustrate further with two more selections, one very successful and the other a colossal failure. Here is the first:

This light which we speake of, This knowledge of God, and means of salvation, is in the highest exaltation. In the state of nature, we consider this light, as the Sunne, to be risen at the Moluccae, in the farthest East; In the state of the law, we consider it, as the Sunne comes to Ormus, the first Quadrant; But in the Gospel, to be come to the Canaries, the fortunate Ilands, the first Meridian. Now, whatsoever is beyond this, is Westward, towards a Declination. If we will goe farther then to be Christians, . . . we depart from the true glory and serenity, from the lustre and splendor of this Sunne (VII, No. 12, ll. 354–66).

Donne's contribution to the very traditional figure of the rising sun is the addition of the place names, which he uses frequently, less for the sensuous power that they have in Milton than for a precision both intellectual and imaginative. By this addition he creates a tension similar to that produced in his "Lecture upon the Shadow,"[5] in forcing the realization that, unlike the natural sun, this sun rises to its height and then stops. In the second part of the passage, capacity for movement is transferred from the sun to "we." As before, his insistence upon likeness wreaks havoc upon the natural world. The abstraction is trapped into following a precise geographical course— but there is conflict because no natural course is adequate to explain it.

My next example is sometimes quoted against Donne as illustrative of the fantastic or ingenious metaphor, and I would certainly agree that it is not successful. It is interesting, however, as definitive of the extreme to which the same imagination could go:

Amongst *naturall Creatures,* because howsoever they differ in bignesse, yet they have some proportion to one another, we consider that some very little creatures, contemptible in themselves, are yet called enemies to great creatures, as the Mouse is to the Elephant. (For the greatest Creature is not *Infinite,* nor the least is not *Nothing.*) But shall man, betweene whom and nothing, there went but a word, *Let us make Man,* That Nothing which is infinitely lesse then a Mathematicall point, then an imaginary Atome, shall this Man, this yesterdayes Nothing, this to morrow worse then Nothing, be capable of that honour, that *dishonourable honour,* that confounding honour, to be the enemy of God, of God who is not onely a multiplied Elephant, millions of Elephants multiplied into one, but a multiplied World, a multiplied All, All that can be conceived by us, infinite many times over; Nay (if we may dare to say so,) a multiplyed God, a God that hath the Millions of the Heathens gods in himselfe alone, shall this man be an enemy to this God? (X, No. 5, ll. 570–85)

Despite its oddity, the figure is really constructed on the same prin-

ciples that shaped that of the rising sun. Donne takes a commonplace idea, the discrepancy between man and God, and tries to make
it intellectually and imaginatively apprehensible. But here the abstraction cannot survive in the image, for the image is too vividly
incoherent and ludicrous. The abstraction is forced out, and the
comic figure remains.

There also seems to be in these figures some conflict between the
emotion attached to, or evoked by, the naturalistic image, and the
intellectual interest in the abstraction. The precision of Donne's
metaphor ordinarily allows each faculty to be gratified to some extent, for the emotion can find some sensory pleasure in the concrete-
ness of the image, while the intellect finds in the same precision an
analogical validity. Sometimes there seems to be a real union between
the two, but more often, I think, in Donne's imagery, one is aware
of their coexistence, and of a certain surrender of rights on the part
of each. So in the sun image, the intellect agrees to accept the fact
that the analogy is imperfect, while the emotions agree to accept a
limitation of sensation. The truce is not an easy one.

The quarrel between abstraction and image summarizes one important aspect of Donne's artistic world view. Another concerns
what we have often been told is a baroque emphasis on fragmentation, or many-sidedness, and the elusive nature of reality. Donne's
frequent use of words like "glass" and "light" is bound up with a
whole complex of figures having to do with seeing, which at least
purport to explain his position. The world was dimmed by Adam's
fall; man sees through a glass darkly.[6] Vision and perspective need
continual refocusing in order for man always to see himself and the
world as clearly as he can. Donne uses every kind of glass known
in his time[7] to describe the various ways in which sight, or understanding, can be renewed, and employs some specific disorders of the
eye to parallel disorders of the heart. By urging men to look through
glasses, he reminds them that the sense impressions given by the eyes
to the memory are not always accurately reflected; man cannot see
except with glasses and the glasses themselves are a reminder that
there is always a barrier between the understanding and the object

regarded. Different kinds of glasses reflect different aspects of the ambiguous world.

God's glass is truest: "when we see sin through that spectacle, through an *angry God,* it appears great, and red, and fearefull unto us" (II, No. 4, ll. 200–202); "He seeth all the way, and at *thy last gaspe,* he will make thee see too, through the multiplying Glasse, the Spectacle of *Desperation*" (IV, No. 5, ll. 175–76). There are other glasses available in this life: "God made the Sun, and Moon, and Stars, glorious lights for man to see by; but mans infirmity requires *spectacles;* and affliction does that office" (IV, No. 6, ll. 306–8). Only on the day of judgment will man really see clearly: "here I never saw my selfe, but in disguises" (IX, No. 4, ll. 738–39). This is the Christian rationale for the baroque preoccupation with metamorphosis, disguise, illusion. The spectacles with which Donne supplies his congregation are also baroque.

Here is a portrait of the man in the pew:

There is a squint eye, that lookes side-long; to looke upon riches, and honor, on the left hand, and long life here, on the right, is a squint eye. There is a squint eye, that lookes upwards and downwards; to looke after God and Mammon, is a squint eye. There are squint eyes, that looke upon one another; to looke upon ones own beauty, or wisedome, or power, is a squint eye. The direct looke is to looke inward upon thine own Conscience (III, No. 10, ll. 142–48).

For these squint-eyed, or cross-eyed people, whose vision is fragmented, Donne has many characteristic images. His explicit purpose is to use the operation of the eye as analogy to inner vision, by constructing a parallel between the focusing of the eye and the unification of the mind. These images appear to be very strongly controlled and, one might say, unevocative. Because he is trying to focus man's attention upon himself, to recollect these thoughts that have splintered away from wholeness, his figures are made to move inward rather than outward like normal imagery—that is, in a sense, they begin at fullest expansion and are immediately caught and drawn in toward the center. Thus, talking about the conflicting doubts that may besiege a man, he says, "If one Milstone fell from the North-

Pole, and another from the South, they would meet, and they would rest in the Centre; Nature would con-centre them. Not to be able to con-centre those doubts, which arise in my self, in a resolution at last . . . is rather a vertiginous giddiness, then a wise circumspection, or wariness" (IX, No. 7, ll. 227–32). Given these very specific details, the two poles and the millstones, and nothing else, however, one must continue to have some doubts about what happens in between. Between separation or distraction, and unity there is a space, which is not accounted for.

The recurrent image of the flat map does possess sufficient acknowledgment of process to quiet some doubts, and perhaps the only tension here is the strain involved in making the abstraction fit the figure:

In a flat Map, there goes no more, to make West East, though they be distant in an extremity, but to paste that flat Map upon a round body, and then West and East are all one. In a flat soule, in a dejected conscience, in a troubled spirit, there goes no more to the making of that trouble, peace, then to apply that trouble to the body of the Merits, to the body of the Gospel of Christ Jesus, and conforme thee to him, and thy West is East, thy Trouble of spirit is Tranquility of spirit (VI, No. 1, ll. 726–33).

He uses East and West again to describe God's infinity, for once daring the eye to take its usual course, to try to move farther outward than it has already gone. "What eye can fixe it selfe upon East and West at once? And he must see more than East and West, that sees God, for God spreads infinitely beyond both" (IX, No. 5, ll. 102–4). Several times, he takes two distant parts of the earth as poles for focusing upon God:

Here is a new Mathematiques; without change of Elevation, or parallax, I that live in this Climate, and stand under this Meridian, looke up and fixe my self upon God, And they that are under my feete, looke up to that place, which is above them, And as divers, as contrary as our places are, we all fixe at once upon one God, and meet in one Center (VII, No. 12, ll. 250–55).

We can now make some further generalizations about Donne's metaphor. He has a tendency to make use of natural objects in an unnatural or nonexistent setting. Millstones are common enough, but

millstones falling toward each other through space are not. His metaphor generally involves geographical location, size, weight, proportion, and transformation. The isolation of the figures makes them
seem bolder, sharper, and more surprising than they might otherwise
be. Donne habitually manipulates his figures, expanding, contracting, revising them as by remote control. He sets the two millstones
apart and brings them together; he flattens the map and then makes
it circular. Spiritual conditions are objectified in clearly bounded objects, and if he cannot entirely subdue the abstractions involved, he
does have complete and obvious power over the movement of the
image. His figures are characteristically mobile rather than quiescent.
His manipulation of them makes them seem somewhat mechanical,
somewhat artificial; at the same time, their precision and lean boldness gives them a good deal of vigor and brilliancy. The fact that
the figures describe a process puts the emphasis more on the effort
toward wholeness than on the unification or reconcilation that is the
desired end.

Another and even more characteristic means by which Donne
gathers in the attention is somewhat more copious in expression and
less clinically exact in definition. I have already discussed his use of
the curt style, which is apt, in a series of asyndetic clauses, to repeat
the same thought in several different ways. An analogous device is
his piling up of several different metaphors with the same underly-
ing meaning. This permits sufficient repetition for emphasis, without
the risk of monotony; as a pedagogical device, it also increases the
preacher's opportunity to reach different sorts of people in the congregation. It works very much as the figures that I have just been describing do, forcing a number of apparently radically different, specifically described things toward a single meaning. The following
passage is a brief example: "when God comes to that particular, *veni
ergo ut mittam te,* Come therefore that I may send thee, him into
Egypt, *Moses* to *Pharaoh,* this was a Rock in his Sea, and a Remora
upon his Ship, a Hill in his way, and a Snake in his path" (VIII, No.
5, ll. 325–28). The dramatic effect is very clear here, the scene provided with minimal props and uncluttered by shading detail. It is to

some extent true that this device produces a massive emotional effect which can then be centered upon the question in hand. But it is also true that this effect is made up of three specific analogies, which lay hold on the imagination and remain in the consciousness, so that one's reaction to the situation Donne describes is really a multiple reaction. With a longer group, there is often some kind of resolution at the end. The following is a particularly good illustration, because it explicitly states his intentions:

God is *the Lord of hosts,* and he can proceed by Martial Law: he can hang thee upon the next tree; he can choak thee with a crum, with a drop, at a voluptuous feast; he can sink down the Stage and the Player, The bed of wantonness, and the wanton actor, into the jaws of the earth, into the mouth of hell: he can surprise thee, even in the act of sin; and dost thou long for such a speedy execution, for such an expedition? Thou canst not lack Examples, that he hath done so upon others, and will no proof serve thee, but a speedy judgement upon thy self? Scatter thy thoughts no farther then, contract them in thy self, and consider Gods speedy execution upon thy soul, and upon thy body, and upon thy soul and body together (I, No. 2, ll. 317–27).

Here, as in so much of his metaphor, Donne's ultimate purpose is to recollect the scattered imagination and turn it upon the self. The examples are intended to draw the mind from pleasure in violence, in feasting, in the theater, without permitting the attention to dwell upon them; the generalized idea of destruction in the midst of life is the important thing, and generates the important emotion, which is then applied to the single soul. The divided vision is to be united. Yet certainly, in both these types of imagery, that in which two widely separated things become one, and that in which a series of metaphors or illustrations is applied to a single case, the fusion is a very unsteady one because the separation or the vivid example is so precise and so intensely felt, because the mind continues to move outward, resisting Donne's didactic attempt to pull it in, and because his description of the fusion is often more abstract and less compelling than the separate instances; the resultant tension is in itself a statement about the world, and helps to create the esthetic distinctiveness of his imagery.

Donne also characteristically plays with unlikenesses and disproportions; not only are like things to be reconciled, brought into harmony, but violently unlike things as well. Erasmus, in discussing the
preacher's use of hyperbole and comparison, observed that the business of Ecclesiastes is to describe things as they are, which is not as
the world sees them.[8] Erasmus' intention was to distinguish the
preacher from the forensic orator, but his words are also in contrast
to the Platonic esthetic, and the ideal of showing things as they
ought to be. To show things as they are, to a Christian in Donne's
tradition, required taking violent liberties with the reality that one
sees; long before Donne's time such descriptions had been provided
in Christian hyperbole and stiffened into convention in the emblem
books. Donne reminds us of some of these conventional figures in
his quotations, as when he repeats what Jerome's ghost said to Augustine: "yet he said no more of that, but this, *Quid quaeris brevi
immittere vasculo totum mare?* Canst thou hope to poure the whole
Sea into a thimble, or to take the whole world into thy hand? And
yet, that is easier, then to comprehend the joy and the glory of
heaven in this life" (IV, No. 2, ll. 873–77). Whether or not he acknowledges the source, Donne's disproportion figures are among his
most traditional, but they are extremely vivid to begin with, and his
methods of working with them often provide new shock and tension.

From several Bible metaphors concerning weighing and balancing
came numerous images common in Christian literature and in the
emblem books. There are, for example, emblems depicting a pair of
scales, with the world on one side and a soap bubble on the other—
and the bubble weighs down the world.[9] Thus all the weighing
metaphors in Donne: "And yet *Ille illis,* to this man comes this God,
God that is infinitely more then all, to man that is infinitely lesse
then nothing, which was our first disproportion, and the first exaltation of his mercy" (IX, No. 5, ll. 224–27); "what is a drop upon
the bucket, to a river, to a sea, to the waters above the firmament?
Man to God? *Man is . . . As small dust upon the balance*" (IX,
No. 5, ll. 182–85); "If you value God, weigh God, you cannot give
him halfe his weight; for, you can put nothing into the balance, to

weigh him withall, but all this world; and there is no single sand in the sea, no single dust upon the earth, no single atome in the ayre, that is not likelyer to weigh down all the world, then all the world is to counterpose God" (III, No. 3, ll. 156–61).[10] It is easy to see why Donne was fascinated by these emblems, rather than others. They deal in the concrete, the specific—and recognition of their own inadequacy is built into them. There is both a tension of disproportion in the figure itself and the tension of inequality between image and abstraction. Donne tightens the screws by insisting that the disproportion did not always exist, and that equipoise will be effected. This balance is brought about in typical fashion in the Christmas sermon from which two of the quotations cited here are taken. The words *ille illis* are made a symbol of reconciliation during the course of the sermon, and the paragraphs describing the disproportions consistently end in sentences using these words, which by their likeness in sound, as well as by their meaning, stress renewal of proportion and harmony.

Nor, despite its apparently colorless nature, can the importance of this kind of conciliating device be overestimated. Father Ong has shown the importance of wordplay to description of Christian mysteries in medieval hymns, and it is this same tradition that is so alive in the Anglo-Catholic preachers. Here symbolic wordplay is balanced against visual analogies, and poetic rhythm against concrete hyperbolic disproportion, so that there is the feel of an argument conducted on two different levels, with the harmonies of one gradually overriding the stresses of the other.

In other disproportion imagery, Donne the manipulator plays a greater role. The crucified Christ spans eternity in "the extension of those sinews, and ligaments which tyed heaven, and earth together" (III, No. 3, ll. 452–53).[11] "Those hands that reached to the ends of the world, in creating it, & span the world in preserving it, and stretched over all in redeeming it, those hands have I manacled, that they cannot open unto me" (V, No. 3, ll. 504–7). The free playing with proportions that goes into this second quotation reinvigorates the traditional image. The figure of Christ first seen as spanning the macrocosm and then as manacled by the infinitely small microcosm that is man, requires a double shift in perspective.

In those meditations upon death which have been advanced as a sign of morbidity in some discussions of Donne's prose, the device by which far separate things are united is combined with this sort of play. When he considers the dust of men swept out of the church-yard into the street, blown into the river, tumbled into the sea, washed to the four corners of the earth, he gives the undisciplined imagination room to travel far, but only that he may increase the sense of man's finiteness, and, again, refocus vision as he pictures the body's reunion with itself:

Shall I imagine a difficulty in my body, because I have lost an Arme in the East, and a leg in the West? because I have left some bloud in the North, and some bones in the South? Doe but remember, with what ease you have sate in the chaire, casting an account, and made a shilling on one hand, a pound on the other, or five shillings below, ten above, because all these lay easily within your reach. Consider how much lesse, all this earth is to him, that sits in heaven, and spans all this world, and reunites in an instant armes, and legs, bloud, and bones, in what corners so ever they be scattered (III, No. 3, ll. 668–77).

The same diminishing and reextension of proportion is employed here, as the world pictured in the opening questions is reduced almost to nothing in the analogy and finally restored to full size and at the same time viewed in proportion to the infinite being that is Donne's God.

This is a good illustration of Donne's use of the homely image. Another writer would either have chosen some different vehicle, or carried out the whole discussion through it. Donne is unusual in combining the immediate and the remote in just this way, flashing back and forth from one to the other. We read Donne wrong when we do not follow his metaphors to their conclusions, and it is easy not to, because the whole figure is sometimes lengthy, and we are not accustomed to imagery so lively and yet at the same time so tautly controlled; nor are we accustomed to imagery that, while it expands and contracts, moves toward resolution in this fashion. The simple thing is to dwell upon the picture of the scattered body, which, in some of Donne's other figures has much more precise detail than here; but this picture is only the farthest edge of the figure, to catch the scattered mind and bring it to wholeness. Thus his use of this same figure in a marriage sermon, where some readers have been distressed to find it,[12] is in a sense singularly appropriate. One theme that remains constant through all Donne's writing is the search for unity in a world that manifests disunion and disproportion everywhere. Yet for him contrast and opposition were the very stuff of life and poetry, and the opposite pulls in his figures were certainly to him a matter of esthetic delight as much as a comment on fallen humanity.

In discussing these images of fragmentation, opposition, and disproportion, we have noticed only indirectly his war with abstractions. One final aspect of his metaphor which I want to point out here is centrally concerned with this problem. It has to do with change, specifically with changes in man's spiritual life, and its main purpose is to make spiritual growth, or regression, physical and immediate.

Abstractions given physical attributes are by no means new, and Donne is merely utilizing a convention when he talks of the "plowing, and weeding, and worming a conscience" (II, No. 3, ll. 457–58), of "the wetting of our foot in sin" (II, No. 3, ll. 510), of mercy as a pillow to rest the soul upon (IX, No. 4, ll. 663–64). He is particularly apt to attribute physical dimensions to sin, for he thinks of it as something which grows like the human organism, and which, if not extirpated, can get completely out of control: "as the Apostle says of the Naturall body, *There are many members, but one body,* so we may say of our sin, it hath a wanton eye, a griping hand, an itching ear, an insatiable heart, and feet swift to shed blood, and yet it is but one body of sin" (II, No. 2, ll. 619–22). The chief difference between this and such metaphors used conventionally (for example, Richard III's "My conscience hath a thousand several tongues")[13] is Donne's stress on the continual progress or regression intrinsic to moral behavior and on the extent to which virtue or vice can become the body in which one lives and the atmosphere he breathes. What Donne calls the natural body is not forgotten; it is, rather, possessed and overwhelmed by what it has fostered—the figures, in this context, then stand for something other than the natural, but identical with what is real. This body of sin then reaches out to transform its surroundings. Everywhere in Donne we find psychological landscapes—Aetnas of lust, mountains and valleys of presumptive sins and inordinate melancholy, a cloud of poverty or death, a North of adversity and a West of despair. In an early sermon preached at Lincoln's Inn, he says that his purpose is to make the sinner see his sin (II, No. 4, ll. 1–6), and he does it in this way, showing how it creeps outward from the soul, and, feeding on the sinner's life, gains sufficient life of its own to become the whole environment of man.

The life of the spirit is a physical life. Sin must be rooted out (VI, No. 9, ll. 251–52), and the seed of God nourished. There are not two worlds, but one; earth and heaven are gallery and bedchamber in the same palace (IV, No. 9, ll. 125–30). It takes movement, it takes a kind of transformation to get from one to the other. Nearly a third of Donne's sermon texts deal with change—with building metaphors, for example. Donne loved this figure because, by use of the word "edify," he could make it a metaphor of itself, describing spiritual and physical building as if they were the same thing (II, No. 10, ll. 251–53; VIII, No. 2, ll. 283–84).

Two most interesting growth metaphors, common in Christian thought, concern assimilation and physical transformation. From Bernard's homilies on the Song of Songs come both the figure of indigestion arising from overintellectualism and the figure of spiritual assimilation of Christian truth as physical digestion.[14] Keckermann and Erasmus, continuing the tradition, stress the assimilation of truth as a way of distinguishing between the effects of superficial knowledge and real wisdom. Keckermann quotes Beza as having said that the age has too much *scientia* and not enough *conscientia;* the world is like a man who has drunk too much wine without digesting it.[15] Erasmus makes a similar distinction between *scire* and *sapere:*

Sapiens est qui didicit non omnia, sed ea quae ad veram felicitatem pertinent, & iis quae didicit, adficitur, ac transfiguratus est. Hoc sit, quoties cibus Evangelicae doctrinae cum plena fide sumtus, trajectus est in animi viscera, & in habitum ac robur spiritus transiit.[16]

In one of the sermons that some critics have thought overingenious, Donne preaches on the text, "Hast thou found honey? Eat so much as is sufficient for thee, lest thou be filled therewith, and vomit it." Here, in his first section, he takes the honey to mean all man's wordly interests, and says of the man who has been excessively greedy for superficial things, "His honey was his soule, and that being vomited, he is now but a rotten and abhorred carkass" (III, No. 10, ll. 454–55). The man became what he ate. In like manner, feeding on faith and Scriptures, whose sweetness, said Bernard, excels that of honey,[17] leads to true assimilation:

But yet, as though our bodily hand reach to our temporal food, yet the mouth and the stomach must do their office too; and so that meat must be distributed into all parts of the body, and assimilated to them; so though our faith draw this salvation neer us, yet when our mouth is imployed, that we have a delight to glorifie God in our discourses, and to declare his wonderfull works to the sons of men, in our thankfulness: And when this faith of ours is distributed over all the body, that the body of Christs Church is edified, and alienated by our good life and sanctification, then is this Salvation neerer us, that is, safelier seal'd to us, then when we believed only (II, No. 12, ll. 471–81).

And the final degree of assimilation is the union of the soul with God:

As my meat is assimilated to my flesh, and made one flesh with it; as my soul is assimilated to my God, and *made partaker of the divine nature,* and *Idem Spiritus,* the same Spirit with it; so, there my flesh shall be assimilated to the flesh of my Saviour, and made the same flesh with him too (III, No. 3, ll. 799–803).

In an article on Marvell's "Nymph Complaining for the Death of her Fawn," Leo Spitzer suggests that the idea of physical transformation, in its materialization of spiritual value, is at the basis of metaphysical wit.[18] The fawn's increasing purity and holy passion is expressed by his transformation into the roses and lilies upon which he feeds. Spitzer finds here a meeting point between classical Ovidian metamorphosis and the Christian myth of spiritual change. Although he does not say so, the technique is certainly given impetus by the central actions of Christianity: the Incarnation, the Last Supper, the Resurrection, and the Transfiguration. The assimilation figures employ this pattern—the worldly man *becomes* his honey; the pure soul becomes a looking glass (I, No. 3, ll. 589–91)—and vary it in their suggestion that faith and learning are transformed into physical substance.

Very similar too is the kind of metamorphosis that expresses for Donne the operation of the Holy Ghost upon man's nature, invariably in terms of the making of a work of art. In one sermon, for example, he says, "The moving of the holy Ghost upon me, is, as the moving of the minde of an Artificer, upon that piece of work that is then under his hand" (IX, No. 3, ll. 350–52), and goes on to develop an analogy with a jeweler shaping a ruby or an emerald into an artificial figure. In a sermon on the calling of Peter and Andrew, he describes at length the inadequacy of these men, as they were, to be disciples of Christ, and again by use of analogies, explains Christ's effect upon them as the success of an artist with rough or unhewn materials:

In a rough stone, a cunning Lapidary will easily foresee, what his cutting, and his polishing, and his art will bring that stone to. A cunning Statuary discerns in a Marble-stone under his feet, where there will arise an Eye, and an Eare, and a Hand, and other lineaments to make it a perfect Statue. Much more did our Saviour Christ . . . foresee in these fishermen, an inclinablenesse to become usefull in that great service of his Church. . . . Hee tooke them weatherbeaten with North and South winds, and rough-cast with foame, and mud; but he sent them back soupled, and smoothed, and levigated, quickned, and inanimated with that Spirit, which he had breathed into them (II, No. 13, ll. 242–54).

Translation metaphors are still more sudden. Just as his sermon texts so often deal with change, so among the most frequently recurring words in Donne's vocabulary are "translation," "transmutation," "transmigration," "renewal," and "regeneration." The following passage well describes his view of the constant changes that man and his world endure:

In the Elements themselves, of which all sub-elementary things are composed, there is no acquiescence, but a vicissitudinary transmutation into one another; Ayre condensed becomes water, a more solid body, And Ayre rarified becomes fire, a body more disputable, and in-apparant. It is so in the Conditions of men too; A Merchant condensed, kneaded and packed up in a great estate, becomes a Lord; And a Merchant rarified, blown up by a perfidious Factor, or by a riotous Sonne, evaporates into ayre, into nothing, and is not seen (VII, No. 10, ll. 530–37).

These are good examples of the kind of thing that leads Spitzer to suggest this type of metaphor as illustrative of Bergson's theory of the comic. It is a kind of mechanization of spiritual process that is indicated by such words as "condensed, kneaded and packed up." And it is much like that characteristic of Donne's metaphor that I have already pointed out—his use of concrete figures that he can manipulate, making spiritual things and spiritual process external, objective, defined. Description of transformation can also eliminate the process, and bring together only the "before" and "after" stages in sharp contrast. Thus he frequently speaks of the transmutation of animals into men, penitent sinners re-enacting the Circe myth; the wolf, the goat, and the fox in the congregation are offered a metamorphosis and "new Creation in Christ Jesus . . . to become *Semen Dei*" (VII, No. 4, ll. 623–25):

. . . join mine Ordinance (your preaching) with my Spirit, (says God to us) and so make man. Preach the oppressor, and preach the wanton, and preach the calumniator into another nature. Make that ravening Wolfe a Man, that licentious Goate a man, that insinuating Serpent a man, by thy preaching (IX, No. 1, ll. 407–11).[19]

Progressive transmutations bring the soul nearer and nearer to God until the last transmigration and translation into heaven.

For sheer brilliancy and fascination, the types of imagery represented by the figures discussed in this chapter probably outstrip any of the others in Donne's sermons. But they are occasional figures, seldom essential to the structure of a sermon, and seldom very far extended. They are flashes of light, and for sustained eloquence, even, perhaps, for his most serious eloquence, we must look elsewhere. At the same time, these frequently used figures certainly have a pronounced effect upon the whole texture of the prose, supplying it with hardness, vigor, tension, and wit that are characteristic Donne, and which a reader of his poems will recognize more readily than he will recognize much of what makes up the sermons. Many of them are trick figures, figures that Donne can manipulate at will, and by means of which he presumably also managed to manipulate the minds of his congregation to spiritual pliancy and spiritual compliance. We have also seen here, in his wordplays particularly, evidence of what is a more comprehensive kind of imagery in his prose, the symbolic and incarnational coincidence of metaphor and abstraction in a single, simple, and natural vehicle whose tensions, such as they are, seem inherent, not manufactured or mechanized.

Most of Donne's images, in poetry and prose, can be found in earlier writings, as I have shown in several instances here. Gregory compared bodily resurrection to the spring; Tertullian talked of gold beaten to airy thinness; there are glass images in Bernard; Chrysostom and Gregory of Nyssa used the Circe myth. But from all the kinds of images that were available, Donne chose *these,* and he chose to use them always in certain peculiar ways. One final point may help to solidify our understanding of the special texture of his metaphor. In very many cases, these are mobile figures, and figures in motion do not move themselves. Our consciousness of the preacher, forced upon us because Donne so often talks in his sermons about how and why he preaches, is intensified by the necessary recognition that he is the mechanic or operator who sets these images in motion and controls their behavior, expanding and contracting them like rubber bands, slamming together abstraction and vehicle, guiding the transformation of spirit into flesh. So, as with the sentence structure, where the mind of the meditator bridges the grammatical gaps, the interaction of the artist with his art is part of the art itself.

The Preacher's Voice

When John Donne preached at Paul's, according to contemporary accounts, children dropped their toys, old men crept from their corners, women fainted, and brave men wept. For an hour on Sunday, as far as his voice and influence could reach, the world belonged to the hoarse Dean.[1] To know how he did it, we must know the sensibility of the man, the texture of the prose. Dylan Thomas once said that it is a matter of spaces left between words and lines, spaces where genius can find room to come in.[2] The worst critics of style, I know, are the word-counters; the best, even when they appear very scientific, operate on intuition at least fifty per cent of the time. Recognizing all this, we must still hold as firmly as possible to the language of the texts before us, for impressionistic criticism is as unreliable as word-counting alone is meaningless. One way to find out something about those uncharted spaces is to place ourselves for a time upon the frontier between technique and attitude, to analyze as rigorously as possible the *tone of voice* that we seem to hear when we read the sermons. Of course we do catch most of it when we consider word order, sentence structure, imagery, and organization, but there is much that still escapes unless we aim directly at it and bluntly say that we mean to consider Donne's humor, his irony, his use of horror, his immediacy, and his theatricality. Afterwards, we can turn again, somewhat wiser I hope, to more conventional methods.

There is throughout the sermons a good deal of gentle humor partly at Donne's own expense, intended to put the congregation into a receptive frame of mind. It occurs particularly at the beginning of a sermon or, especially when he has overrun his allotted hour, near the end: "This is the third time that I have *entertained* you (in a businesse of this nature, intended for Gods service, and your edification, I must not say, *troubled* you) with this Text" (IV, No. 8, ll. 1–3); "If there be a minute of sand left, (There is not) If there be a minute of patience left, heare me say" (VII, No. 14, ll. 716–18). In some of the early sermons, there are traces of a particularly robust kind of humor made of sheer hyperbole: "God can raise up children out of the stones of the street, and therefore he might be as liberal as he would of his people, and suffer them to be sold for old shoes; but Christ will not sell his birth-right" (I, No. 1, ll. 195–98); such humor does not seem to be in evidence in sermons preached after he left Lincoln's Inn. These early sermons (after all, they are preached to bold young men) also contain examples of a kind of bold ironic humor directed against the congregation: "But if thou could'st consider that every sin is a Crucifying of Christ, and every sin is a precipitation of thy self from a Pinacle; were it a convenient phrase to say, in every little sin, that thou would'st *Crucifie Christ a little,* or break thy neck a little?" (I, No. 3, ll. 474–78). In later sermons we may find simple understatement: "We have a convenient Embleme of Liberality in a Torch, that wasts it selfe to enlighten others; But for a Torch to set another mans house on fire, to enlighten me, were no good Embleme of Liberality" (VIII, No. 10, ll. 150–53). Both humor and irony may be brought into play for ridicule of any idea:

. . . they take the word here (as in many other places of Scripture it does) to signifie onely a *winde,* and then that that addition of the name of *God (The Spirit of God)* which is in their Language a denotation of a vehemency, of a high degree, of a superlative, (as when it is said of *Saul, Sopor Domini, A sleepe of God* was upon him, it is intended of a deepe, a dead sleepe) inforces, induces no more but that a very strong winde blew upon the face of the waters, and so in a great part dryed them up. And this opinion I should let flye away with the winde, if onely the Jews had said it. But *Theodoret* hath said it too, and therefore we afford it so much answer, That it is a strange anticipation, that Winde, which is a mixt Meteor, to the making whereof, divers occasions concurre with exhalations, should be thus imagined, before any of these causes of Winds were created, or produced, and that there should be an effect before a cause, is somewhat irregular (IX, No. 3, ll. 145–59).

The presence of this humor in Donne's irony is an important and distinguishing characteristic of the controversial passages in his sermons. These passages, as J. B. Leishman has pointed out, are very numerous.[3] The ecclesiastical rhetoricians disapproved of pulpit controversy on the grounds that it was a source of confusion and danger to the common hearer;[4] but they were thinking especially of the kind of controversy that deals with doubtful points. James I, in his instructions to preachers, put forth different policies at different times,[5] but it was always made clear that on subjects important to salvation the preacher might rightfully speak out. And Donne did so, with irony, with wit, and with a pertinence not limited to temporary and topical disputes. Almost always he attacks through his specific targets the vain imagination, the faculty in man that permits excesses of all kinds, most reprehensibly when they are perpetrated in the name of religion:

What is mediocrity? Or where is it? In the Hierarchy of the Roman Church they never thought of this mediocrity; They go very high, and very low, but there is no meane station; . . . In one degree you finde embroydered shooes, for Kings to kisse, and in another degree bare feet; we finde an Order of the *Society of Iesus;* and that is very high, for, Society implies community, partnership; And we finde low descents, *Minorits,* men lesse then others, and *Minims,* least of all men; and lower then all them, *Nullans,* men that call themselves, *Nothing;* And truly, this Order, best of all others hath answered and justified the name, for, very soone, they came to nothing. Wee finde all extreames amongst them, even in their names, but none denominated from this mediocrity (VI, No. 15, ll. 570–83).

Leishman has spoken of Donne's power to define, to draw the mean between two extremes;[6] Donne uses the Roman Catholics and all other groups which he regards as "enthusiastic" to illustrate the dangers of emotionally charged aberrations of the mind and to clarify the position of his own church, the church of the middle way. And the means by which larger issues are figured in the lesser ones help to make these passages not mere excrescences, but statements of philosophical and psychological consequence, transcending sectarian argument.

Leishman finds in this aspect of Donne's prose a "Miltonic savagery,"[7] but on the whole I do not find the comparison illuminating. It is not just that Milton, unlike Donne, is at his best in sustained polemical oratory, in pleas for external, concrete, and political reform, or that his writing is more entirely directed at an audience that is to be converted by persuasive means to specific and indignant revolutionary action. Perhaps it is that Milton's savagery so often springs from a sense of personal injury and from a high and humorless belief in his own calling, which, while it changed from the church to poetics, he had twice to lay aside. His style is passionate, robust, and fierce, though not always grand; the irony which he called grim humor[8] is, in comparison with Donne's, gross and unrestrained. Speaking from within the established church, Donne was almost always able to be slightly amused by his opponents, as I do not think Milton ever was; the behavior of Milton's enemies made him retch.

And, despite its frequent appearance, polemics is a minor note in Donne, supplying a certain amount of exterior toughness to a style principally devoted to analysis of the inner and spiritual life of man. Seldom is a sermon wholly argumentative. His diatribe against the Jesuits at the end of one Christmas sermon (IV, No. 11) comes as a surprise, because he almost never builds to so negative a conclusion. Partly, I suppose, because he had more sense of literary propriety than most of his fellow preachers, his longing for a united church comes out most strongly in the conclusions of his sermons, where his descriptions of the church triumphant supersede all temporal differences.

This is the Anglican preacher of the middle way. His worldly security—the security that comes of being politically and ecclesiastically on the right side—was really his chief stability, and in this one area he not only desired but knew moderation. Inner balance was much harder to achieve. Traditionally, it was understood that man's greatest sins were pride (we might say self-satisfaction or egoism) and despair. Donne was keenly aware that these conditions can coexist in a man, and much of the contrast in his sermons is his attempt to hit both at the same time.

His use of horror is particularly relevant here. A morbid exploitation of the macabre has long been supposed to be a central aspect of Donne's prose style, although the arguments advanced have not been especially convincing. For one thing, they have been based on anthology passages, taken out of context.[9] For another, they have been advanced by critics considering Donne's prose as a whole out of context, without reference to other meditational or homiletic literature of the period. Clay Hunt, for example, sets beside Donne's paragraphs selections from Nashe, Peele, and Shakespeare, from Vaughan, Browne, and Herbert;[10] but one cannot expect a sermon to treat death in exactly the same way that a lyric poem or an essay does. There are closer parallels.

Death is certainly a frequent subject in seventeenth-century sermons, as one might expect. However, although the number of descriptions of death in Donne has been much exaggerated,[11] other preachers, whether Anglo-Catholic or Puritan, do not consider the subject so often or with such intensity and immediacy as he does. There is, however, another source to go back to, and fortunately, Louis L. Martz's book, *The Poetry of Meditation*,[12] has given us a better understanding of the handling of death in the spiritual exercises; this is the tradition in which Donne's use of the macabre must be placed. It is certainly not a morbid tradition, either in itself or as Donne employs it. Death, and the death-like aspects of life, are almost always introduced into his writing as prologue to or part of a discussion of resurrection; or, as in meditation, as a device to inspire man with humility, which had always been considered a necessary antecedent to spiritual well-being. It is, however, a particularly vivid and forceful tradition, and Donne's sense of literary effectiveness goes hand in hand with his sense of his own and his auditory's spiritual needs.

There are several macabre situations in particular which he describes more than once during his preaching career, and part of their purpose is to recall the attention of his listeners. But they always have in context a positive end. I have already analyzed his use of one of these situations—what happens at the Resurrection to a man who has lost parts of his body in different parts of the world. A similar problem concerns the man whose body goes a progress through the guts of a fish (IV, No. 13, ll. 94–118); both these support and emphasize the miracle of resurrection. A third is the story in Lamentations of women eating their own children. Observe the context of one mention of this story:

> . . . by the measure of that sorrow, which follows barrennesse, or orbitie, we may proportion that joy, which accompanies Gods miraculous blessings, when *Women receive their dead raised to life againe.* In all the secular, and prophane Writers in the world, in the whole bodie of Story, you shall not finde such an expressing of the misery of a famine, as that of the Holy Ghost in the Lamentations; *That women eate Palmares filios;* We translate it, *Their children of a span long;* that is, that they procured abortions and untimely births of those children, which were in their bodies, that they might have so much flesh to eate. As that is proposed for the greatest misery, that ever was, women to destroy their children so, so is this for the highest accumulation of Joy, to have dead children brought to life againe (VII, No. 15, ll. 164–76).

The paragraph continues, listing several examples of imagined joy— what St. Augustine might have felt if his son had been restored to life, the joy of any parent at the recovery of a sick child, the joy of any man at the coming of spring after winter. The first example— the enforced cannibalism—clearly need not have been given, and Donne has gone out of his way to produce a startling illustration. But the context shows that he has used it to stir up the imaginations of his hearers, to make them feel the horror or despair of death at its worst, from the viewpoint of the survivors, in order to let them experience, with the immediacy of real relief an emotional rather than a simply pious acceptance of resurrection. For this aspect of Donne's use of the macabre, one might use his own phrase for one of the preacher's functions; it is a "shaking the soul" (IV, No. 8, l. 46). It is followed here, as always, by an elevation of the shaken soul to happier thoughts.

Meditational literature generally takes humility as the first step of the way toward the mystic's contemplation or toward the turning of the whole mind upon God. In Meres's translation of Luis de Granada's *Spiritual and Heavenly Exercises,* the first meditation, on the miseries in which man is created, summarizes the thoughts of

Hugh of St. Victor, Augustine, and Bernard. Here man is called a "stinking and detestable worm," "froth and fome made flesh," a "putrified carkasse," "an uncleane sperme, a sack of dunge, and food for wormes."[13] Since these or similar pages of earnest invective were certainly familiar to his auditors, Donne could only arrange old thoughts in a new way to make his point:

Behold God hath walled us with mud walls, and wet mud walls, that waste away faster, then God meant at first, they should. . . . Thou seemest, in the eye of the world, to walk in *silks,* and thou doest but walke in *searcloth;* Thou hast a desire to please some *eyes,* when thou hast much to do, not to displease every *Nose;* and thou wilt solicite an adulterous entrance into their beds, who, if they should but see thee goe into thine own bed, would need no other mortification, nor answer to thy solicitation. Thou pursuest the works of the flesh, and hast none, for thy flesh is but dust held together by plaisters; Dissolution and putrefaction is gone over thee alive; Thou has[t] over liv'd thine own death, and art become thine own ghost, and thine own hell (II, No. 2, ll. 396–411).

The preacher's business, said Erasmus, is to describe things as they are, and such description Augustine and Bernard and Hugh had tried to achieve. In this passage, which may be characterized with Donne's phrase "elegant horror" (II, No. 18, l. 199), it is only the elegance that is new, revitalizing an old tradition. The sermon from which this passage is taken is preached on the text, "There is no soundnesse in my flesh, because of thine anger, neither is there any rest in my bones, because of my sinne" (II, No. 2). In its development, there can be no immediate contrast with joy. But near the end of the sermon, Donne says that although he has had to insist here upon misery and sin, he will dismiss the congregation with a consolation, and knowledge of God's cure (ll. 711–24). The whole sweep of his sermons is often from earthly misery to heavenly joy, and all the macabre passages are part of this large pattern.

Donne is humorous, ironic, macabre, exalted. He is also urgent, immediate, dramatic. He uses all kinds of impersonation and dialogue, for example, to make his sermons more vivid. These stage techniques have some odd as well as some obvious characteristics. The apostrophe is probably the most emotionally charged of all these, and the least used. Except for the omnipresent "Beloved," and one apostrophe in the commemoration sermon for Lady Danvers, in which he addresses her and asks her to appear in the memories of those present (VIII, No. 2, ll. 820–39), it is ordinarily a concentrated attack upon some particular sin, directed at a hypothetical member of the congregation. It is used in accordance with his own comment that all the sermon is not meant for everyone; a preacher with a multitude of different people before him cannot hope to reach everyone every time. The apostrophe is really an attempt to score a lucky hit, to reach by violence a soul that cannot be moved by gentler forms of persuasion. His famous apostrophe to the atheist is one of these, and exemplifies not only the apostrophe, but also several of the other devices that I want to stress in this section.

The paragraph begins abruptly with two exclamations:

Poore intricated soule! Riddling, perplexed, labyrinthicall soule! Thou couldest not say, that thou beleevest not in God, if there were no God; Thou couldest not beleeve in God, if there were no God; If there were no God, thou couldest not speake, thou couldest not thinke, not a word, not a thought, no not against God; Thou couldest not blaspheme the Name of God, thou couldest not sweare, if there were no God: For, all thy faculties, how ever depraved, and perverted by thee, are from him; and except thou canst seriously beleeve, that thou art nothing, thou canst not beleeve that there is no God (VIII, No. 14, ll. 740–48).

The circling of the rapid flow of words around the word "God" creates an atmosphere dominated by the thought of God to stand in irony against the atheist's position and to provide the emotional setting of the passage. The paragraph then moves into a colloquy between Donne and the atheist, in which several further scenes are suggested:

If I should aske thee at a Tragedy, where thou shouldest see him that had drawne blood, lie weltring, and surrounded in his owne blood, Is there a God now? If thou couldst answer me, No, These are but Inventions, and Representations of men, and I beleeve a God never the more for this; If I should ask thee at a Sermon, where thou shouldest heare the Judgements of God formerly denounced, and executed, re-denounced, and applied to present occasions, Is there a God now? If thou couldest answer me, No, These are but Inventions of State, to souple and regulate Congregations, and keep people in order, and I beleeve a God never the more for this; Bee as confident as thou canst, in company; for company is the Atheists Sanctuary; I respit thee not till the day of Judgement, when I may see thee upon thy knees, upon thy face, begging of the hills, that they would fall downe and cover thee from the fierce wrath of God, to aske thee then, Is there a God now? I respit thee not till the day of thine own death, when thou shalt have evidence enough, that there is a God, though no other evidence, but to finde a Devill, and evidence enough, that there is a Heaven, though no other evidence, but to feele Hell; To aske thee then, Is there a God now? I respit thee but a few houres, but six houres, but till midnight. Wake then; and then darke, and alone, Heare God aske thee then, remember that I asked thee now, Is there a God? and if thou darest, say No (VIII, No. 14, ll. 748–70).

A great many of Donne's favorite techniques are crowded together in this passage. The chief unifying device is, of course, the repetition that runs, with constant variations, through the whole paragraph. The stiffness of the dialogue is characteristic; Donne tries to make his colloquies not realistically individual, but typical, and by means of formality he achieves this equivalent of symbolism. He is also, of course, enabled to increase the emotional volume of the passage by the repetitiveness that contributes both to the formality of the dialogue and to the regularity of the paragraph.

It is also important that among the best proofs of God he can think of, and the first that come to his mind, are two forms of human art, and these two the secular play and the sermon. Between the stage villain weltering in artificial blood and the atheist living out his tragedy, Donne sees little difference, for both are emblems of his moral vision. And the sermon too is an emblem, in its character of sacrament inanimated by the Holy Ghost; the apostrophe to the atheist exists inside one of its own proofs for God's existence. This is the first occasion I have had to notice Donne's use of art terms; their effect is to lessen the distinction between art and life, calling attention to Donne's belief that everything in the world is God's art, and strengthening the view that the life of art is the spiritual reality of which the art of life is the visible manifestation.

I shall want to come back again both to this and to his use of midnight. To him the time has a psychological and symbolic meaning signifying the utter helplessness of the man to whom physical deprivation of light corresponds to internal darkness. All these techniques meet in this apostrophe, whose form provides scope for an address in which passionate immediacy of tone is combined with a use of formal rhetoric and technical art that raises the immediacy to broad symbolic expressiveness.

The dialogue of the apostrophe is one illustration of Donne's many uses of dramatic speech, in impersonation of things or people other than himself. He does not employ this technique often in an extended form, but conversation and monologue scattered through the pages of the sermons do cumulatively help to give dramatic immediacy to his preaching. Once, he mentions dialogue as a legitimate form, even for a whole sermon, and although he never begins to make such extensive use of it, the passage shows his awareness of the propriety of the method: "*Damascen* hath a Sermon of the Assumption of the blessed Virgin, which whole Sermon is but a Dialogue, in which *Eve* acts the first part, and the blessed Virgin another; It is but a Dialogue, yet it is a Sermon. If I should insist upon this Dialogue, between God and *David, Tu me, Tu me,* Doe thou worke upon me, it would not be the lesse a profitable part of a Sermon for that" (V, No. 15, ll. 329–34).

Sometimes Donne rearranges Scripture in some creative fashion to shape a scene, or equates a Scriptural speaker or one of the Fathers with members of the congregation, giving his people, like actors, their scripts. In a sermon preached at Whitehall in 1621, he envisages Christ's arrival in heaven by imagining the conversation that would take place between him and the angels, taking a passage from Isaiah to use as dialogue:

. . . the highest of the highest orders of Angels, were amaz'd at Christs coming up in the Flesh; it was a new and unexpected thing . . . There they say with amazement, *Quis iste? Who is this that cometh from Edom, with dyed garments from Bozrah?* And Christ answers there, *Ego, it is I, I that speak in righteousness, I that am mighty to save.* The Angels reply, *Wherefore are thy garments red, like him that treadeth the wine-press?* and Christ gives them satisfaction, *calcavi;* You mistake not the matter, . . . *I have trodden the wine-press alone, and of the people there was none with me* (III, No. 9, ll. 394–404).

Taking the idea from Dionysius and most of the words from the Bible, Donne cut some phrases and translated others into his own idiom; the repetitions, the stage directions, and the one dialogue phrase not underlined are his work.

He also frequently enlarges upon a Biblical quotation, as in the following illustration, where the Christian is given Christ's lines for Peter with Donne's additions: "Take heed what you heare; and be but able to say to Satan then, as Christ said to *Peter,* in his name, *Vade retro Satan, come after me Satan,* come after me *to morrow;* come a minute after my soule is departed from this body, come to me, where I shall be then" (VII, No. 16, ll. 750–54). One notices in all these passages that Donne makes no attempt to preserve or create an idiom different from his own; the Bible and the Fathers are translated or extended into Donne, and all things given voice in his sermons speak in his manner. Yet enough of the original remains to give the old passage a new and revivifying context; the device had been known to homilists for centuries (compare Alfred's refurbishing of Augustine with homely metaphors) [14] as a means by which Christian writings could be brought home to an audience born in a different country and in a later age.

There are a few techniques by which Donne, in context, distinguishes the feigned speech of others from his own when, by means of dialogue or monologue, he characterizes an attitude in order to satirize or refute it; and they are some of the same techniques that I have pointed out in his sentence structure, adapted to this particular use. Repetition and refrain are heavily employed with a gracelessness that can almost be thought of as a parody of his usual style, and the effect is of flurried and stereotyped speech, connoting the uneasy unoriginality of the sinner's nature. An illustration is the following passage from a sermon on a text from Amos, where he imitates the somewhat frantic self-righteousness of the prophet's hearers:

... to the Prophets themselves they were come to say, You your selves live parched and macerated in a starved and penurious fortune, and therefore you cry out that all we must die of famine too, you your selves have not a foot of land among all the Tribes, and therfore you cry out that all the Tribes must be carried into another Land in Captivity. That which you call the Day of the Lord is come upon you, beggery, and nakednesse, and hunger, contempt, and affliction, and imprisonment is come upon you, and therefore you will needs extend this day upon the whole State, but *desideramus,* we would fain see any such thing come to passe, we would fain see God goe about to do any such thing, as that the State should not be wise enough to prevent him (II, No. 18, ll. 102–13).

The passage continues in a torrent of language until, at the close of the paragraph, the last sentence quoted recurs again, "We would fain see such a time, we would fain see such a God as were much too hard for us."

At times the repetitiveness assumes the position of refrain in a paragraph, for it should be clear by now that this is literary speech, patterned as carefully as poetry. Another pattern reveals itself in a second characteristic of this device; Donne uses it to buttress an attack of his own. The technique is related to an older catechistical tradition, in which the writer creates a dialogue, putting questions into the mouths of his audience in order to answer them;[15] but it is in Donne's variation clearly more dramatic and creates in this violent opposition of viewpoints a greater tension and climax when the two meet; especially when they are tied together within a single sentence: "Neither say to your selves, we shall have preparatives enough, warnings enough, many more Sermons before it come to that, and so it is too soon yet; you are not sure you shall have more; not sure you shall have all this; not sure you shall be affected with any" (VIII, No. 7, ll. 15–19); "wilt thou say with that man in the Gospell, *Omnia haec à juventute,* I have kept all this Law from my youth? From thy youth? remember thy youth well" (II, No. 18, ll. 292–94). The device may be used simply for contrast of viewpoint, as in this exceptionally macabre passage where he pits the supernatural resurrection of the body against its condition in this world:

Here a bullet will aske a man, where's your arme; and a Wolf wil ask a woman, where's your breast? A sentence in the Star-chamber will aske him, Where's your ear, and a months close prison will aske him, where's your flesh? a fever will aske him, where's your Red, and a morphew will aske him, where's your white? But when after all this . . . *I shall see God,* I shall see him in my flesh (III, No. 3, ll. 814–20).

In all these instances, dramatic speech is a quality of the prose, not something independently presented. While it contributes immediacy and urgency, its poetic character removes it somewhat from the atmosphere of common reality, and the situations described become types of human experience.

Hypotyposis is the term used by the rhetoricians to describe the technique of bringing an imagined scene directly before the listener's eyes.[16] It is comparable to the composition of place suggested by the spiritual exercises, except that these often suggest that the meditator think of himself as actually in the scene that he has conceived.[17] Donne's use of the technique is often closer to the second kind of thing, but it has further characteristics of his own devising. The scene is sometimes not visual at all, and sometimes its visual elements are only manifestations of a psychological or spiritual environment. It is always symbolic rather than realistic, and during the course of this discussion we will see much more evidence of his use of art terms. Finally, the scene generally has much more relevance to the life of the individual soul than to anything else; he employs the usual descriptions of Biblical events only when they can be made directly applicable to the soul's welfare. Five particular kinds of scenes are most frequent and best illustrate his practice. The first two make use of time—the present moment and midnight. The others illustrate the progress of the soul, beginning with self-analysis, proceeding to application of Christ's merits to the soul, and ending with description of Christian death.

The present moment is made a surrounding symbol as the moment that may, for some, become eternity. The connection between timelessness and time, or between God and man, is for Donne that each of man's minutes can reflect and expand into God's eternal now, so that every given moment is potentially the moment of redemption and grace: "his grace is renewed to me every minute" (VIII, No. 16, ll. 481); "God . . . is fitting the robe of Christs righteousness to me now, this minute" (IX, No. 1, ll. 585–88); "Lord put this swiftnesse into our sins, that in this one minute, in which our eyes are open towards thee, and thine eares towards us, our sins, all our sins, even from the *impertinent frowardnesse of our childhood,* to the *unsufferable frowardnesse of our age,* may meet in our present *confessions,* and *repentances,* and never appear more" (II, No. 1, ll. 784–89); "now God comes to thee, not as in the dawning of the day, not as in the bud of the spring, but as the Sun at noon to illustrate all shadowes, as the sheaves in harvest, to fill all penuries, all occasions invite his mercies, and all times are his seasons" (VI, No. 8, ll. 149–52). The emphasis on God's eternal Now, so constantly repeated in the sermons, both imparts urgency to their general tone and, as we shall see, creates the scene for meditation.

The moment is explicitly made a doorway to the spiritual or heavenly life in such passages as the following, in which the congregation is asked to make this minute their return to God:

If there be a minute of patience left, heare me say, This minute that is left, is that eternitie which we speake of; upon this minute dependeth that eternity: And this minute, God is in this Congregation, and puts his eare to every one of your hearts, and hearkens what you will bid him say to your selves: whether he shall blesse you for your acceptation, or curse you for your refusall of him this minute: for this minute makes up your *Century,* your hundred yeares, your eternity, because it may be your last minute (VII, No. 14, ll. 717–25).

The concept of the meaninglessness of human time, except as it becomes an eternal Now, before God, enables Donne to treat past time as immediately present. This is a device which he uses rather moderately, however; he is more likely to make parts of the past into symbols than to suggest that some past scene is immediately present before his listeners. And when he does employ the technique, it is to find types of the present in the past:

And so, for matter of Action, and Protection, come not home to your selves, stay not in your selves, not in a confidence in your owne power, and wisedome, but *Ite,* goe forth, goe forth into Ægypt, goe forth into Babylon, and look who delivered your Predecessors, (predecessors in Affliction, predecessors in Mercy) and that God, who is *Yesterday, and to day, and the same for ever,* shall doe the same things, which he did yesterday, to day, and for ever (VIII, No. 4, ll. 455–62).

From here to incorporation of the past into the present is only a step: "We need not put on spectacles to search Maps for this Land of the *Gergesens;* God knows we dwell in it" (X, No. 2, ll. 61–62).

Consideration of the present moment as future is most fully exploited as dramatic device in references to the last judgment, which he says can be anticipated in the present: "this is one great benefit from the present contemplation of the future judgement, that whosoever does truly, and advisedly believe, that ever he shall come to that judgement, is at it now" (VIII, No. 15, ll. 308–11). The question "are you reconciled? durst you heare the trumpet nowe?" (II, No. 6, l. 205) states explicitly what is always in his mind in poetry as well as prose; it expresses his sense of the Christian's need for shock tactics in conversion. Each moment is crucial, bordering on eternity:

> Now, in respect of the time after this judgement, (which is Eternity) the time between this and it cannot be a minute; and therefore think thy self at that Tribunall, that judgement now: Where thou shalt not onely heare all thy sinfull workes, and words, and thoughts repeated, which thou thy selfe hadst utterly forgot, but thou shalt heare thy good works, thine almes, thy comming to Church, thy hearing of Sermons given in evidence against thee, because they had hypocrisie mingled in them; yea thou shalt finde even thy repentence to condemne thee, because thou madest that but a doore to a relapse. There thou shalt see, to thine inexpressible terror, some others cast downe into hell, for thy sins; for those sins which they would not have done, but upon thy provocation. There thou shalt see some that occasioned thy sins, and accompanied thee in them, and sinned them in a greater measure then thou didst, taken up into heaven, because in the way, they remembred the end, and thou shalt sink under a lesse waight, because thou never lookedst towards him that would have eased thee of it. *Quis non cogitans haec in desperationis rotetur abyssum?* Who can once thinke of this and not be tumbled into desperation? But who can think of it twice, maturely, and by the Holy Ghost, and not finde comfort in it, when the same light that shewes mee the judgement, shewes me the Judge too? (VII, No. 8, ll. 737–57)

The passage may be compared with the "Hymn to God the Father," which it echoes, and with "At the round worlds imagin'd corners," which also anticipates the last judgment. The sermon passage, far less compressed, and giving less weight to individual words, still maintains much of the cumulative power of the sonnet. However, since it is distanced by use of the future tense, greater elaboration, and some moral commentary, the symbolizing of and emphasis upon the moment gain importance as the chief means by which he does give urgency to the meditation, warning his readers to live always so as to be able to say, "come Lord Jesu come quickly, and be glad if at the going out of these dores, we might meet him coming in the clouds" (I, No. 9, ll. 220–22). The imposition of subjective time upon external reality enables Donne to give his hearers a meditational environment which they themselves have shaped; and to concentrate within the moment a world of meaning.

Another time that he often returns to in his sermons and to which he gives extended treatment is midnight. Here the scene is less immediate; there is no suggestion that midnight is now, and the second person is not always used. However, there is the same use of time as symbol and setting, this time for psychological drama. For Donne midnight has several connotations that enrich its meaning. It was of course the time suggested by St. Ignatius for the first of a series of meditations. Donne also thinks of it in relation to two particular Biblical passages. The first is Amos 8:9: "And it shall come to pass in that day, saith the Lord God, that I will cause the sun to go down at noon, and I will darken the earth in the clear day." The second is the New Testament parable of the rich man in Luke 12:16–21:

And he spake a parable unto them, saying, The ground of a certain rich man brought forth plentifully: And he thought within himself, saying, What shall I do, because I have no room where to bestow my fruits? And he said, This will I do: I will pull down my barns, and build greater, and there will I bestow all my fruits and my goods.
And I will say to my soul, Soul, thou hast much goods laid up for many years; take thine ease, eat, drink, and be merry.
But God said unto him, Thou fool, this night thy soul shall be required of thee: then whose shall those things be, which thou hast provided?
So is he that layeth up treasure for himself, and is not rich toward God.

It is also possible that Donne associated the time with the final scene of *Dr. Faustus,* for passages in the sermons seem to echo the play, and it has been conjectured that he knew it.[18] His own association of midnight with depression and horror, however, is personal and could only have been reinforced by these passages. He thinks of midnight as a time when the self, deprived of reliance upon all external things, is thrown back upon its own resources and is entirely subject both to awareness of God's justice or mercy and to the consequences of its own spiritual emptiness or well-being. Thus, he uses the word first as a psychological figure, when he talks of "a melancholy midnight of dejection of spirit" (VIII, No. 8, ll. 545–46), the "midnight of afflictions and tribulations" (VIII, No. 1, l. 600), or the "midnight of sadnesse, and dejection" (V, No. 14, l. 902). In longer considerations of the time, he thinks of the heightening of fear and terror that darkness and isolation can bring to the sinner:

> . . . every midnight shall be a day of judgement to him, and keepe him awake; and when consternation, and lassitude lend him, or conterfait to him a sleep, so S. *Basil* sayes of the righteous, *Etiam somnia justorum preces sunt,* That even their Dreames are prayers, so this incorrigible sinners Dreames shall be, not onely presages of his future, but acts of his present condemnation (VI, No. 1, ll. 816–21).

The actual night merges in his thought with the night of the dying man, which is no different, though more final:

> Remember then, and remember now; *In Die,* in the day; . . . for in the night, in our last night, those thoughts that fall upon us, they are rather dreams, then true remembrings; we do rather dream that we repent, then repent indeed, upon our death-bed. To him that travails by night a bush seems a tree, and a tree seems a man, and a man a spirit; nothing hath the true shape to him; to him that repents by night, on his death-bed, neither his own sins, nor the mercies of God have their true proportion. Fool, saies Christ, this night they will fetch away thy soul (II, No. 11, ll. 153–64).

Atheism is in particular his target in meditation on midnight, for this sin above all others he considers possible only in company. "Whom do I tremble at, and sweat under, at midnight, . . . if there be no God?" (VIII, No. 9, ll. 225–26). Surely here, the reader may say, is the baroque spirit, the baroque macabre. Yes. Here also are the contrast, the becomingness, the transformation of an art that seldom ends with the rattling of the bones or the "metaphysical shudder": "For even midnight is noone in the sight of God, and when your candles are put out, his Sunne shines still" (IX, No. 1, ll. 452–53); "But even in the depth of any spirituall night, in the shadow of death, in the midnight of afflictions and tribulations, God brings light out of darknesse, and gives his Saints occasion of glorifying him. . . . Nay, they see God better in the dark, then they did in the light" (VIII, No. 1, ll. 599–608). Within the moment that can be eternity, midnight and noon both potentially exist; man's meditational environment, and his exterior life, are conditioned by his spiritual state. The urgency that the constant use of the moment gives to the tone of the sermons is colored by the equally constant use of despair and joy, darkness and light.

The progress of the soul is given considerable space in the sermons and does to some extent differentiate Donne's preaching from that of other Anglicans, who are less concerned than he with intensive self-analysis. The method varies, from professional attacks upon the soul's sinfulness, where imagery is less used to create a real scene than to provide a probing tool; through very vivid meditational description of the soul's entrance into the life of Christ; to somewhat formal emblematic deathbed tableaux, where the moment of transition from earth to heaven is represented by a cessation of motion and a kind of suspension of time often accompanied by use of art terms.

In Donne's pleas to his congregation to descend into themselves, the most important images to assist concentration upon inner being are those dealing with law, with anatomy, and with healing. It has not, I think, been sufficiently observed that his legal metaphors are not simply the result of his education at Lincoln's Inn, nor only the result of his desire to appeal to the experience of the Lincoln's Inn benchers, to whom he preached most of his early sermons. They play an important part in the development of his thought.[19] As a man young in religion, he added them to the logical paraphernalia of his early poetry, to use as a kind of defense against a God with whom he was not quite comfortable and as a way of trying to make the justice of God intelligible in human terms. In the sermons the legal words are frequently used to suggest a court scene—the trial

of the soul; even when a trial is not vividly described, the terminology implies the existence of such a setting. And even in the later
sermons, these words still appear, centered for the most part on his
thoughts of the Last Judgment, and his desire to teach his people
how to anticipate that judgment in the present, to try themselves:

> He that is afraid to be brought to the last judgement, hath but one Refuge,
> but one Sanctuary, *Ascendat Tribunal Mentis suae & constituat se ante seip-
> sum;* Let him cite himself before himself, give evidence himself against him-
> self; and so guilty as he is found here, so innocent he shall stand there (VIII,
> No. 15, ll. 317–21).

There are other figures which, although they are not legal, present
the same analytic tone, the same urging toward self-examination.
The anatomist, in particular, also strips the soul:

> But we may better discern our selves *in singulis,* then *in omnibus;* better
> by taking ourselves in pieces, then altogether, we understand the frame of
> mans body, better when we see him naked, than apparrelled, howsoever; and
> better by seeing him cut up, than by seeing him do any exercise alive; one
> desection, one Anatomy teaches more of that, than the marching, or drilling
> of a whole army of living men. Let every one of us therefore dissect and cut
> up himself, and consider what he was before God raised him friends (I,
> No. 7, ll. 188–95).

This meditation proceeds by peeling the self like an onion, reducing
it first from its acquired endowments to its original solitary ignorance, then to its life before it had a soul, and then to its uncreated
state. The memory works back toward what a modern writer might
describe as racial consciousness. Self-dissection is a learning to understand Man, and as Donne says elsewhere, the Christian may find
sympathy and kinship with others in the knowledge of himself.

Does this far-from-new imagery add anything to our understanding of Donne's prose? I think it does. It belongs with all the legalistic and analytic passages in his sermons; together they contribute
a sense of precision, and intellectual and spiritual anxiety to his
prose. Further, the treatment of the soul as a thing, to be brought
to court, or cut up and analyzed is another instance of physical
handling of spiritual fact which will come out more clearly in the
next illustration.

There are numerous images of healing, of curing the sickness one finds in the process of self-analysis.[20] The soul, for Donne, is the receptacle for the image of God. A sick soul is described as frozen, benumbed, or, occasionally, inflamed, and so not translucent but opaque, whereas a soul in which the image of God is clear is a mirror or glass through which God himself may be known. In passages using these figures, the meditator is again asked to descend into himself to heal the disorder:

Thou hast a gate into Heaven in thy selfe; If thou beest not sensible of other mens poverties, and distresses, yet *Miserere animae tuae,* have mercy on thine owne soule; thou hast a poor guest, an Inmate, a sojourner, within these mudwals, this corrupt body of thine; be mercifull and compassionate to that Soule; cloath that Soul, which is stripp'd and left naked, of all her originall righteousnesse; feed that Soule, which thou hast starv'd; purge that Soule, which thou hast infected; warm, and thaw that Soul, which thou hast frozen with indevotion; coole, and quench that Soul, which thou has inflamed with licentiousness; *Miserere animae tuae,* begin with thine own Soule; be charitable to thy self first, and thou wilt remember, that God hath made of one bloud, all Mankind, and thou wilt find out thy selfe, in every other poor Man, and thou wilt find Christ Jesus himselfe in them all (II, No. 10, ll. 83–96).

These are the most important techniques used for concentration upon the soul and the self as it is in isolation. The second step—the application of Christ's merits to the soul—involves vivid sensory description and comprises Donne's closest approximation to the traditional composition of place. Through applying Christ's merits to the soul in meditation, he says that the Christian can "come to a conformity with Christ" (II, No. 9, ll. 548–49). The "liberality," the real goodness of the preacher, is to insist upon exactly what he enforces in illustration in the following passage:

To finde a languishing wretch in a sordid corner, not onely in a penurious fortune, but in an oppressed conscience, His eyes under a diverse suffocation, smothered with smoake, and smothered with teares, His eares estranged from all salutations, and visits, and all sounds, but his own sighes, and the stormes and thunders and earthquakes of his owne despaire, To enable this man to open his eyes, and see that Christ Jesus stands before him, and sayes, *Behold and see, if ever there were any sorrow, like my sorrow,* and my sorrow is overcome, why is not thine? . . . To bow downe those Heavens, and bring them into his sad Chamber, To set Christ Jesus before him, to out-sigh him, out-weepe him, out-bleed him, out-dye him, To transferre all the fasts, all the scornes, all the scourges, all the nailes, all the speares of Christ Jesus upon him, and so, making him the Crucified man in the sight of the Father, because all the actions, and passions of the Son, are appropriated to him, . . . to comfort this sad soule so, as that he shall beleeve, and by beleeving finde all Christ to be his, this is that Liberality which we speake of now (VIII, No. 10, ll. 340–60).

Here there is for the first time a real stage setting; and in it, heaven and earth are boldly juxtaposed, a small room required to hold the cosmos. The union of finite with infinite is also expressed in the conformity of the mortal man to Christ, to the point of actual identification with Christ's suffering and death. The use of the small material room as receptacle for heaven thus parallels the use of man as receptacle for Christ's infinite suffering, and infinite reward; he is again using physical shock to emphasize the wonder of the spiritual transformation.

In the next illustration, the "I" is brought to the same identification with Christ. He is preaching on the verses in St. Matthew that describe Christ's calling of Peter and Andrew, and in the second sermon on the text he discusses the means by which the Christian may follow Christ. The material is divided into four sections: "Our Saviour saith, *Hee that will follow me, let him take up his crosse, and follow me.* You see foure stages, foure resting, baiting places in this progresse. It must bee a *crosse,* And it must be *my crosse,* And then it must be *taken up by me,* And with this crosse of mine, thus taken up by me, I must *follow Christ,* that is, carry my crosse to his" (II, No. 14, ll. 463–68). The first section then proceeds as follows:

First it must bee a *Crosse, Tollat crucem;* for every man hath afflictions, but every man hath not crosses. Onely those afflictions are crosses, *whereby the world is crucified to us, and we to the world.* . . . And when I am come to that conformity with my Saviour, as to *fulfill his sufferings in my flesh,* (as I am, when I glorifie him in a Christian constancy and cheerfulnesse in my afflictions) then I am crucified with him, carried up to his Crosse: And as *Elisha* in raysing the *Shunamits* dead child, put his mouth upon the childs mouth, his eyes, and his hands, upon the hands, and eyes of the child; so when my crosses have carried mee up to my Saviours Crosse, I put my hands into his hands, and hang upon his nailes, I put mine eyes upon his, and wash off all my former unchast looks, and receive a soveraigne tincture, and a lively verdure, and a new life into my dead teares, from his teares. I put my mouth upon his mouth, and it is I that say, *My God, my God, why hast thou forsaken me?* and it is I that recover againe, and say, *Into thy hands, O Lord, I commend my spirit.* Thus my afflictions are truly a crosse, when those afflictions doe truely crucifie me, and souple me, and mellow me, and knead me, and roll me out, to a conformity with Christ. It must be this *Crosse,* and then it must be *my crosse* that I must take up, *Tollat suam* (ll. 469–91).

The passage coincides with Donne's outline of the points to be covered in a sermon division, which points, represented as the stages of a royal progress, are the stages in the carrying to Christ's cross of the cross which is developed as a symbol during the course of the division. Thus the image is analyzed within a dramatic framework; and the meditational drama here is employed in partial support of the analysis. The first stage of the progress presents the tableau of the crucified Christ. It also describes the conformation of the soul to Christ in terms of the art of pastry-making—a very clear example of the slightly comic aspect of the materialization of spiritual meaning in metaphysical wit. This device corresponds as emphasis to the supporting use of the small room in the previous selection; both startlingly describe in physical, somewhat mechanical terms the spiritual process that follows the imaginative physical juxtaposition of the Christian with Christ.

The tableau deathbed scenes which occur rather often in the sermons are of course an expression of a highly traditional theme, expressed everywhere from Seneca to Montaigne; it is the *Ars Moriendi* theme,[21] and in Donne's case one must be very conscious of that particular tradition, for his scenes are frequently either explicitly presented as art, like the *Ars Moriendi* engravings, or ordered in such a way that they approximate the effect of painting and sculpture. They are deathbed scenes because such a setting enables him to bring together those dramatic or pictorial devices which most fully depict several of his chief concerns. The Resurrection was always to him the central fact of Christianity, as it symbolizes the meeting of earth and heaven, the final cleansing and unification of the personality, resurrection from sin, the reunion of soul and body, and the expansion of time into eternity. Granada's translator expresses, in a way that Donne would have approved, this telescoping of the two worlds, when he says of the soul at the point of death: "Looking backwardes, it shall see all her life time, as the tract and step of one pace. And looking forwards, seeing so everlasting an age of eternity, it shall howll and cry out, that in so short a time it did not purchase that great glory, which the Saintes shall enjoy for ever and ever."[22] But the accent in Donne is more often on joy than on despair.

In a Lenten sermon preached at Whitehall in 1627, he presents, toward the end, a formal diptych, parallel pictures of a sinner's and of a Christian's death. The pair is introduced in these words: "Here I shall only present to you two Pictures, two pictures in little: two pictures of dying men" (VIII, No. 7, ll. 518–19). And the picture of the Christian's death begins thus:

Bee pleased to remember that those Pictures which are deliver'd in a minute, from a print upon a paper, had many dayes, weeks, Moneths time for the graving of those Pictures in the Copper; So this Picture of that dying Man, that dies in Christ, that dies the death of the Righteous, that embraces Death as a Sleepe, was graving all his life; All his publique actions were the lights, and all his private the shadowes of this Picture. And when this Picture comes to the Presse, this Man to the streights and agonies of Death, thus he lies, thus he looks, this he is (VIII, No. 7, ll. 587–95).

The picture which follows is less visual than psychological, a description of a man whose memory, will, and understanding are united and fixed upon Christ. The use of art frames the description, makes it seem tangible, and suggests the completion of earthly endeavor, in the completion of the picture which represents the spirit of the man. The use of the present tense with the artistic terminology creates an effect of frozen motion, the symbolizing of an instant of time whose significance for this man reaches into eternity.

The moment of death may also symbolize the soul's transfer from earthly to heavenly existence as the sort of pause that is the overlapping of an end with a beginning, before either the mortal or the immortal life has ascendancy. Again, the present tense and art are among the techniques used, and the immediacy is heightened by employment of the second person:

The sun is setting to thee, and that for ever; thy houses and furnitures, thy gardens and orchards, thy titles and offices, thy wife and children are depart- ing from thee, and that for ever; a cloud of faintnesse is come over thine eyes, and a cloud of sorrow over all theirs; when his hand that loves thee best hangs tremblingly over thee to close thine eyes, *Ecce Salvator tuus venit,* behold then a new light, thy Saviours hand shall open thine eyes, and in his light thou shalt see light; and thus shalt see, that though in the eyes of men thou lye upon that bed, as a Statue on a Tomb, yet in the eyes of God, thou standest as a *Colossus,* one foot in one, another in another land; one foot in the grave, but the other in heaven; one hand in the womb of the earth, and the other in *Abrahams* bosome (II, No. 12, ll. 618–29).

There is perhaps more tenderness here in the sense of loss ex- pressed than is usual in the *Ars Moriendi* tradition; it is reminiscent of the sadness of the exile in Latin literature.[23] And the juxtaposi- tion of that and of the pious gesture of closing the dead man's eyes, with the Christian conception of immediate passage into God's presence is startling and effective. More important to the present discussion is the fact that the coincidence of earthly with heavenly being is symbolized in sculpture as tomb statue and colossus. And although a number of things are happening in the paragraph, there is no real movement, for the duality of action reinforces the use of art terms in the suppression of all action.

Some generalizations can be made about Donne's tracing in ex- tended treatment through the sermons of these three stages of Chris- tian development. In all three, he considers the soul as an objective "thing," with substance and dimensions of its own. Those self-analy- ses in which the soul is considered as something diseased and sinful treat it half-professionally, half-mechanically, as a piece of matter to be dissected or healed, or as a case, a prisoner, to which legal attention must be given. At the same time there is an attempt to make this thing conscious of itself; the meditator is made both doc- tor and lawyer to probe the disease and guilt; and the patient and sinner is forced by analysis to feel the pain of which he has not been aware. In scenes describing the soul's conformity to Christ, the soul has become sufficiently conscious of itself to guide its own actions, and what changes are wrought upon it are a result of its successful identification with Christ. These changes are physical, mechanized transformations. The deathbed scenes symbolize the completion of the work of art that, through its own effort and the action of Christ, the soul has been made. The whole process is supposed to be a renewal of the image of God in man.

Donne thinks of the soul, as St. Bernard did, as a receptacle for the image of God that is so irrevocably stamped in man that it can never be burnt out by sin or punishment. The soul is "the Gallery for this Picture, the Arch for this Statue, the Table, and frame and shrine for this Image of God," and the body is the outer case: "as you see some Pictures, to which the very tables are Jewells; some Watches, to which the very cases are Jewells, and therefore they have outward cases too; and so the Picture, and the Watch is in that outward case, of what meaner stuff soever that be: so is this Image in this body as in an outward case" (IX, No. 2, ll. 424–26, ll. 407–12). The meditations and scenes which discuss the progress of the Christian life are qualified as drama by the use of art for description of the renewal of the tarnished image, and the transformation of body and soul into emblems of spiritual meaning.

But for what reason does Donne choose such images as these? Here, where he describes matters that are central to the spiritual exercises, one might expect from a man like him more blood and thunder, more gnashing of teeth, and less of the calm that art, used in this way, provides. I have supposedly been talking about techniques of immediacy, yet many of these illustrations could be used to exemplify esthetic distance. The answer to this question will become clearer in the next chapter, but I shall make some tentative generalizations now. The artistic terminology frees the figures from time, and makes the actual symbolic. Donne as artist and as preacher sees everything as emblems; art seems to be as real to him personally as the world around him. These devices are closely related to the physical transformation that has already been discussed. And Donne the artificer controls their movement.

His use of the first person, while it is another subject, eventually provides the most extraordinary illustrations of this kind of artistry. There would seem to be something immediate to the point of flamboyancy about the style of a man who so often speaks for himself in the pulpit. It is true that the ecclesiastical rhetoricians considered and approved the minister's inclusion of himself with his congregation,[24] citing the authority of St. Paul, but preachers of the time spoke very rarely of themselves. Donne frequently justifies his preaching of himself, referring to Plato as well as Paul, and noting the possibility of a *persona* as well as direct self-confession. Donne's *persona* is simply his pulpit self; as he assumes that a judge is a different person upon the bench than he is at home (and, interestingly, uses the point as analogous to the difference between ordinary and sacramental bread), so he assumes that he is a different man in the pulpit, as preacher of God's word. Thus his use of the first person combines the immediacy of the "I," in varying degrees, with the ceremonial and symbolic nature that he attributes to himself as intermediary between God and man. He uses the "I" for purposes ranging from simple convenience to meditational drama and symbolism.

At its simplest, the "I" simply facilitates the making of a point, as in the two or three instances when he uses illustrations from his own experience as *exempla* (II, No. 3, ll. 635ff; IV, No. 7, ll. 893ff), or in the five sermons preached upon the five psalms assigned to him as prebend of St. Paul's, when he uses his personal interest in these psalms as a way of getting into the sermon. Such uses of the first person give added immediacy to the material under discussion, because they demonstrate Donne's personal connection with it. The "I" is also used in a general way, to show how men think or behave; examples of this are passages beginning as follows: "When I pray to be delivered, and beginne to thinke that God hath bound himselfe by his promise to give me the issue with the temptation" (II, No. 6, ll. 72–74); "When I pray in my chamber, I build a Temple there, that houre; And, that minute, when I cast out a prayer, in the street, I build a Temple there" (VII, No. 11, ll. 459–61). The first person is still but a convenience, yet even so, it is a convenience that few preachers employed so frequently; it lends support to other, more interesting uses, and it has its own immediacy as well.

Very often, he speaks as representative of all men in a far more comprehensive sense, making himself a symbol of *man*. Passages beginning as follows are representative of numerous examples throughout the sermons: "God found me nothing, and of that nothing made me; *Adam* left me worse than God found me" (VII, No. 4, ll. 654–55); "And here the *aeternum* is enlarged; in the secular mariage it was an eternity considered onely in this life; but this eternity is not begun in this world, but from all eternity in the Book of life, in Gods eternall Decree for my election, there Christ was maried to my soul" (III, No. 11, ll. 421–24). The "I" speaking is the soul of man objectified in the person and words of John Donne, and it is a timeless "I," which incorporates the whole history of mankind into itself. Thus, this first important use of the first person is also another way, besides his explicit employment of time, of making a limited thing—Donne in the pulpit—a means of denying the importance of chronological time measured in generations, and compressing all human experience into a point that symbolizes the indwelling of an eternal God in a temporal world.

Such a use of the "I" seems to give an exaggerated importance to the individual because it is so bold a device for the speaker to make himself his own symbol, but I think that many writers (though not, generally, in the pulpit) were experimenting with this device at this time. Montaigne does it; so does Thomas Browne. It was not possible in the late Renaissance for a man to think of himself as a unique and lonely romantic figure. An abundant egotism and individualism still willingly involved in tradition is *part* of what creates the now-you-see-it-now-you-don't character of the baroque; you are almost never really sure which is the actor or writer, and which his mask.

In all the instances given so far, Donne has obeyed the rhetoricians' advice to include himself with his hearers by using the first person. There are other passages where, although the use of the

"I" heralds no specific references to himself, a scene is described with such immediacy and vividness of detail that we must suppose him to be acting out his own part. These passages, perhaps more than any others to be discussed, are self-dramatizations. The great passage beginning "That God should let my soule fall out of his hand" is one; the following is another:

But when I lye under the hands of that enemie, that hath reserved himselfe to the last, to my last bed, then when I shall be able to stir no limbe in any other measure then a Feaver or a Palsie shall shake them, when everlasting darknesse shall have an inchoation in the present dimnesse of mine eyes, and the everlasting gnashing in the present chattering of my teeth, and the everlasting worme in the present gnawing of the Agonies of my body, and anguishes of my minde, when the last enemie shall watch my remedilesse body, and my disconsolate soule there, there, where not the Physitian, in his way, perchance not the Priest in his, shall be able to give any assistance, And when he hath sported himselfe with my misery upon that stage, my deathbed, shall shift the Scene, and throw me from that bed, into the grave, and there triumph over me, God knowes, how many generations, till the Redeemer, my Redeemer, the Redeemer of all me, body as well as soule, come againe (IV, No. 1, ll. 394–408).

The passage includes one of a number of stage metaphors that run through the sermons, in which the concept of man as actor on God's or the devil's stage is developed.[25] The Donne who dramatizes himself in such passages as this is the same Donne who lay in his grave-clothes for his portrait to be made. But the figure of the stage should remind us that when he thinks of men, and of himself, as actors, his attitude can be thought of as a peculiar blending of self-consciousness with self-effacement. The actor whose life is in the hands of God is the outer shell of the soul whose willingness to belong to God determines the actor's fate. The emblem that Donne made of himself as he posed on his deathbed, and the emblem scene that he makes of himself here are analogous. And here again comes in the optical illusion. The conscious use of one's own body as a religious symbol is both a vain and a pious thing.

In some particularly interesting passages, Donne is clearly thinking of his own individual life and soul. He may present himself simply, often in a personal outburst which has behind it the force of passion, and is rarely more than a brief exclamation: "I doubt not of mine own salvation; and in whom can I have so much occasion of doubt, as in my self? When I come to heaven, shall I be able to say to any there, Lord! how got you hither? Was any man lesse likely to come thither then I?" (VIII, No. 16, ll. 595–99). Sometimes he so completely identifies himself with a Biblical character that he elaborates a quotation in his own words, and from his own thoughts. A notable instance is a passage remarked upon by Evelyn Simpson (II, p. 19), where only the first four lines quoted have any connection with Jeremiah:

Jeremy was angry because his Prophesie was like to be performed; he preached heavy Doctrin, and therfore his Auditory hated him; *Woe is me, my Mother,* says he, *that thou hast born me a man of strife, and a man of contention to the whole earth!* I preach but the messages of God; (and *vae mihi si non,* wo be unto me if I preach not them) I preach but the sense of Gods indignation upon mine own soul, in a conscience of mine own sins, I impute nothing to another, that I confesse not of my selfe, I call none of you to confession to me, I doe but confesse my self to God, and you, I rack no mans memory, what he did last year, last week, last night, I onely gather into my memory, and powr out in the presence of my God, and his Church, the sinfull history of mine own *youth* (II, No. 1, ll. 131–43).

Not only does he use himself as a specific example of a point simply expressed; at times he makes of his own life a symbol and a poem in developing a meditation that is entirely his own. The following illustration is taken from a very long passage:

First, The Militant Church shall transmit me to the Triumphant, with her recommendation, That I lived in the obedience of the Church of God, That I dyed in the faith of the Sonne of God. . . . So the Militant Church shall transmit me to the Triumphant, with this praise, this testimony, this recommendation. And then, if I have done any good to any of Gods servants . . . If I have but comforted a sad soule, or instructed an ignorant soule, If I have but preached a Sermon, and then printed that Sermon, that is, first preached it, and then lived according to it, . . . All those things that I have done for Gods glory, shall follow me . . . .
This shall be my praise to Heaven, my recommendation thither; And then, my praise in Heaven, shall be my preferment in Heaven. That those blessed Angels, that rejoyced at my Conversion before, shall praise my perseverance in that profession, and admit me to a part in all their Hymns and Hosannaes,

and Hallelujahs; which *Hallelujah* is a word produced from the very word of this Text, *Halal;* My *Hallelujah* shall be my *Halal,* my praising of God shall be my praise. . . . And when he hath sealed me with his *Euge,* and accepted my service, who shall stamp a *Vae quod non,* upon me? who shall say, Woe be unto thee, that thou didst not preach, this or that day, in this or that place? When he shall have styled me *Bone & fidelis, Good and faith-full servant,* who shall upbraid me with a late undertaking this Calling, or a slack pursuing, or a lazy intermitting the function thereof? When he shall have *entred me into my Masters joy,* what fortune, what sin can cast any Cloud of sadnesse upon me? This is that that makes Heaven, Heaven, That this Retribution, which is future now, shall be present then, and when it is then present, it shall be future againe, and present and future for ever, ever enjoyed, and expected ever (VII, No. 9, ll. 648–99).

He has begun with a generalized "I," developing the text, "And all the upright in heart shall glory." The Halal-Hallelujah comment has been explained earlier in the sermon, so that in context it seems here not so much a pedantic digression as a refrain, though here it also has the effect of tying the meditation to the words of the text, making it literary. The theme of the meditation is that the upright in heart, although they may be despised on earth, will both praise and be praised in heaven, and it is with this in mind that he begins, in the first person, the description of the passage of the upright soul into the eternal life. But he puts himself so much into the description that more and more his illustrations are taken from his own calling, so that, as it develops, it is clearly Donne himself experiencing this transmigration, and the meditation becomes something which the audience could only have shared vicariously and not with the immediacy of more generally elaborated passages. The congregation is really put into the position of an audience listening to a very moving soliloquy, and not to something which they can enter into. The pulpit here is a stage.

But not the final stage. In the last kind of usage of the "I," Donne turns himself into a symbol:

I will give God a Cup, a cup of my blood, that whereas to me the meanest of Gods servants it is honor enough to be believed for Gods sake: God should be believed for my sake, and his Gospel the better accepted, because the seal of my blood is set to it; that that dew which should water his plants, the plants of his Paradise, his Church, should drop from my veines, and that sea, that red sea, which should carry up his bark, his Ark, to the heavenly Jerusalem, should flow from me: This is that that poures joy even into my gladness, and glory even into mine honor, and peace even into my security; that exaltes and improves every good thing, every blessing that was in me before, and makes even my creation glorious, and my redemption precious; and puts a farther value upon things inestimable before, that I shall fulfill the sufferings of Christ in my flesh, and that I shall be offerd up for his Church, though not for the purchasing of it, yet for the fencing of it (VIII, No. 7, ll. 415–29).

Here he thinks of himself so completely in his function as mediator between God and man that his human qualities are wholly submissive to this symbolic portrayal. The spiritual qualities that are poured into him—joy and glory and peace—are made to seem to change him physically into something more than man. The "I," like the soul, has undergone a transformation.

Therefore we now can keep in mind these things about Donne the preacher. Irony gives his sermons a toughness of fiber, and helps to focus the importance of all he has to say, in the warning against enthusiasm which it presents. It reminds us that we are dealing with a conservative, a man who wants to preserve old truths; it encourages steadiness and singleness of mind. He uses the macabre as another kind of antidote—against complacency; its figures are intended to startle and arouse the imagination to recognition of the human state. The dark thread that the macabre gives to the sermons is utilized to strengthen by contrast their stronger note of hope and joy. Several kinds of dramatic speech add immediacy and of course drama to the sermons, but the fact that they are incorporated into paragraphs as a quality of the prose controls their realism and makes them types of human experience. Emphasis upon the moment gives the sermons urgency and provides a setting for immediate meditation upon the expansion of the moment into eternal life. This setting is colored by use of midnight and noon as symbols of the potential despair or joy that exists within the expanding minute; and juxtaposition of light and dark summarizes the slower movement of almost all the sermons from a negative to a positive tone.

The mingling of art and realism in most of the meditational

scenes is perhaps the most interesting and distinctive characteristic. It springs from Donne's literary vision—his inability or refusal to distinguish between art and life in their relation to things of the spirit. We may know very well why he does it, but when he interpolates an etymological aside into a hymn of joy, when he talks of "shifting the scene" from a sickbed to the grave, when he uses drama as a proof of God and describes death in terms of a tableau or sculpture grouping, our reaction is inevitably different from what it would be if his meditations were more apparently natural or realistic.

Modern dramatists, like Pirandello and Genet, purposely confuse life and art, the player and his role, or present apparently incompatible views of the same subject in order to involve the audience, soften the borderline between reality and artifice, and undermine the spectators' notions about absolute truth. But the ambiguity of the baroque is different from contemporary ambiguity because the intention of the artist makes it different. The Catholic baroque, even through its ambiguities, is intended to illustrate an absolute Christian world view. Bernini's famous statue of St. Teresa, for example, has been called theatrical because the walls of her chapel are lined with prie-dieus containing statues of the donor's family. If they are her audience, then they represent life and she represents art. But the chapel is built in such a way that they cannot see her; her audience consists of two very enthusiastic skeletons represented by insets in the floor, and the denizens of a heaven painted into the vault overhead. To supernatural beings, both "life" and "art," both the saint in ecstasy and the restless characters in the prie-dieu are part of one scene.[26]

It is the concept of eternity which makes Donne's mingling of life and art, and his own apparent theatricality justifiable. To us the justification may seem a thin excuse. The question resolves itself into a large issue—to what extent ought we to have to revise our own sensibilities in order to appreciate the art of another age, and must we appreciate it in the way in which the author intended? It is my belief that the tension of a dual perspective has to be a part of our reading of Donne. If we look at him both through Izaak

Walton's eyes and through our own, we will never quite trust him, but I think we will know more about his preaching than Walton did, and more about the texture of baroque than the Council of Trent ever dreamed would go into the art it recommended.

There is also the related and intrusive problem of Donne's own personality. He preached himself and so did St. Paul. Both had been worldly, self-seeking men. But Paul's new career began when he was knocked off his horse by a flash of light. Donne was forced by economic necessity to accede to the wishes of King James. He preached himself in imitation of St. Paul, and in imitation of Augustine. He was certainly sincere. There can be no doubt whatsoever that he believed everything that he preached. Nor can one doubt that he believed it best when he could make it all into art, and assign himself a central role in the drama. And he found ways, in the rhythms of his sentences, the pulls in his imagery, and in his use of the "I" to admit continuously that he needed his own thunder as much as anyone in the congregation did.

V

Word and World

The Anglo-Catholic clergy were reproached for preaching the wisdom of words, as opposed to the Word of wisdom,[1] and thus the Puritans officially ranged themselves on the side of content in the confused but perennial battle over form and meaning. But Donne was lucky to find himself in a tradition where this dichotomy, whether viewed from a literary or a nonliterary position, was simply not meaningful. In his dealings with language as such, although he continues to use techniques that we have already observed, he achieves a real unity of vision.

The Anglicans, and especially Donne, were much more preoccupied with the indwelling power of words than the Puritans were; it was in fact in a literary way that they went about magnifying the Word. Donne's view of language is intimately connected with the traditional concept of the Word, which not only inspires the sacramental treatment of Scripture, but is also closely related to the symbolic reading of the world that, coming over from Platonism into Christianity, helped to shape the metaphor of medieval theology and homiletics. In his writing the idea of the word does not constitute a philosophy; he does not think of the Logos of Philo Judaeus or Plotinus or John Scotus Erigena, and what he shares with Gregory of Nyssa, whose thought and style are sometimes very like his own,[2] is still primarily a literary and not a philosophical view. The important thing for Donne is that almost everything in the world made by God is a word of God, and as much encompassing theory as there is behind this notion can be quite simply expressed.

First of all, Donne characterizes all three persons of the Trinity as the essential Word (VIII, No. 4, ll. 324–28; VII, No. 18, ll.

519–20; III, No. 14, ll. 1–56). This Word, manifesting itself differently in Father, Son, and Holy Ghost, utters other words. The Father, or creator, spoke at the creation the words that are incarnate in the Book of the Creatures, the world. The Holy Ghost spoke in tongues of flame to the apostles, in bestowing upon them the gift of languages; and he is also the author of the written word, the Scriptures. The Son was incarnate (Word made word) in the flesh of Christ, and uttered himself again in Scripture by means of the Holy Ghost: "Christ was . . . not onely the Essentiall Word, which was always with God, but the very written word too; Christ was the Scripture, and therefore, when he refers them [the Apostles] to himselfe, he refers them to the Scriptures" (VII, No. 16, ll. 257–60; bracketed words added). The primary distinction to be made, then, in dealing with the stuff of reality, is between the Essential Word, which is unknowable to human senses and is the cause of all order in experience, and the words that are the effects and sensible extensions of the Word, which are as close to truth in their presentation of order as man can come.

Although Donne makes the usual Renaissance distinction between words and things (*verba* and *res*);[3] and although the words of Scripture are signs of things, many of which in turn are signs of other things, both the treatment of things in the world as words and the assumption of the Bible's superiority to the Book of Creatures tend to minimize the distinction between the printed and the natural world. And the extreme importance which Donne, like St. Bernard,[4] assigned to every word and syllable of Scripture gave to some of it a direct significance. The linguistic signs of abstractions, for example, are as immediately symbolic as the things of the world; and syntax and poetic form also have intrinsic significance. The application of exegetical techniques to both Word and world, through Scriptural exegesis on the one hand, and through emblematic interpretation on the other, also helps to equate the two; and the resultant intermingling in Donne of realism with technical rhetoric increases the literary character of the artistic texture discussed in the previous chapter.

I have spoken so far only of man's reading of God's words. But of course man, who has the image of the Trinity stamped upon him, is also a dispenser of words, which, like God's, are at least thought to be the outermost expression of the self, the sensible extension and embodiment of the soul. "Let us put on lineaments and apparel upon our Devotions," Donne says, "and digest the Meditations of the heart, into words of the mouth. God came to us *in verbo,* In the word; for Christ is, The word that was made flesh. Let us, that are Christians, go to God so, too" (VIII, No. 15, ll. 127–31).[5] His appreciation of the orderliness of God's presentation of himself through his words has, together with his distrust of enthusiasm, much to do with his dislike of extemporal preaching, for with his sacramental view of the Word, he sees the sermon as a point of connection between God and man. Not only is the sermon a channel of grace, as the preacher is the instrument of the Holy Ghost; it is also a symbolic joining of God with man in the union of the preacher's words with those of Scripture. Donne, assuredly still a poet in the pulpit, gladly accepts whatever justification he can find for serious handling of language. He recognized, of course, that words can lead man's imagination far astray, but there is much regret in his acknowledgment that sacrament as outward sign is but sign and not cause of God's presence (VI, No. 8, ll. 596–602), or in his praise of the compelling force of any moving image, as when he remarks that Irenaeus so well said that the Son of God is sown in every furrow in Scripture that "it is almost pity, if it be not true" (III, No. 5, ll. 239–40). What he can do to make language both accurate and impressive, he does.

Symbolic readings of the word were commonplace in the early seventeenth century,[6] but Donne is unusual in so stressing that most familiar commonplace, the Book of the Creatures, as continually to imply that man is a word speaking words, a book within a book. The world has infinite volumes (IV, No. 6, ll. 148–51); man too is a volume (VII, No. 15, ll. 732–33), an illustration of nature (VII, No. 10, ll. 543–46), an index or abridgment of the Book of Creatures (IV, No. 8, l. 620; IX, No. 2, l. 564), a library (IX, No. 7,

l. 455; II, No. 6, ll. 41–42). There are such concomitant figures as
the description of skin as vellum or parchment (III, No. 3, ll. 469–
70), man's life as preface to the book of life (VI, No. 14, ll. 207–
9), editions of God's election printed first in the Scriptures and second in man's conscience (VIII, No. 2, ll. 260–62), or the books of
histories men compose in their lives and actions (VII, No. 9, ll. 118–
23). It is inevitable that Donne should think of the preacher as his
own sermon (as Milton believed the poet should be himself a
poem),[7] and describe as printing a sermon the business of practicing what one has heard preached (VII, No. 9, ll. 663–66).

The numerous images based on rhetorical terms spring in part
from the exegetical custom of using rhetoric to illuminate the meaning of Scriptural passages. Such a handling of rhetoric tended to
give such figures as exclamation, interrogation, and repetition specific meanings listed in the preaching manuals,[8] and so made them
more available for use in metaphor. Ordinary homiletic procedure is
illustrated in such comments as this: "And therefore having so many
Occasions to speak to God, and to speak of God, *David* ingeminates
that, and his ingemination implies a wonder, *O that men would*
(And it is strange if Men will not) . . . *O that men would praise
the Lord*" (VIII, No. 15, ll. 148–53). From this, imagery is only an
easy step away: "The Scriptures are Gods Voyce; The Church is his
Eccho; a redoubling, a repeating of some particular syllables, and
accents of the same voice" (VI, No. 11, ll. 5–7). The Incarnation is
an obscure piece of writing, a "hard Style" (III, No. 14, ll. 205–8);
life is an alphabet (II, No. 8, l. 28); time is an accumulation of
words which cannot "make up one syllable, towards this *Eternity,
the period of this blessednesse*" (IX, No. 4, ll. 115–20).

Grammatical figures also have their source in exegetical practice:
"It is S. *Hieromes* note, That when God in the Scriptures speakes of
divers things in the singular number, it is ever in things of grace;
And it is S. *Augustins* note, that when he speaks of any one thing
in the plurall Number, it is of heavy and sorrowfull things" (III,
No. 10, ll. 123–27). In his own creative use of the singular and
plural he varies the use of the figure, and especially likes to think

of God in these terms: "God is a plurall God, and offers himselfe to all, collectively; God is a singular God, and offers himselfe to every man, distributively" (IX, No. 5, ll. 341–43). Active and passive voice become figures of speech: "The Devils grammar is . . . to apply Actives to Passives; where he sees an inclination, to subminister a temptation; where he seeth a froward choler, to blow in a curse. And Gods grammar is to *change* Actives into Passives: whereas man delights in cursing, to make that man accursed" (VII, No. 14, ll. 664–69). God's blessings and man's responsibility are assumed into grammatical cases:

There is not a better Grammar to learne, then to learne how to blesse God, and therefore it may be no levity, to use some Grammar termes herein. God blesses man *Dativè,* He gives good to him; man blesses God *Optativè,* He wishes well to him; and he blesses him *Vocativè,* He speaks well of him (III, No. 12, ll. 98–102).

Donne's knowledge of Hebrew was very slight indeed; most of his references to the language, as Don Cameron Allen has pointed out, could have been taken from glosses available to him.[9] Thus it is indicative of the kind of thing that had interested the exegetes, as well as of his own preoccupations, that his most frequent citations have to do with Hebrew grammar, particularly the symbolic meanings of certain limitations in the syntax. He associates the Hebrew closely with immediate revelation; it is to him the language in which God spoke, and his references seem to assume that every aspect of the language was contrived as symbol. Over and over, he recalls, for example, that Hebrew has no present tense, and he takes this as a sign of God's eternity (all times are the same to him), and of the future nature of the Christian life: "In the Hebrew there is no Present tense; In that language wherein God spake, it could not be said, *The upright in heart, Are praised;* Many times they are not. But God speaks in the future" (VII, No. 9, ll. 562–64). And he also notes the absence of the superlative, as a sign that in all that God promises, "in all that he hath spoken, his mercy hath no superlative" (VI, No. 8, ll. 239–42).

By describing the world as grammar and rhetoric, Donne is able to convey the impression that instead of writing about ideas and things, one writes the ideas and things themselves. What really happens is of course rather different; because he assumes that words and combinations of words have a validity nearly equal to that of things, he can make any word or construction or grammatical term into a symbol as meaningful as anything in the physical world. The wisdom in words, or the spirit in the letter, prevents this enforcement of close attention to period and syllable, and the assumption of the whole world into period and syllable, from becoming sterile.

The literary view of the world was fostered not only by the church Fathers, but also by some of the authors of the emblem books so popular in Donne's time. Signor Praz, following G. S. Haight, notes, for example, the nearness of this passage from Sylvester's translation of Du Bartas's *Divine Weeks* to the whole emblematic approach to reality:

> The World's a Book in Folio, printed all
> With God's great Works in letters Capitall:
> Each Creature is a Page; and each Effect
> A faire Character void of all defect.[10]

The emblem proper is a symbolic picture usually accompanied by a short poem or quotation. These pictures range from the very simple type of Geoffrey Whitney's *A Choice of Emblemes,* which are really only illustrated moral precepts, to the immensely complex and crowded emblems of some of the Jesuit books, where different parts of the picture are lettered and a key to the letters supplied below.[11] It was, however, generally agreed that the emblem should embody in picture a public moral intuition whose "soul" the motto supplied; in expression the emblem was a good deal freer than the *impresa,* which was intended to apply only to the person for whom it was made, and for which numerous rather strict rules were drawn up. Part of the importance of the emblem was a result of the common belief that the hieroglyph, from which it was derived, had been the language of revelation before letters were invented.[12]

A number of Donne's emblems and hieroglyphs are only narrowly symbolic, simple pictures of abstractions, as when he says that a lamb is a hieroglyph of patience (VII, No. 12, ll. 824–25), a torch the emblem of liberality (VIII, No. 10, ll. 150–51), the pigeon and the turtle dove emblems of fecundity and chaste widowhood (VII, No. 11, ll. 110–11). Such figures, however, underline his literary approach to the world; he is not here making symbols that directly affect his own art; rather he is reaching out to describe the world in terms of art, and again diminishing the distinction between word and thing.

When he derives his emblems from actions or conditions of men, he comes much closer to the generally accepted definition of emblem as a form that symbolizes a universal truth about something. In comparison, those emblems already mentioned are all only hieroglyphs or simple characters. In God's clothing of Adam and Eve in the skins of dead animals and in the daily funerals of London citizens, he sees emblems of mortality (IV, No. 1, ll. 263–71). Clearly, he is still describing the world in terms of art, and he can impose upon it whatever set of emblems may conform to any general theme with which he may be concerned, as when, writing his poem "The Crosse," he sees emblems of crosses everywhere.[13] Thus, in the following passage, all things remind him of the brevity of life; "every thing is a remembrancer, every thing is a Judge upon me, and pronounces, I *must* dye" (III, No. 8, ll. 555–56):

If thou looke up into the aire, *remember that thy life is but a winde,* If thou see a cloud in the aire, aske St. *James* his question, *what is your life?* and give St. *James* his answer, *It is a vapour that appeareth and vanisheth away.* If thou behold a *Tree,* then *Job* gives thee a comparison of thy selfe; A *Tree* is an *embleme* of thy selfe; nay a Tree is the *originall,* thou art but the *copy,* thou art not so good as it: for, *There is hope of a tree.* . . . Looke upon the *water,* and we are as that, and as that spilt upon the ground: Looke to the *earth,* and we are not like that, but we are earth it self (III, No. 8, ll. 560–66, ll. 569–71).

The passage is taken from a sermon on a text in Job, "Loe, though he slay me, yet will I trust in him"; and it is clear, I think, in an over-all reading of Donne's sermons, that texts with poetic contexts, like Job or the Psalms, or particularly imaginative texts from any book of the Bible are most likely to inspire in Donne an extension of the poetry, in his own literary mode. This particular sermon begins with a discussion of the style of God's manifestation of himself to the world, and is throughout replete with close readings of words, and with imagery requiring a strong awareness of the mechanics of language. The emblems here are completely in line with the practice of religious emblematists, accompanying the picture or body (wind, cloud, tree, water, earth) with Bible tags. Here the emblem does begin to be important to sermon structure as well as to world view, for it can be seen as one way of fixing the meditation that is the sermon, upon a central subject, and bringing in the wandering attention by forcing its every object to lead toward the same consideration. The emblem imagery becomes integral to the theme of the sermon, for it brings to life a central abstraction.

In her discussion of the English emblem books, Rosemary Freeman points out the fact that ordinary emblems have by no means the strength of what modern criticism calls symbols, because there is no identification of emblem and thing.[14] The emblem, she says, was chosen first, and then its points of resemblance to a moral idea were imposed upon it; it has therefore a stiffness, even a forced quality in comparison to the free organic action of the kind of symbolism that Blake, for example, uses in his sunflower poem. In one chapter of her book, she analyzes Herbert's use of the emblematic method, and shows that, while at the outset of his poems, the connection between emblem and idea is arbitrary, during the course of the poem, the reader is convinced of the significance of the analogy, and without losing its emblematic quality it becomes more organic, for illustration and moral are fused.[15]

Donne's method of sermon writing sometimes partakes of this emblematic technique. For example, he once chose as organizing figure the letter Y, which he made an emblem of the two courses of life open to men. And he does share with the emblem writers the custom, inevitable in a sermon, of explaining his images very fully. However, in all the sermons which have emblems as central figures he begins, not with the emblem but with the text, and the emblem does not dictate the idea but embodies it. The sermon referring to

Adam's clothes and London funerals was preached at Whitehall in 1621 on a text from Corinthians, "The last Enemie that shall be destroyed is Death." The emblems which he chooses for enlargement of this text are war as a sign of misery and household harmony as a sign of peace and goodness: "As peace is of all goodnesse, so warre is an embleme, a Hieroglyphique, of all misery" (IV, No. 1, ll. 119–20). It is quite clear that these emblems are much more abstract than those more common ones cited earlier, and more amenable to creative and organic development. Throughout the sermon, he reiterates the idea that the Holy Ghost chose the metaphors of war and enmity to keep men from fastening upon earthly things for hope of happiness; war as a real thing to be read as an emblem in the world thus corresponds to war as a metaphor in the text.

He then continues in a paragraph both interesting and typical:

Militia and *Malitia,* are words of so neare a sound, as that the vulgat Edition takes them as one. For where the Prophet speaking of the miseries that Hierusalem had suffered, sayes, *Finita militia ejus,* Let her *warfare* be at an end, they reade, *Finita malitia ejus,* Let her *misery* be at an end; War and Misery is all one thing (IV, No. 1, ll. 188–93).

Thus he brings emblem and abstraction together, identifying the two by means of a play on words. The whole state of the world is subsumed into rhetoric, and the wordplay becomes a passionately serious thing. Yet, one must add, the esthetic value of this kind of expression is peculiarly limited. Given the background of rhetoric, and its use in expression of religious thought, that many of his auditors had, there were still hearers who could not be so moved by words as the poet Donne. The sensibility that gives to literature so unique an immediacy is incomprehensible to minds not similarly oriented; there will always be, as there were then, men who complain of the wisdom of words. And from any sympathetic reader today, this kind of writing, in its near-denial of the distinction between life and language, requires some readjustment of ear and mind.

There follows a paragraph which again depends entirely on emblems for its development, and in which there seems to be a purposeful recession into the popular and abstract hieroglyph of the circle:

> *Surge & descende in domum figuli,* sayes the Prophet *Ieremy,* that is, say
> the Expositors, to the consideration of thy Mortality. It is *Surge, descende,*
> *Arise and go down:* A descent with an ascension: Our grave is upward, and
> our heart is upon *Iacobs* Ladder, in the way, and nearer to heaven. Our
> daily Funerals are some Emblemes of that; for though we be laid down in
> the earth after, yet we are lifted up upon mens shoulders before. We rise in
> the descent to death, and so we do in the descent to the contemplation of it.
> In all the Potters house, is there one vessell made of better stuffe then clay?
> There is his matter. And of all formes, a Circle is the perfectest, and art thou
> loath to make up that Circle, with returning to the earth again? (IV, No. 1,
> ll. 235–46)

The paradox of *"surge & descende"* is the motto for the emblem that
develops from it (emblem coming from motto, as usual in Donne),
and then, characteristically, he resolves the paradox by use of a
more perfect figure, turning the rising and falling of life and death
and resurrection into the circle. Circle is identified naturally with its
meaning, not isolated from it; simile is the figure of the emblem
writers, but it is not that of Donne.

Donne's use of emblems is also modified by the fact that, on their
most serious and significant level, they merge in his thought with
signs, in the Biblical sense, as one of the ways by which God manifests himself to men. Donne acknowledges several kinds of signs.
There are, first of all, the great natural signs, sun, moon and stars,
thunder and hail. These are both functional in nature and indicative
of God's purpose toward men. There are ceremonial signs, established in the church as sacrament and ritual. And there are particular signs, given at definite times to specific men. All these different
kinds of signs are brought together in a single sermon preached at
St. Paul's on Christmas Day, 1624, on the text, "Therefore the Lord
shall give you a signe; behold, a virgin shall conceive, and beare a
son, and shall call his name Immanuel" (VI, No. 8). He here explains signs as given to all men, both to the natural man, who is composed not of reason only, but of reason and sense, and to the Christian,
who is composed not of faith only, but of faith and reason. One
purpose of the sign, then, is to give a tangible and credible illustra-

tion of an intangible and often incredible truth. But the sign can
also be a vehicle for truth. This is the case with the natural signs,
which Donne here identifies with emblems: created "for signes, as
well as for seasons" (l. 267), "His Sun, and Moone, and Starres,
(Emblemes and Instruments of his Blessings) move circularly, and
communicate themselves to all." "His hailestones, and his thunder-
bolts, and his showres of bloud (emblemes and instruments of his
Judgements) fall downe in a direct line, and affect and strike some
one person, or place" (ll. 192–97). These celestial characters are
symbolic in their representation of God's blessings and judgments,
but they are also the vehicles of specific blessings and judgments;
thus, they are both emblem and sign, and sign as outward expression
of grace or damnation is sacramental.

In his mention of ceremonial signs, he links natural signs with
sacraments, beginning a paragraph with mention of sun and moon
as signs and concluding with emphasis upon the importance of ritual
and sacrament:

He disobeyes God, in the way of contumacy, who refuses his signes, his outward assistances, his ceremonies which are induced by his authority, derived
from him, upon men, in his Church, and so made a part, or a help, of his
ordinary service, as Sacraments and Sacramentall things are (VI, No. 8,
ll. 281–85).

Sermon and sacrament are very close in Donne's mind, and his use
of emblem and sign is one important way in which he extends the
sacramental power of the text, building paragraph and sermon from
a word or phrase that in its emblematic or significatory function
combines letter with spirit, outer sense with inner grace.

There is one clear limitation in Donne's use of emblem and sign,
and that is that it is primarily employed as a means of reading the
world; although, as I have shown it can also become important in
sermon development, that is not its first function. It is relevant for
us in showing us how Donne looked at the world and in demonstrating once more the intermingling of art and common reality that
has so great an effect upon his sermons. By his use of grammatical
and rhetorical figures and by use of emblem and sign, he equates

word and thing and gives the world a literary meaning that, while it gives order and literary value to *things,* increases the life of literature.

Perhaps the bookishness of Donne's metaphor—that is, its reliance upon actual literary sources—has not even yet been sufficiently recognized, and W. Frazer Mitchell's statement that it is impossible to tell whether Donne is ever really original[16] (though Mitchell uses the word in a modern sense) should be kept in mind by everyone who works with the sermons. Donne's genius often manifests itself as that kind of originality which belongs to men whose intense vision of ideal unity or absolute truth can work itself out most fruitfully in a creative synthesis of the experiences of others. Mitchell has pointed out that zeal for commonplace books must have helped to inspire the enthusiasm for quotation that is observable in much Anglican preaching of the time,[17] but this is a rather barren kind of parallel. Much more important is the recognition of tradition upon which the Anglican church laid its claim to authority; and the recognition of the dangers inherent in extemporaneity and enthusiasm. Such views as these impelled Laud to try to preserve an old order,[18] Andrewes to compose his famous prayers almost entirely of sentences and phrases taken from the Fathers and from the Book of Common Prayer, and almost all the Anglican clergy to advise their congregations of the great value of the disciplined devotion provided by the church.[19] Finally, and perhaps most important, it was felt that a sermon purporting to be inspired by the Holy Ghost could best manifest this inspiration by close adherence either to the words of the Scriptural text or to the words of the church Fathers, who were accepted as inspired interpreters of church doctrine.[20] More of Donne's imagery than the casual reader would guess is dependent in this way for inspiration and development upon the Scriptures, and upon such Fathers as made use of metaphor for elaboration of text or doctrine, among whom, in particular and in illustration of the range of his borrowings, may be mentioned Tertullian, Jerome, Gregory of Nyssa, Gregory the Great, and Bernard of Clairvaux.[21] Augustine, so much Donne's guide everywhere else, is less important here, for Augustine's mind is much more freely intellectual, abstract, and mystical; he did not need, as Donne did, to cling to the concrete, and he uses relatively little imagery in his writing.

Donne frequently pulls together a number of references from all parts of the Bible, achieving vitality by unexpected juxtapositions as well as by the forceful rhetorical and literary devices that mark his own style. Preaching on building a chapel, he develops the idea that every man is in fact his own church; the apparent paradoxes that result are really only attention-getting devices to ensure the reception of his point:

> The Church of God should be built upon a Rock, and yet *Job* had his Church upon a Dunghill; The bed is a scene, and an embleme of wantonnesse, and yet *Hezekiah* had his Church in his Bed; The Church is to be placed upon the top of a Hill, and yet the Prophet *Jeremy* had his Church *in Luto,* in a miry Dungeon; Constancy, and setlednesse belongs to the Church, and yet *Jonah* had his Church in the Whales belly; The Lyon that roares, and seeks whom he may devour, is an enemy to this Church, and yet *Daniel* had his Church in the Lions den; *Aquae quietudinum,* the waters of rest in the Psalme, were a figure of the Church, and yet the three children had their Church in the fiery furnace; Liberty and life appertaine to the Church, and yet *Peter,* and *Paul* had their Church in prison, and the thiefe had his Church upon the Crosse. Every particular man is himselfe *Templum Spiritus sancti,* a Temple of the holy Ghost (II, No. 10, ll. 116–30).

Donne's handling of these Scriptural paraphrases and allusions is particularly complex, for most of the statements in the first halves of the pairs are metaphorical, and many can be applied to inner character rather than to outer condition (for example, the source of the first paraphrase, "Thou art Peter, and upon this rock I will build my church"—the rock being ordinarily taken to signify Peter's faith); the apparent paradox is created by juxtaposing in the second halves of the pairs metaphorical with literal statement; that is to say, the churches spoken of are in every case the spiritual edifices of men's hearts, but the dunghill, the lion, and the bed are both literal and symbolic, since they represent both the actual things surrounding the men spoken of, and symbolically, the condition of a world that is perpetually dangerous, seductive, and inconstant, but cannot injure the stable heart. Bringing together a great number of Scriptural references, Donne has shaped them into superficial paradoxes to focus the attention of his auditors upon a spiritual truth, no paradox, which all these references have in common.

A passage from one of the Fathers is less likely to be central to a sermon or major division; more often he uses it to add vitality to a point developed from Scripture or conceived by himself. Miss Wallerstein has pointed out a passage in the sermons where a rich and elaborate metaphor is unfolded by movement from one Father to another within the scope of a single image of God's mercy as the medicine that cures all the ills of the soul.[22] A comparable illustration occurs in a sermon on two verses of Psalm 6, of which the relevant portion is, "All the night make I my bed to swim, I water my couch with my teares" (VIII, No. 8). The sermon is strongly literary throughout, and several passages in it might serve as well as this one. He begins with his own image of concupiscence: "The concupiscencies of man, are naturally dry powder, combustible easily, easily apt to take fire; but teares dampe them." There follows a reference to David as author of the text, joined with a quotation from Hilary: "*David* had laboured hard; first *Ad ruborem,* as Physitians advise, to a rednesse, to a blushing, to a shame of his sin; And now *Ad sudorem,* he had laboured to a sweat; for *Lacrymae sudor animae moerentis,* Teares are the sweat of a labouring soule." He develops this image, contrasting it with his own symbolizing of the condition preceding such sweat, and this brings him to the next stage, which commences with a new quotation, this time from Gregory Nazianzanus, "But *Lacrymae diluvium, & evehunt animam,* These teares carry up our soule, as the flood carried up the Arke, higher then any hils" (VIII, No. 8, ll. 280–95). This citation is in turn elaborated and is followed by a literal passage from Judges, and then one from Samuel, which, with a final reference to Rabbi Oziel, is made into a new image.

Of course, the whole passage, like most of the sermon, is organized around the word "tears," which becomes the controlling symbol. But the fact that the symbol is built up partly by these references to the Fathers and to the Bible is central to its whole nature.

First, by taking his symbol from a verse of the Bible and by developing it with the assistance of commentators from various periods in church history, he tries to give it something of the timelessness of the essential Word, which according to him informs the words of Scripture; and he makes himself not an individual voice, but what he would have liked to think of as part of a consort. Second, even from a wholly secular viewpoint, one can see that the literary nature of the sermons, which I have stressed so far, is reinforced by this method of making symbols out of other literature, and that the life of the letter is guaranteed by the resulting sense of a symbol growing in force through the recurrent temporal affirmations that perpetuate what we may wish to think of as its representation of a kind of eternal life. The great commonplaces of literary symbolism —the rose or the ruined building, for example—preserve their evocative power in exactly the same way. A poet working with less familiar terms or with a less obvious point to make, or a homilist wishing to strengthen a sense of tradition in his audience, will work his sources into his own poem, as Donne does here, or as T. S. Eliot does, quite differently, in *The Wasteland.*

By means of these techniques, Donne makes language of both the world around him and the history of which he is a part. He goes on to give life and complex, even palpable reality to his own words as they unfold and share the sense of the Scriptual texts upon which he builds his sermons.

The words of the text are real things to begin with. The traditional sense of Scripture as food or as perfume emitting a sweet savor is important in Donne, who often refers to it in this way in his prose.[23] He also thinks of the text as a compression of something expanded in the sermon into a solid structure. Or, again, he considers the sermon as a living thing, growing up out of the words of the text. Toward the end of a late sermon, for example, he speaks of "the last beating of the pulse of this text" (IX, No. 5, l. 834); he frequently compares the sermon to a growing tree or to a limb of the body that is the Scriptures (IX, No. 7, l. 32). Occasionally he sees it broadening out into a whole landscape in which every word, every flower has significance. And there are innumerable instances

of the life of individual words—his appreciation, for instance, of
Luther's endowment of the word "why" with a stubborn and dangerous character of its own (VI, No. 9, ll. 91–93), or his use of
"this flowing and extensive word *Now*" (II, No. 12, ll. 32–33) to
set up the divisions of a text. These are the techniques that balance
his consideration of the world as a book and allow him to move
easily from one to the other, for if the world is a text, the Scriptures
are a world; and sound and syntax mingle with tangible reality.

One very important technique by which Donne gives added depth
and meaning to his own words is his use of that kind of wordplay
in which the word is apparently made a metaphor of itself. Thus,
discussing the psychology of sin, he makes extensive use of the
word "habit," taking it to mean both settled custom and covering
garment. The settled custom is the perpetuated sin; the garment is
its symbol. Elaborating upon the custom of sin as garment, he points
out the concealment that accompanies it, not only because the habit
disguises the sin from others, but also because it becomes so habitual that the wearer, the sinner, ceases to notice it. He doubles
the metaphor by adding to this habit that of impenitence, which is
also symbolized as a garment. And finally he suggests a remedy, in
the same terms—putting on Christ, with the habit of good actions;
and he also suggests that if "*Love covereth all sins,* much more
shall God, who is *Love* it selfe, cover our sins so, as he covered the
Egyptians, in a red Sea, in the application of his blood, by visible
meanes in his Church" (IX, No. 11, ll. 775–77).

I have already mentioned his use of the word "edify" to mean
both outward building and inward raising of the spirit, and his
plays on "Sun" and "Son" are too well known to need comment.
Other instances are his mention of the brackish and engulfing Sea
of Rome (VII, No. 16, ll. 182–84); his description of the dying
Christian as an engraving whose picture had been "graving" all his
life (VIII, No. 7, ll. 590–92);[24] his use of the word "state" as inner condition and political body (VII, No. 13, l. 580), and of the
word "favor" as grace and countenance (V, No. 17, ll. 93–98).
Since he habitually thinks of preaching as thunder, the phrase, "the
ordinance of preaching," readily supplies its own metaphor: "And

in this Church, his Ordinance is Ordinance indeed; his Ordinance of preaching batters the soule, and by that breach, the Spirit enters" (VII, No. 16, ll. 113–15). The suggestion of the power and depth that a single word can have, implicit in the opening out of long passages from these wordplays, recalls the symbolism that Donne sees in all the words of God, meaning standing behind meaning, abstraction supplying its own incarnation.

In this connection, we may also note the quite traditional stress he puts on etymology and names,[25] as symbolic much as the Hebrew language is taken to be symbolic, although many of these names have no connection in his mind with revelation. He is interested, for example, in Naomi's rejection of her name: *"Call not me Naomi,* says she there; *Naomi* is lovely, and loving, and beloved; *But call me Mara,* says she, *Mara* is bitternesse" (VIII, No. 14, ll. 214–16); he justifies his identification of prayer with praise by reference to the similarity of their Hebrew names (V, No. 14, ll. 79–85); and he distinguishes between the words "Matza" and "matzah" (between a legitimate calling and a desire for worldly satisfaction) by pointing out the significance of the letter H as "an aspiration, a breathing, a panting after the things of this world" (III, No. 10, ll. 212–15).

When Donne's stress on the importance of the word and on the world as language begins to affect the structure of his sermons, the way in which he develops the words of the text is the most important thing to be considered. I have already noted Dennis Quinn's comment that when no metaphor presents itself in the text, Donne will work with ordinary words instead, and turn them into images.[26] This is a central insight into the method of Donne's work; it springs from his belief that there can be no idle word in Scripture; each has significance. And while he is always insistent upon staying with the literal meaning of the text, and adverse toward those interpreters who, like Origen, pushed allegorical readings very far, when the right interpretation of a text is not at stake, he likes to expand upon the meaning of words, to give them more extensive import than is explicitly suggested by their context. Thus he notes the frequency of the word "blessed" in the Psalms or the word "all" in

the whole Bible: "There is no one word so often in the Bible, as
this, *Omne, All.* Neither hath God spread the word more liberally
upon all the lines of this Booke, then he hath his gracious purposes
upon all the soules of men" (VII, No. 9, ll. 390–93). Often such an ob-
servation leads him to develop a symbol in an extended passage, as
in the following quotation, where he notices two words characteristic of the conversation of Christ: "I thinke we find no words in
Christs mouth so often, as *vae,* and *Amen.* Each of them hath two
significations; as almost all Christs words, and actions have; consolation, and commination." The passage continues, elaborating upon
the words, until they have become symbols that can be used almost
independently:

And this seale, this Amen, as Amen is *Fiat,* is always set to his *vae,* as his *vae*
is *vox minantis;* . . . God threatens nothing *in terrorem* onely, onely to
frighten us; every *vae* hath his *Amen,* every Judgement denounced, a purpose
of execution . . . if the first condition, that is *Innocency,* and the second,
that is *Repentance,* be rebelliously broken, then every man hath his *vae,* and
every *vae* hath his *Amen* (III, No. 6, ll. 283–357).

The passage is particularly illuminating as it shows not only the
facility with which Donne can make a symbol of any word, but also
the duality involved in so much of his symbolism. As justice and
mercy are the characteristics of God to which he most frequently
returns, so much of his symbolism, whether built up from metaphor
or common word, portrays this double meaning. Two symbols, for
example, which dominate all others in his imagery are the sea and
the circle: the sea is both a sea of misery and a sea of grace; the
circle is both the closed circle of man's ignorance or his circuitous
progress from womb to grave, and the circle of God's infinity.[27] He
says in his *Devotions* that there are two qualities imprinted by God
in all things,[28] and Donne sees them always as extreme opposites—
which in God and in God's symbols are both the means of grace.

    When the text itself gives him easy access to symbolic develop-
ment, the whole sermon can be organized to give full extension to
a single word. Such a sermon is one preached before the Countess of
Montgomery on February 21, 1619, on a rather forbidding text,
Matthew 21:44: "Whosoever shall fall on this stone, shall be

broken; but on whomsoever it shall fall, it will grinde him to powder" (II, No. 8). What he actually does is to make the stone a symbol of the same sort that the *vae* and *amen* of the passage previously quoted are, encompassing both the justice and the mercy of God. He begins by collating passages in the Bible in which Christ is called a stone, and then develops these in turn to show that Christ is a foundation stone, a cornerstone, a stone that can be a place of rest (Jacob's pillow), a stone of defense against enmity (David and Goliath), and a rock of firmness and certainty. He then goes on to interpret the two statements of the text as meaning, first, that he who falls upon that stone shall be broken of sin and reconciled with God, and second, that at the last judgment the unreclaimable sinner will be damned. At the end of the sermon he circles back again to the promise of forgiveness and joy with which he began.

Within the structure of the sermon the symbol is organic but not radiant. That is, in Rosemary Freeman's terms, although we are certainly convinced of the validity of the comparison between Christ and the stone, the comparison is so fully and elaborately made that there is no room within the sermon for the symbol to radiate of itself, or to take on implications that Donne himself has not explicitly stated. However, we can, I think, take the whole sermon as an image which, seen as a whole, has power to extend beyond itself. I can clarify this distinction by reference to a completely different kind of art, a verse satire by the young John Donne. The famous third satire's most famous lines are these:

> On a huge hill,
> Cragged, and steep, Truth stands, and hee that will
> Reach her, about must, and about must goe;
> And what the hills suddennes resists, winne so;[29]

The whole poem is about religious differences and about doubt and the ways to faith and knowledge, and Donne's thoughts on these subjects are made with the support of such symbols as that of the hill, which are not carefully explained, but identified implicitly with what they stand for. The symbol of the stone, on the other hand, is most carefully and fully explained within the context of the sermon. The third satire is not itself symbol, but statement, although it uses symbols to make its statement clear. Conversely, the sermon is not a statement at all, but a symbol of the justice and mercy of God, and when we look at it as a whole, we have the sense of compression and radiant meaning that a symbol ought to provide. We do not see this as we trace the development of each sentence and paragraph, because they are limited to close readings and extensions of one Biblical text supplemented by others. It is only when the sermon as a whole is held in the mind that we can see how far it reaches beyond its apparent limitations, in the many Scriptural passages that it embraces and in the different meanings that the stone takes on. And the sermon is meant to be like the stone, in its effect upon the congregation.

Donne's writing in poetry and prose had always depended heavily on the analogy, on the depiction of relationships between things. But in his sermons, he turns more and more toward symbolism, which insofar as it can be distinguished from the analogy which is its basis, either presents a closer identity between thing and abstraction than the ordinary analogy does or includes within its boundaries complex references to an extended context outside itself.[30] The closeness between symbol and abstraction is evident in the treatment of things as sacramental, as signs of what they themselves are, as in Donne's discussion of natural signs like hail and sun, in the concept of words as the outer extension of thought, and in word-plays, where literal and metaphorical meanings combine. All this presents us with the same attitudes or habits that inform other techniques, and yet the result feels somewhat different. When Donne can completely transform the world into language and work with it as such, it behaves better for him; he understands it better and feels more at home in it. Many readers will still find here the baroque ambiguity, the uncertainty about whether one is dealing with life or art and about whether either one is real. But I doubt that with this aspect of his work there is any uncertainty in Donne's mind. This really literary universe is his place, where he is most serene and cool. And in it he finds materials for the organization, the buildings of his sermons.

VI

The Model of the Whole

The text is to the sermon, said Donne, as the soul is to the body and the honey to the honey-comb. This compact theory is really a better explanation of the structure of his sermons than any rules we can find in the rhetoric books. But because the ecclesiastical rhetoricians did emphasize organization, it is interesting to compare Donne's practice with their teaching. They are aware of the possibility of using the rules of classical rhetoric to build a sermon, and most of their outlines are roughly patterned after the oration's division into *exordium, narratio, explicatio, confirmatio, confutatio,* and *conclusio.* Typical headings under which the parts of the sermon are discussed are, for example, exordium, division, explanation of doctrine, confirmation, application, and conclusion. The division of the text would ordinarily necessitate repetition of explanation, confirmation, and application in each respective part. This could and often did lead to extremely rigid and mechanical homilies. But most of the writers are conscious of the dangers of excessive complication; they caution the preacher to strive for simplicity and apparent artlessness.[1] It is suggested, for example, that the exordium may be entirely dispensed with,[2] that a simple text need not be divided at all and that sermon divisions should never exceed three or four,[3] that the preacher should not burden his auditors with numerous subdivisions, quotations, or illustrations,[4] and that the application can best be merged with explanation and confirmation of the text.[5] The importance of smooth transitions joining elaboration of a few memorable points is very strongly emphasized.[6]

Beyond question, many of these (for the most part) Puritan

rhetoricians would have objected to Donne's obvious artfulness, his displays of learning, his quotations, and his long, involved, and sometimes artificial metaphors. But the basic rules for a simplified framework are applicable to his sermons. His exordia are brief and generally have an immediate connection with the text; they are apt to resemble what Keckermann calls textual precognition,[7] an advance survey of text and context, and may include comment on such traditional topics as the time, place, and persons involved. He organizes the remainder of the sermon under two or three clear headings, and while these headings may include numerous subdivisions, he takes pains to prevent them from becoming confused by allowing them to fall into some such natural sequence as chronological order, the order of the words of the text, or esthetic and logical climax. Amplification of each division consists of an explanation of the text that merges at almost every point with application—which is generally not so much application to the particular congregation before him as symbolic or literal generalization that can include all men. Generally there is some recapitulation of theme at the end, an exhortation more specifically intended for occasion and audience, and a final prayer.

Thus, he avoids the extreme complexity generally associated with scholastic preaching,[8] but his sermons do differ in other important ways from those which the rhetoricians advocated and which the Puritans preached. The Puritans were at this time on the defensive; they required a medium for instruction in a religion that had no established tradition to recommend it. The Bible was a necessary source of argument—a history and an instructional manual—and such a conception of it is not conducive to symbolism. When the Puritan preachers were willing to go beyond strictly utilitarian and logical exposition, they favored combinations of allegory, homely metaphor, and realism for the depiction of the struggle between good and evil in man and his world (in the Bible as well as in contemporary time), and of the Christian wayfarer or soldier travelling through a land possessed by the enemy.[9] Much of the immediacy of their sermons is a reflection of the belief that the war of the spirit could be won then and there against real and specific enemies who represented for them the eternal adversary. Their sources or parallels can all be found in the medieval vernacular homilies, which, like theirs, were written against a background of warfare, and made to appeal simply and urgently to the common man.[10] Some of their techniques of immediacy are also those of the Roman Catholics and of the spiritual exercises, depicting the struggles of the soul in terms meant to awaken and terrify.

The position of the Anglicans of Donne's time was quite different; prevention of warfare was to their benefit; their purpose was to hold to an old order and to make their congregations aware and appreciative of its vitality and worth. The Anglican preacher could also assume that his audience had been born and brought up in the faith he preached and that instruction was far less necessary than awakening. Thus, for Donne, "The art of *salvation,* is but the art of *memory*" (II, No. 2, l. 52); the preacher's office is not that of a teacher, but that of an arouser, a reminder, an official conscience. The Puritan sermons move in the direction of lectures or parables, while Donne's move in the direction of poems or meditations.

The evident learning and sophistication of the Anglican sermon does in general preclude a particular kind of immediacy—that of a simple, vigorous, or homely dramatic realization of a text. Many of the sermons of Laud, Andrewes, or Donne are very hard work for us, because they assume an ease and an eagerness in religious matters that cannot be assumed by anyone today, and because they are often written for religious intellectuals, whose idea of an enjoyable discourse was different from what ours is. The Puritan sermons are likely to be more fun now, although they were not then. They simply appealed to different audiences and fulfilled different purposes.

Donne's sermons are, on the whole, less intellectual and more dramatic than those of Laud and Andrewes, because he put particular stress on the importance of the memory, because he distrusted logic, and because he was by nature a poet and an extremist. There is also in Donne something of the immediacy of the spiritual exercises: the stripping of the soul before God, or the total involvement of the soul in a vividly realized scene, is more characteristic of Puritan and Roman Catholic than of Anglican writing. But Donne's vividness, as we have seen, is qualified by obvious artifice.

Knowing that the Puritans commonly thought of preaching as sacramental, we might want to say that Donne is Puritan in his treatment of the Word as sacramental and in his concern to make the discourse seem to grow out of the text—but this same sense of the power of Scripture was very common, if not always so clearly expressed, in Anglican preaching.[11] Actually, I think, it is not the general concept but its particular interpretation and development which is important here. The Puritans used the words of the text chiefly as a way of getting at the spirit; despite their very great veneration for Scripture, their attitude toward sacraments in general was on the whole more casual than that of the Anglicans, and they made a much sharper distinction between the printed or spoken word and its meaning. For Donne the sermon exists inside the letter of the text, while for the Puritan it exists inside the spirit; in Donne's view, reverence for the letter insures the spirit's power.

When Donne develops a text by expansion of a symbol that he finds in it, he believes that he is preserving its literal sense, but for him this means not just a narrow historical or moral meaning, but a timeless one. For him, as for many of the clergy in both camps, the literal sense, whether expressed in metaphorical or explicitly literal language, was the principal intention of the Holy Ghost in that place.[12] But as Dennis Quinn has pointed out,[13] such a reading undertaken by the Puritans was likely to make Job, for example, a merely historical figure, where for Donne it made him a type of Christ and of modern man. Although Donne moves very early in the sermons from a literal-historical interpretation to a moral-universal one, and although he would have said that his broadest interpretations are not strictly literal,[14] the sustained use of the historical person or situation, as depicted in the very words of the text, as symbol, gives the widest expansion of the meaning a great deal of authority. The Puritan rhetorics, lacking this notion of continuity, sometimes suggest moral interpretations that cannot be applied to the original context.[15] Donne's moral is invariably possible in context as well as in his larger application, and this fact, together with the coherence of the symbol, makes it difficult to mark in his sermons any real break between amplification and application of the text.

Millar Maclure, in his book on the Paul's Cross sermons, has described Anglican preaching as a commentary or gloss upon the text.[16] For the best-known preachers, at least, such a definition is extremely inadequate, but such commentary does often exist in Donne's sermons, side by side with the development of the symbol, limiting its function. And there are times when scholasticism completely overwhelms felicity of expression, and the homily becomes a dry point-by-point or word-by-word exposition of his theme (for example, VIII, No. 6; II, Nos. 15 and 16). To such methods, I shall devote only passing attention, for their products do not lie within the province of literature. I should like to point out, however, that in the reliance of the commentary on the Christian tradition, especially the church Fathers, Donne's sermons are in part distinguished from those of the Puritans and made vehicles of an orderly and established religion. What the sermon loses in immediacy it sometimes gains in depth, in its sense of the continuity of the meaning of thought and symbol.

I may also say that there are many sermons in which the point-by-point explanation of the symbol limits its function to that of an emblem which has no radiant life of its own. On the other hand, even when this is the case, the sermon itself may become a symbol because it is not instruction, not statement, but simply the expansion of a figure which achieves by sheer repetition and emphasis a place in the listener's mind that permits it to work, beyond the temporalities of its delivery, upon the imagination. And since Donne conceives of the Word as sacramental, he constructs all his sermons to imitate the action of a sacrament, to be the outward expression or even the doorway of spiritual grace.

Donne used symbolism to get the sermon out of the text, and the world into the sermon. Being a poet, he had a particular concern with the meaning of the phrase "the rhetoric of the spirit," and with the ways in which Biblical rhetoric is different from secular prose. His sermon structure invites the world into the text and at the same time keeps the text literary; that is, he turns the very letter of the Scripture into palpable drama without ever forgetting that it is made of words. The sermon becomes a spiritual-literary adventure.

The adventure begins with an exordium or precognition of the text, for whose special spirit in Donne the term proem (which carries the double meaning of exordium and poem) is perhaps more congenial. In proem and sermon division, a special effort is made to provide the listener with a kind of doorway. By means of symbol and metaphor, the sermon itself is presented as a penetrable thing. It is distinctly suggested that the listener can enter and move about within its borders, to explore the content of a text, or to participate in the unfolding of a symbol. The proem may also be used to attune the listener to concentration upon the literary nature of text and sermon, and to a religious rather than a secular appreciation of their merits.

The proem begins with a declarative sentence, often strikingly forceful and direct, reminiscent of the famous openings of many of his poems: "He that will dy with Christ upon Good-Friday, must hear his own bell toll all Lent" (VIII, No. 7); "Never such a frame, so soon set up, as this, in this Chapter" (IX, No. 1); "Peace is in *Sion*; Gods whole Quire is in tune" (VII, No. 14). The boldness and suddenness of the figures instantly command the attention; and the statement is frequently sufficiently enigmatic to assure the listener's continued response. The figure or symbol introduced in this sentence is ordinarily developed in the rest of the proem.

The function and length of the proem vary a good deal with the sermon text. Except upon occasions of unusual importance or solemnity, the opening is very short, in keeping with the advice of the rhetoric books, whose authors indicated that its original persuasive function was obviated by the fact that no man does "for the most part, set his foote toward the church, but that he is already persuaded that he shal heare those things, that he ought worthilye and greedily to learne."[17] According to Keckermann, the exordium should contain something beautiful to delight and arouse the hearers' minds; it should be like the vestibule of a house to lure the listener in. Variety, he says, is important; the matter of the exordium may consist of a summary of the preceding sermon if it is closely connected with the one to follow; discussion of the occasion of the text—the person, place, or reason of it; praise of the text; mention of some outstanding and relevant saying of Christ; or comment upon the time—the occasion upon which the sermon is preached, if the time is especially relevant.[18] Donne uses all these suggestions at one time or another, most frequently adopting the practical approach of giving the context or occasion of the text to be discussed. And if this were all that could be said about his exordia, we might better call them prefaces or precognitions of the text, indicating thereby, as some of the ecclesiastical rhetoricians did, a rather business-like opening. But discussion of the context is often combined in the proems with material suggested only by Keckermann's description of the exordium as a vestibule and by his grudging reference to use of time. Because I see a very close relationship between this aspect of the proem, and the sermon division and transitions, I should like to discuss these parts of the sermon together as they are shaped by his technical use of three characteristic subjects—time, space, and music or literary style. These, let me emphasize, are not necessarily the subjects of the proems; they are used as supporting devices in Donne's effort to make a symbol of the sermon and to set the tone of his discourse.

A survey of Donne's sermons in Potter and Simpson's chronological edition reveals that in his middle and later years of preaching, he was more and more apt to use time as a way of getting into the matter of his sermon, and as a way of equating the day commemorated with the present day, the action commemorated with the action to be performed by the Christian listener. And in all his preaching, his proems and sermon divisions rely a good deal on the ordinary time by which men live, calling the listeners' attention to the relationship between minute, hour, or year, and eternity. His idea of time is in part derived from the orthodox medieval tradition which saw all time as having been fulfilled in the life of Christ, all other time being one with that as type or copy. And it is much affected by the ritual observance of the Christian calendar. Time is for Donne a series of symbols, reflecting the central events of Christ's life as they are re-enacted in the Christian year; it is important only in relation to the spiritual life and to eternity: one Easter is as important as, and no different from, another. And one moment is potentially all time and eternity. This whole conception, of course, differentiates his preaching sharply from that of the Puritans, whose desire for reformation without tarrying involved them inextricably in temporal progress, and whose reaction against all things Roman or ceremonial led them to play down or completely ignore the Christian festivals.[19]

It is not surprising to find that Donne enjoys playing with time, making it into something physical and manipulable. That man's life is a span is a commonplace, but Donne carries the commonplace farther than usual: "we know our life to be but a span, and yet we can wash away one inche in ryot, we can burn away one inch in lust," (I, No. 1, ll. 248–52); "If my span of life become a mile of life, . . . my acre a sheere; . . . if there be nothing of the next world at the end, . . . still all is but *nothing* multiplied" (IV, No. 6, ll. 297–300). The sermon attempts to portray what is infinite in the *space* of an hour: "We are then upon the contemplation of the joyes of heaven, which are everlasting, and must we wring them into the discourse of an *houre*? of the glory of heaven which is intire, and must we divide it into *parts*? we must; we will; we doe; into two parts" (VI, No. 7, ll. 35–38). Conversely, and most spectacularly, space is turned into time:

But if I had a Secular Glass, a Glass that would run an age; if the two Hemispheres of the World were composed in the form of such a Glass, and all the World calcin'd and burnt to ashes, and all the ashes, and sands, and atoms of the World put into that Glass, it would not be enough to tell the godly man what his Treasure, and the Object of his Heart is (IX, No. 7, ll. 6–12).

The sermon, being spatialized, is made into a violently compressed symbol of that which is timeless and infinite, imitating the original symbol of the timeless God born in time. In a lighter mood, in an earlier sermon, where he develops the symbol of Christ's tears as a sea, he prefaces the third section with the words, "Those teares we called the Sea, but a Sea which must now be bounded with a very little sand" (IV, No. 13, ll. 530–31); the sand of the hourglass is made into the border of the symbol, space and time again being made one to emphasize the miraculousness of any faint realization in space or time of an image whose meaning is infinite. The congregation is invited to enter infinity by participating in a finite sermon.

Donne also makes the sermon a compression of actual time, without the use of space, as when, speaking on the text, "Because thou hast been my helpe, therefore in the shadow of thy wings will I rejoyce," he says that "as the spirit and soule of the whole booke of Psalmes is contracted into this psalme, so is the spirit and soule of this whole psalme contracted into this verse" (VII, No. 1, ll. 27–29). Expansion of the verse then naturally employs time's division into past, present, and future as the divisions of the sermon itself:

So that we have here the whole compasse of Time, Past, Present, and Future; and these three parts of Time, shall be at this time, the three parts of this Exercise; first, what *Davids* distresse put him upon for the present; and that lyes in the Context; secondly, how *David* built his assurance upon that which was past; *(Because thou hast been my help)* And thirdly, what he established to himselfe for the future, *(Therefore in the shadow of thy wings will I rejoyce)* (ll. 35–42).

What he then does with these divisions is also significant. In the first section he discusses the relationship between temporal and spiritual affliction, and the ways in which a limited present event can affect man's spiritual and eternal life. In the second, he shows that past occurrences can be taken as guides for present action, since God's past mercies are eternal; and neither God nor his actions toward a man can change. In the third, he says that the heavenly life is present with men on earth: "we must not onely not decline to a murmuring, that we have no more, no nor rest upon a patience for that which remains, but we must ascend to a holy joy, as if all were done and accomplished"; "The everlastingnesse of the joy is the blessednesse of the next life, but the entring, the inchoation is afforded here" (ll. 503–6, ll. 677–79). Since in each section of the sermon the temporal aspects of eternal meaning are discussed, since the sermon is organized according to the limitations of mortal time but elaborates upon a text which contracts time and for Donne symbolizes eternity, the sermon itself becomes a temporal symbol of the eternal joy that is its chief theme.

The frequency with which he calls attention to the length of the sermon underlines his use of time in the proem as symbol. The sermon, measuring an hour, is itself a unit of time, as well as a vehicle of grace; and a good use of the sermon, and its hour, expands them into all of this life and eternity; but a reformation that lives no longer than the sermon extends in mortal time, is, he says, a short-lived and abortive reformation: "upon every minute of this life, depend millions of yeares in the next, and I shall be glorified eternally, or eternally lost, for my good or ill use of Gods grace offered to me this houre" (III, No. 13, ll. 514–17). Once he apologizes for putting the end of the sermon first by suggesting that neither he nor his congregation knows whether they will live till the end of the hour, and the few moments at the beginning may be crucial (III, No. 10, ll. 39–48).

It is clear that Donne's use of time, as discussed so far, is psychological and symbolic, rather than semirealistic or allegorical. It is not at all the kind of time that the Puritans thought of in their wayfaring pilgrim figures, for example, and if it sacrifices their homely realism and temporal urgency, it gains immediacy and excitement of another kind, by its indication of the violent compression of all time into this one hour, and its promise that by meditation upon and within this hour the Christian may find a release from time in the re-expansion of the symbol into eternity.

These have all been in a sense secular references, the use of times universally understood, as symbols to assist the Christian meditator. Donne also works within the specifically Catholic framework of the

Christian year, which begins with Trinity Sunday rather than with New Year's, and more and more frequently the sermons of his middle and later years are shaped in such a way that they are at least in part meditations upon the symbolic meaning of the day or season celebrated. Thus he says, in the proem to a Lenten sermon, "Make way to an everlasting Easter by a short Lent, to an undeterminable glory, by a temporary humiliation" (IV, No. 1, ll. 10–11); the sermon *Encaenia*, preached at the dedication of the Lincoln's Inn chapel, stresses rededication of the self to Christ (IV, No. 15); a sermon at New Year's, the Feast of the Circumcision, asks for spiritual circumcision of the Christian heart (VI, No. 9). This is the method of interpreting a text applied to the day on which it is preached; that is, he interprets the day both literally and morally, in its original meaning and in its contemporary application. And he brings to this interpretation an immediacy something like that which was more commonly brought to the text, although the ritual nature of the symbol gives it a stiffness in context, which represents the decorum of Christian worship.

His own sense of the significance of the Christian calendar is very clearly explained in *Encaenia*, where he says that on those feast days which God called Sabbaths, He enjoined certain things to be done and remembered, "So that there is one *Moralitie*, that is the soule of all *Sabboths*, of all *Festivalls*; howsoever all *Sabboths* have a ceremoniall part in them, yet there is a *Morall* part that inanimates them all; they are elemented of *Ceremonie*, but they [are] animated with *Moralitie*" (IV, No. 15, ll. 65–69). This is a distinctly sacramental view of time, and I think we can say that most of his uses of time, as well as many of the other devices to be discussed in this chapter, are sacramental. The power of the symbol is in its clear indication of an infinite or timeless spiritual meaning informing it, and in the presentation of the symbol as a perceptible doorway to spiritual truth. The device is explicit in the proem to a sermon preached on a Sunday after the Conversion of St. Paul:

As *S. Augustine* sayes of the Sacrament of Baptisme, that it is *Limen Ecclesiae*, The threshold over which we step into the Church; so is Christmas day, *Limen festorum,* The threshold over which we step into the festivall celebration of some other of Christs actions, and passions, . . . But the Sabbath is not onely *Limen,* or *Ianua Ecclesiae,* The doore by which we enter into the Church, and into the consideration what the Church hath done, but *Limen mundi,* The doore by which we enter into the consideration of the World, how, and when the World was made of nothing, at the Creation (VIII, No. 6, ll. 5–18).

When the day to be celebrated commemorates an event in Christ's life, the idea of the arrival of the fullness of time in Him makes the day a symbol that partakes of this fullness, and enables man to identify himself with Christ's action: "And when we have paced, and passed through all these steps, we shall in some measure have solemnized this day of the Resurrection of Christ; and in some measure have made it the day of our Resurrection too" (IV, No. 14, ll. 47–50). The fullness of time is in a sense the compression of infinity; it means that temporal progress can be forgotten, that, being born in time, Christ freed men from its limitations, allowing them to grow spiritually beyond time through fixed ritual celebrations. To Donne, Christmas or Easter Day offers concrete instances of the eternity of all God's acts, the perpetualness of the redemption of man that occurred during Christ's lifetime. In the fixed days of the church calendar, the opportunity given by Christ is reoffered; the acts of his life are re-enacted; and man's cooperation can this time redeem the time. In the proem to a Whitsunday sermon he says,

Our *Panis quotidianus,* Our daily bread, is that *Iuge sacrificium,* That daily sacrifice of meditating upon God; Our *Panis hodiernus,* This dayes bread, is to meditate upon the holy Ghost. To day if ye will heare his voice, to day ye are with him in Paradise; For, wheresoever the holy Ghost is, he creates a Paradise. The day is not past yet (VI, No. 16, ll. 1–6).

This fixing of the eternal immediacy of the life and the significance of Christ makes the development of the whole sermon on the Scriptural text much more vital, since it concerns something which is happening now, or can happen now to the people in the congregation. The ecclesiastical date can also be employed in such a way as to make the sermon itself an extended symbol of the time, for

Donne often thinks of Christ's saying, "This day is the whole Scripture fulfilled in your ears." Thus, in an Easter sermon on St. Paul's dark glass, he begins the first part as follows:

For the first term, *Now (Now in a glasse, now in part)* is intended most especially of that very act, which we do now at this present, that is, of the Ministery of the Gospell, of declaring God in his Ordinance, of Preaching his words; . . . And then the *Then,* the time of *seeing face to face,* and *knowing as we are knowne,* is intended of that time, which we celebrate this day, the day of Resurrection, the day of Judgement, the day of the actuall possession of the next life. So that this day, this whole Scripture is fulfilled in your eares; for now, (now in this Preaching) you have some sight, and then, (Then when that day comes, which (in the first roote thereof) we celebrate this day) you shall have a perfect sight of all (VIII, No. 9, ll. 11–22).

The relationship of time with the form of the sermon is pointed out even in such incidental comments as one that occurs in the proem to a sermon preached at Christmas, probably in 1629 (IX, No. 5), where he begins by discussing the length of the twelve-day festival of Christ's birth and suggests that properly the sermon too should be longer than at other times.[20] So close an identification of sermon and day suggests again that the hearer is intended to think himself inside the context of the sermon, as, in time, he lives in the day.

Finally, that the whole life of the Christian is intended to be an imitation of the Christian year is discussed at length in the opening to another Christmas sermon, preached at Paul's in 1626, on the Song of Simeon. Epiphany, explained as a manifestation of Christ, is identified with Christmas Day, with the Epiphany celebration of the coming of the Wise Men, with Simeon's sight of Christ, and with the sacrament of Communion received by the congregation of St. Paul's on this specific Christmas. The symbolic day, linking all these things, gives the Christian a freedom from time through ritual, and a fixed pattern to follow through life that will sustain him in spiritual growth:

To be able to conclude to your selves, that because you have had a Christmas-day, a manifestation of Christs birth in your soules, by the Sacrament, you shall have a whole Good-Friday, a crucifying, and a *consummatum est,* a measure of corrections, and joy in those corrections, tentations, and the issue with the tentation; And that you shall have a Resurrection, and an Ascension, an inchoation, and an unremoveable possession of heaven it self in this world (VII, No. 11, ll. 44–50).

If Donne's use of time in the proems, and occasionally in the divisions and transitions of his sermons, provides the listener with a frame or doorway through which to proceed into meditation upon the text that celebrates the time, his use of space supplies the landscape, the scene of the meditation. And because he here indicates the progress of the Christian listener through the points or landmarks which he designates, the figures employing space are somewhat more frequently found in his sermon divisions than in the proems. The landscapes that he describes most often designate the text as a globe, a map, a building, or a garden. In the following proem, the location of the listener within the text is evident:

Some Cosmographers have said, *That there is no land so placed in the world, but that from that land, a man may see other land.* I dispute it not, I defend it not; I accept it, and I apply it; there is scarce any mercy expressed in the Scriptures, but that from that mercy you may see another mercy. Christ sets up a candle now here, onely to lighten that one roome, but as he is *lumen de lumine, light of light,* so he would have more lights lighted at every light of his, and make every former mercy an argument, an earnest, a conveyance of more. Between land and land you may see seas, and seas enraged with tempests; but still, say they, some other land too. Between mercy, and mercy, you may finde Comminations, and Judgements, but still more mercy. For this discovery let *this text be our Mappe.* First we see land, we see mercy in that gracious compellation, Children, *(the Children of Israel)* Then we see sea, then comes a Commination, a Judgement that shall last some time, *(many days shall the Children of Israel suffer)* But there they may see land too, another mercy, even this time of Judgement shall be a *day,* they shall not be benighted, nor left in darkeness in their Judgements; *(many dayes,* all the while, it shall bee day) Then the text opens into a deep Ocean, a spreading Sea, *(They shall bee without a King, and without a Prince, and without a Sacrifice, and without an Image, and without an Ephod, and without Teraphim.)* But even from this Sea, this vast Sea, this Sea of devastation, wee see land; for, in the next verse followes another mercy, *(The Children of Israel shall returne, and shall seeke the Lord their God, and David their King, and shall feare the Lord, and his goodnesse in the later dayes.)* And beyond this land, there is no more Sea; beyond this mercy, no more Judgement, for with this mercy the Chapter ends (VII, No. 17, ll. 1–28).

I have quoted the entire proem to demonstrate how the figure of the map is interwoven with his introduction of the text, to such an extent that the text does seem to become a globe, and sea and land part of the condition of the children of Israel. Because at the outset the listener's perspective is established within the text, so that he sees the world symbolically through the eyes of the Israelites, the body of the sermon can move easily into an identification of the congregation with the children of Israel. The division of the text continues the figure established in the proem: "Consider our text then, as a *whole Globe,* as an *intire Spheare,* and then our *two Hemispheares* of this Globe, our *two parts* of this text, will bee" (ll. 29–31).

This method of division is one which he learned to develop, and appears only infrequently in the early sermons. He could not have learned it from the ecclesiastical rhetorics, which ordinarily spend only enough time on the subject to advise the preacher to use few divisions and to make them memorable. Donne's method is obviously a device to make the sermon seem an extended version of the text itself, with continents and landmarks somewhat more clearly outlined. Like the one above, his sermon proems and divisions typically include such comments as these:

> In this discovery from this Red *Sea,* to this *dead Sea;* from the mercy of God, in the blood of his Son, to the malediction of God, in the blood of the sinner, be pleased to make these the points of your Compasse, and your Land-marks by the way, in those, the two parts of this exercise (VII, No. 14, ll. 74–78).

> The whole journey of a Christian is in these words; and therefore we were better set out early, then ride too fast; better enter presently into the parts, then be forced to passe thorow them too hastily (IV, No. 11, ll. 1–4).

His consideration of the text as a building proceeds in much the same way. The parts of the text are the building itself; the Christian is to walk through the building and observe the way in which Donne furnishes the rooms. The implication, as with his addition of landmarks to the globe-text, is that Donne's part is to clarify or beautify or make more comfortable to the Christian reader a framework of doctrine and knowledge which has already been set up; he does not change the shape of the text, the globe, or the building: "And so you have the *Modell* of the whole frame, and of the partitions; we proceed now to the furnishing of the particular roomes" (IV, No. 10, ll. 82–84).

The word "branch" is used by Donne from the time of his very earliest sermons as a technical term indicating the subdivision of parts. But as he grew more adept at dividing his discourses in this more organic fashion, he began to use the word in a metaphorical sense as well, in connection with his visualization of the text as growing into the parts of the homily. Hence, his consideration of the sermon both as a garden and as a tree, whose fruit it is his task to make available to the congregation. His conception of himself as instrumental in the presentation of the text is clear. He is a guide to the map, not the creator of the globe; a guide or furnisher of rooms, not an architect; and a guide in the garden, not its maker: "For, as you see, the branches are many, and full of fruit, and I can but shake them, and leave every one to gather his own portion, to apply those notes, which may most advance his edification" (IX, No. 13, ll. 89–91).

The use of space to set up the dimensions of the sermon is sometimes strikingly carried through the divisions themselves, and once through two sermons on the same text. Preaching on the twenty-sixth verse of Genesis, "And God said, Let us make man, in our image, after our likenesse" (IX, Nos. 1 and 2), he begins with a consideration of the size of the world, the swiftness with which it was made and can be cast down. "But then," he says, "raise thy selfe to a higher hope againe. God hath made better land, the land of promise; a stronger city, the new *Jerusalem*; and inhabitants for that everlasting city, *Vs*; whom he made, not by saying, let there be men, but by consultation, by deliberation; *God said, Let us make Man in our Image, after our likenesse*" (No. 1, ll. 55–60). He then divides the course of the two sermons according to the points of the compass, East, West, North, and South,[21] symbolizing the little

world of man, and the Christian life. In the division of the first
sermon he explains that two sermons are necessary to complete the
discussion:

But as that Pilot which had harbor'd his ship so farre within land, as that he
must have change of Winds, in all the points of the Compasse, to bring her
out, cannot hope to bring her out in one day: So being to transport you, by
occasion of these words, from this world to the next; and in this world,
through all the Compasse, all the foure quarters thereof; I cannot hope to
make all this voyage to day. To day we shall consider onely our longitude, our
East, and West; and our North and South at another tyde, and another gale
(ll. 125–32).

At the end of the first sermon, whose development is centered on
the symbolic meaning of East and West, he concludes, "so far are
we gone, East, and West; which is halfe our Compasse, and all this
days voiage. For we are strooke upon the sand; and must stay another Tyde, and another gale for our North, and South" (ll. 760–
63). Here the sand of the hourglass again provides him with a subject for useful wit and links the sermon's dimensions, space and
time, together. The following sermon summarizes the preceding
one and continues the voyage and compass figure.

The use of proem and sermon divisions to give the text a status
as time leading into eternity and as space in which the listener can
move around encourages the kind of concentration of all the senses
upon the meditation that was advocated for individual practice in
spiritual exercises. The environment of the congregation during the
course of the sermon is to be the space and time that it represents,
not the physical surrounding of church and fellow-worshippers. If
the immediacy of this motive were maintained consistently during
the course of the sermon, we would have discourses more closely
approaching the dramatic immediacy of the medieval sermon and of
many Puritan homilies. But Donne's sermons are more complex than
this, and even in proems and sermon divisions the attention of the
congregation is called to another point—the literary and musical
nature of the text.

For Donne, beauty, harmony, order, and conformity are all very

closely related to one another. We tend to overlook in the twentieth
century the fact that the great bulk of his writing—the sermons—is
one expression of a philosophy that we easily condemn in his contemporary Laud—the "reactionism" that preferred stability to a
progress in which the Jacobean divines could not believe, and the
sacramental, ritual expression of truth to the more individualized
and extemporal expression of beliefs, subject, in their view, to the
misguidance of enthusiasm and fancy. Music and poetry were for
Donne a means of precision, and confinement of thought, as well
as beautiful forms. Of the hundreds of references to music throughout the pages of his sermons, the great majority express confidence
in the beauty and order of God's universe and in the inevitably harmonious cadences of the visible expression of truth, whether as the
emblems and signs of God's mercy and justice in the world or as
the printed characters of the Bible and the writings of the church
Fathers. God's style includes both: thus he says, "As God hath
spangled the firmament with starres, so hath he his Scriptures with
names, and Metaphors, and denotations of power. Sometimes he
shines out in the name of a *Sword,* and of a *Target,* and of a *Wall,*
and of a *Tower,* and of a *Rocke,* and of a *Hill*; And sometimes in
that glorious and manifold constellation of all together, *Dominus
exercituum, The Lord of Hosts*" (VII, No. 1, ll. 510–15). Donne
does frequently castigate those who come to hear a preacher for his
eloquence alone, and yet for him the rhetoric of the spirit is the
embodiment of truths that cannot be apprehended at all except
through love and penetrating perception of the meaning of their
form. Thus, again and again in the proems, we find him speaking of
the style of the text, partly, at least, to establish its relation to the
whole musical structure of the world. Preaching on the Song of
Deborah in Judges, for example, he begins by saying that God's
words are sweetest when the Holy Ghost expresses them in song,
that this world and the next both began with song—in Adam's song
expressing his peace of conscience after the forgiveness of his transgression; and in the celebration of Christ's coming, in the Magnifi-
cat, the Benedictus, and the Song of Simeon. "And, to Tune us, to

Compose and give us a Harmonie and Concord of affections, in all
perturbations and passions, and discords in the passages of this life,
if we had no more of the same *Musique* in the *Scriptures* . . . this
Song of *Deborah* were enough, abundantly enough, to slumber any
storme, to becalme any tempest" (IV, No. 7, ll. 34–40).

As he himself observes in an early sermon, he loved particularly
to preach on texts taken from the Psalms, because his own love of
poetry coincides in these sermons with his love for order and harmony. "God . . . gives us our instruction in cheerfull forms, not in
a sowre, and sullen, and angry, and unacceptable way, but cheer-
fully, in *Psalms,* which is also a limited, and a restrained form; Not
in an *Oration,* not in *Prose,* but in *Psalms*; which is such a form as
is both curious, and requires diligence in the making, and then when
it is made, can have nothing, no syllable taken from it, nor added to
it" (II, No. 1, ll. 22–31). Such a form, he says, insures our certainty of the content as well as our pleasure. The frequency of such
discussions in the proems helps to justify his concern for words—
in fact, his whole literary approach to the text in the development
of his sermons. Perhaps he also intends, by concentration on the
eloquence of the Holy Ghost, to turn the minds of the congregation
from preoccupation with the eloquence of the preacher, to help them
to see the form of the sermon as participating by extension of the
rhetoric of the Holy Ghost in the sacramental nature of Scripture,
rather than as presenting to them an example of secular rhetoric to
be admired for itself. And by giving attention to the sacramental
function of the ordered beauty of the Scriptures, he wishes to emphasize the importance of ritual in general—in prescribed prayers
and services and sacraments.

The constant mention of music in the proems and throughout the
sermons also prepares the listener for the poetic use of transitions
and themes that occasionally makes of the whole sermon a kind of
poem. The paragraphs and parts of the sermons are most frequently
united by one of three specific devices: question and answer, repetition that builds upon the preceding paragraph, and refrain. All
three of these devices are essentially musical or poetic. The answer-

ing technique of the first moves like the verses of a song; an expectation is built up in the reader, often in the swelling to urgent climax of a whole paragraph, which requires an answer more for esthetic and emotional than for intellectual reasons:

And of all formes, a Circle is the perfectest, and art thou loath to make up that Circle, with returning to the earth again?
    Thou must, though thou be loath (IV, No. 1, ll. 244–47).[22]

The second device repeats at the beginning of the second paragraph a phrase that ends the first, sometimes with variation. It may so much assume the existence of the first that it does not even make sense without it; the two paragraphs are thus welded together by the musical repetition, as in the following example:

God shall be so jealous of him, as that he *shall* see God, he shall be so watchfull upon God, and his motions, as that he *will* see him.
    And more then see him (IV, No. 6, ll. 409–13).

The third device is the most frequent of all. The refrain ending is usually a repetition, with variation, of the words of the text. Any preacher anxious to keep the text before the congregation employs this mnemonic device. But it does not usually, as it sometimes does in Donne, assume the position of a refrain. Consider, for example, a sermon preached upon two verses of Psalm 32: "Many sorrows shall be to the wicked; but he that trusteth in the Lord, mercy shall compasse him about. Be glad in the Lord, and rejoyce yee righteous; and shout for joy all yee that are upright in heart" (IX, No. 18). The sermon is divided between development of "Many sorrows shall be to the wicked," and elaboration of the mercy and joy that are the lot of the righteous. The first three paragraphs of the first part of the sermon all end with "Many sorrows shall be to the wicked." Thereafter, the refrain varies with the subject of the paragraph, but almost always includes at least one word of the text; the final phrase of the paragraph may refer to "many sorrows," "great sorrows," "the wicked," and so forth. The transitional paragraph and the first paragraph of the second part end with the second motif, "mercy shall compasse them," and thereafter a number of the paragraphs end with reference to mercy and joy. I have already discussed Donne's habit of building paragraphs around key words; these refrains emphasize the centrality of sorrow, mercy, or joy to the paragraphs which they conclude. In the last three short paragraphs of this sermon, variations of the word "joy" appear twenty-four times, focusing the emotional climax of the whole homily. And as the sermon began with sorrow, the final line is, "Mercy shall compass him about that trusteth in the Lord."

Donne introduces the text to the congregation most frequently with reference to time, to space, and to music. The apparently very great difference between the first two methods and the third does not prevent him from combining any two, or even all three techniques, in a single opening. What may be inferred, then, is that although he wants to present the text, or sermon, as a penetrable thing, as a room or garden in which the congregation may walk, he does not want his discourse to proceed like a play or like a spiritual exercise; that kind of dramatic immediacy is not his aim. He does want his *words* to be taken seriously as things, with real dimensions. His purpose is to fuse literary with spiritual experience, to emphasize the distinction between secular and ecclesiastical rhetoric by calling attention to the depth of words sacramentally considered. Because the music of the word is for him an emblem of, and a doorway to, the Word, he feels bound to keep his eye on the language, always with an intensity that is partly love of literature, partly love of God's ritual expressions of himself, and partly dissatisfaction with man's inability to know spiritual truth more fully and to be done with the beautiful but never wholly sufficient earthly manifestations of eternity.

As we have seen, the supporting themes of the proems and sermon divisions are often echoed in Donne's method of handling transitions between paragraphs, parts of sermons, and whole sermons. But these are only supporting themes; the main principles involved in his methods of organizing the body of his homilies have yet to be considered. Every sermon is to some extent individual, and it would be impossible to state these principles precisely enough to wholly explain his methods. But we can create enough order to see in general what his thoughts were when he set out to divide the text into parts. The first necessity was to interpret the meaning of the text. His guiding principle here is that which is set forth in all the ecclesiastical rhetorics: the text is to be interpreted according to its literal sense, which is the intention of the Holy Ghost in that place. For Donne, this means primarily two things. First, the literal sense is often more accurately to be called the literary sense. That Christ is a vine, for example, does not mean that Christ is literally a twining plant; the literal sense of this passage can only be derived by interpretation of the metaphor.[23] Determination of the intention of the Holy Ghost is in all essential passages easy when undertaken by the light of faith; when the passage is not absolutely clear, the literal sense is what is consonant with Christianity. Second, Donne ordinarily interprets the text in its broadest possible terms. He has no use for what he considers fanciful or even wild allegorical interpretations; but the broad moral sense which is, partly at least, inherent in the text itself always receives his fullest attention. In very few of his sermons does he spend more time on the historical sense of the text than is necessary to make it understood and to establish the validity of the generalized moral meaning that he intends to draw from it. Even when his sermon division is set up to discuss three senses—application of a Psalm, for example, to David (historical), to all men (moral), and to Christ (allegorical or anagogical)—the second division is in effect the body of the sermon. At other times when the threefold division appears to be a separation of historical, moral, and anagogical senses, a closer examination reveals that what he is actually doing is tracing some aspect of the Christian life, from its narrowest earthly awakening to its fulfillment in the heavenly kingdom; and the three divisions can thus all be considered a moral application of the text. The two chief literary results of his method are these: first, he very easily falls into a symbolic extension of the text—the historical places and personages are made figures of universal meaning; and second, his sermons hardly ever distinguish between amplification and application, since the moral sense is an application of the text to all men, including his present congregation.

The major ways in which he divides his text into parts are these: word-by-word interpretation (X, No. 3; II, No. 11; III, No. 10); discussion of persons involved, their actions, the object of their actions, and so forth (II, Nos. 13 and 14); interpretation of the text according to several senses (II, No. 18); detailed and painstaking interpretation of a difficult symbolic or allegorical text, taking a phrase or word at a time (VIII, No. 1); interpretation of the text followed by its application to the congregation—this is rare (VIII, No. 8); development of a single symbol expressed in the text (II, No. 1); use of a symbol of his own as emblem and organizational device (IX, No. 7); discussion of several points suggested by the text (VI, No. 6); merging of text with occasion by development of a symbol or symbols that apply equally to both (III, No. 11; VI, No. 18). In all these, artistic arrangement of material takes precedence over such other considerations as the order of the words in the text. Donne builds his sermons with a particular kind of climax in mind, shaping the development to open outward, from its narrowest, most particular earthly meaning, to its widest, most fully spiritual sense. If an historical setting must be conveyed, an argument presented or a rebuke administered, this is done early in the sermon. And whatever negative pictures must be painted or unpleasant points made clear, are taken care of early; the movement of the sermon is also likely to be from sorrow to joy. Words of consolation, visions of heaven, prose poems on the eternal life appear at the conclusion of the sermon, so that the words appear to have carried the reader to the farthest reaches of human meaning and experience, and here the sermon is left open.

Detailed consideration of all the different ways in which Donne's sermons are organized would be boring and unnecessary. The more mechanical types of arrangement are available enough to the interested reader and cannot claim the right to literary analysis. The majority of the sermons, probably all of the best ones, are represented in the four patterns I have chosen to discuss here, in less or more detail. The fact that more than one method of development can operate in a single sermon will become clear in the process of these analyses.

There is, first, the sermon which carefully and thoroughly elaborates the meaning of an obscure figurative passage. A sermon preached at St. Dunstan's on Trinity Sunday, 1627 (VIII, No. 1), has as its text Revelation 4:8: "And the foure beasts had each of them six wings about him, and they were full of eyes within; and they rest not day and night, saying, Holy, Holy, Holy, Lord God Almighty, which was, and is, and is to come." Because this is a hard text, considerable space is given in the division and in the first part of the sermon to a consideration of its meaning. The one certain thing is that since these words were appointed by the Church to be read upon Trinity Sunday, "we are sure, that in the notion, and apprehension, and construction of our Church, these words appertaine to the Trinity" (ll. 56–57). In the opening to the first part of the sermon, he concludes, in view of the multiplicity of past interpretations and the evident obscurity of the text, that "since wee cannot give *Sensum adaequatum,* Any such Interpretation of these foure creatures, but that another, as probable as it, may be given, it may be sufficient, and it is best, (as in all cases of like intricacy) to choose such a sense, as may most advance the generall purpose, and intention of the place; which is, in this place, The celebration of the Trinity" (ll. 106–11). When he has to work with such texts as this, particularly those taken from Revelation, Donne is likely to develop the sermon by means of a full and elaborate interpretation of the probable or most edifying meaning of the words. The method is like the method of the emblem writers, the text standing for the picture, and the body of the sermon for the explanation, which even in emblem books was sometimes a very lengthy affair. The sermon is divided into two parts, dealing with the persons and their actions, and each of these parts is further divided into three sections. The first part considers who the persons are, what their wings are, and what their eyes are. The second considers their profession of zeal in God's service, their assiduity, and their celebration of the Trinity.

The first section of the first part determines that the four beasts stand for the four evangelists, but he immediately enlarges this interpretation to include all Christian ministers, and this larger sense is really the subject of the sermon. From this point on, the organization of the sermon depends on a detailed analysis of the emblem: as the four beasts had the faces of a lion, an ox, a man, and an eagle, so the Christian minister must combine the courage of a lion, the labor of an ox, the keen-sightedness of the eagle, and the persuasive reason of a man. The sermon is interesting chiefly because it demonstrates Donne's conception of the office and duties of the Christian minister, and because it contains some very imaginative and moving passages on the preacher's ability to lift his people from the earth toward spiritual life and vision. In these places he transcends a mere mechanical development. There is also one final point of great interest. The last section of the sermon is extended to a seven-page discussion of the nature of the Trinity. It is really a sermon within a sermon; Donne is no longer interpreting a text but preaching the Christian religion, and in so doing he must have been conscious that he was making himself an illustration of the Christian minister whose duties he had just been so eloquently discussing. This is one of many instances in which he makes external life—in this case himself—part and symbol of his text.

Some of Donne's very best sermons were preached early in his ministry at Lincoln's Inn, in a course of sermons on the Thirty-eighth Psalm. He spoke often of his love for the Psalms, which for him, as poetry, represented the order and beauty of religion. And he does also seem to identify himself with David more nearly than with any other Old Testament figure, so that almost all his sermons on the Psalms have an urgent immediacy that distinguishes their tone from that of others. There is a closer grappling with the symbols involved, and less tendency to explain their meaning than to experience them directly. Some of these are among the numerous sermons which develop a single figure found in the text.

The first sermon of the course was preached on the second verse of the Thirty-eighth Psalm: "For thine arrowes stick fast in me, and thy hand presseth me sore."[24] The sermon is divided into two parts; the first considers "how it may become a godly man, to limit God so far, as to present and oppose *Reasons* against his declared purpose, and proceedings" (II, No. 1, ll. 61–63). This part is a very short summary of some of the occasions that moved Biblical characters to complaint, and of the greater instances of triumph over hardship, and rejoicing in the midst of difficulty. This section completed, he turns to an intensive examination of the word "arrows," which he takes to mean temptations. The headings under which they are discussed are both the characteristics of arrows in general and the conditions expressed in the text. The arrows are shot by others; they are swift, scarcely visible, and numerous; they stick in him and stick fast and in all his parts, and the hand which shot them presses him sore; but they are God's arrows, and shot from God's hand; they bring with them the balsamum of mercy.

Despite this careful enumeration of the subdivisions, the sermon is not drily developed, and there is little point-for-point interpretation of the symbol; rather, the figure of the shooting arrow is simply consistently and extensively used to describe what Dennis Quinn defines as the "mechanics of temptation,"[25] as the following passages show:

And then, these arrows *stick in us;* the raine fals, but that cold sweat hangs not upon us; Hail beats us, but it leaves no pock-holes in our skin. These arrows doe not so fall about us, as that they misse us; nor so hit us, as they rebound back without hurting us (ll. 489–92).

They stick, and they *stick fast; altè infixae;* every syllable aggravates our misery. Now for the most part, experimentally, we know not whether they stick fast or no, for we never goe about to pull them out: these arrows, these tentations, come, and welcome: we are so far from offering to pull them out, that we fix them faster and faster in us; we assist our tentations: . . . And he that does in some measure, soberly and religiously, goe about to draw out these arrows, yet never consummates, never perfects his own work; He pulls back the arrow a little way, and he sees *blood,* and he feels *spirit* to goe out with it, and he lets it alone (ll. 542–54).

Dennis Quinn says of this sermon that temptations become arrows and arrows temptations, that the fusion of image and abstraction is complete. If this is true, it is because Donne thinks of both image and abstraction as *words,* and he thinks of words as things. Hence, "every syllable aggravates our misery." "Temptation" is a word; so is "arrow," and Bible words are shot like arrows. The use of very short, stabbing sentences throughout the sermon supports the intensity created by the driving insistence upon this single symbol, and by Donne's willingness almost to let his symbol alone. In no passage in the sermons do his figures have more freedom than they have here to become something of themselves, unlimited by much interpretation. But this sermon may stand as typical of this course of six, of a number of his other sermons on the Psalms, and of a much smaller number of sermons on texts whose metaphors Donne found particularly compelling.

In this sermon, and in the others in this course, another ostensible method of development is employed. The passage is to be applied to David, to all men, and to Christ. At the beginning of the second part here, he considers the possible meanings of the arrows in David's case, summarizing the suggestions of previous commentators. "But," he goes on to say, "these *Psalmes* were made, not onely to vent *Davids* present holy passion, but to serve the Church of God, to the worlds end. . . . Extend this *Man,* to all *Mankind;* carry *Davids* History up to *Adams* History, and consider us in that state, which wee inherit from *him,* and we shall see *arrows* fly about our ears" (ll. 229–34). In application of the text to all men, he resolves the conflict and finds the sense which is to be carried through the sermon.

In the last long paragraph of the sermon, he applies the text to Christ; and the transition here is interesting enough, as regards Donne's whole sense of the text and method of interpretation, to deserve quotation in full:

To end all, and to dismisse you with such a re-collection, as you may carry away with you; literally, primarily, this text concerns *David:* He by *tentations* to sin, by *tribulations* for sin, by *comminations,* and *increpations* upon sin, was bodily, and ghostly become a quiver of arrows of all sorts; they *stook,* and stook *fast,* and stook *full* in him, in *all* him. The Psalm hath a *retrospect* too, it looks back to *Adam,* and to every particular man in his loines, and so, *Davids* case is our case, and all these arrowes stick in all us. But the Psalm and the text hath also a *prospect,* and hath a *propheticall* relation from *David* to our Saviour Christ Jesus. And of him, and of the multiplicity of these arrows upon him in the exinanition, and evacuation of himself, in this world for us, have many of the *Ancients* interpreted these words literally, and as in their first and primary signification; Turne we therefore to *him,* before we goe, and he shall return home with us (ll. 747–61).

The clinging of the literal sense to all three interpretations is clear; and his typical use of the text as a compression of all time is also evident. Now, rather than lose the sense of climax that has been built to, and the sense of peace achieved by the final discussion of the arrows as both temptation and remedy for temptation, he turns this final section into a colloquy and prayer, alternately speaking and praying to Christ. The device is utilitarian in its simultaneous application of the text to Christ and indirect exhortation of the congregation; and its heightened tone, together with increasing mention of the heavenly life, provides the kind of open, high conclusion for which Donne always strove. The closing pair will serve as illustration:

And lastly, thine arrows were followed, and *pressed with the hand of God; The hand of God pressed upon thee,* in that *eternall decree,* in that *irrevocable contract,* between thy *Father* and *thee,* in that *Oportuit pati, That all that thou must suffer, and so enter into thy glory.* Establish us, O Lord, in all occasions of diffidences here; and when thy hand presses our arrows upon us, enable us to see, that *that* very hand, hath from all eternity written, and written in thine own blood, a *decree* of the *issue,* as well, and as soon, as of the *tentation.* In which confidence of which decree, as men, in the virtue thereof already in possession of heaven, we joyn with that Quire in that service, in that *Anthem, Blessing, and glory, and wisdome, and thanksgiving, and honour, and power, and might, be unto our God for ever, and ever,* Amen (ll. 821–33).

The proportionate lengths of time spent on David, all men, and Christ in this sermon are typical of his method of handling these three senses. He uses David to open, and sometimes resolve, the meaning of the text. He comes to Christ in conclusion. But his major endeavor is to show the application of the moral to all men.

A Lenten sermon preached to the King at Whitehall (IX, No. 7) illustrates Donne's use of subsidiary patterns within his own organizing symbol. The text is Matthew 6:21: "For, where your treasure is, there will your heart be also." In the division he takes to symbolize sermon and text the letter Y, "that hath first a stalk, a stem to fix it self, and then spreads into two Beams" (ll. 41–42). The letter then becomes both the shape of the sermon as it divides into three parts, and an emblem[26] of the two courses that man may take in life. The sermon illustrates his occasional rearrangement of the text to suit the climax he wants, for he takes up the last part of the verse at the beginning.

The first part of the sermon, the stem of the letter Y, is a consideration of the constant and of the wayward heart, with full elaboration of the impediments to Christian constancy. The second part takes up the word "treasure" and elaborates upon the significance of the term to the worldly man, as he lays up for himself a treasure of sinfulness. In this section and the next, the meaning of the word "treasure" changes constantly, not so much because it is being developed as symbol as because Donne places it in several different contexts, varying its meaning by shifts in tone and surrounding metaphor. Thus, although the sermon in these two sections is centered around the word, the organization is quite different from that of the preceding sermon. There by intense concentration upon the function of temptations as arrows, Donne vividly realizes a spiritual condition with an almost dramatic immediacy. The consistent development of the meaning of the symbol is the structure of the sermon. The formal structure of this sermon depends upon the filling in of the simple and pre-established emblem, the letter Y. Within this structure, discussion centers around the words "heart" and "treasure," but they are used as *motifs* rather than as symbols, recurring in rapidly shifting contexts as Donne rings the changes on his theme. After associating the word "treasure" with the broad beam of the letter Y, with greed and the evanescence of worldly goods, and with the piling up of a treasure of sin, Donne shifts the point of view and describes God's answer to the worldly man. God treasures up these sins in "the Treasury of his judgements" (l. 400), pours out upon the world "his Treasures of Snow, and Treasures of

Hail" (ll. 401–2), war and dearth and sickness, and still retains in his treasury "Weapons of Indignation for the World to come" (ll. 437–38). A tone of strong irony emphasizes the very frequent repetitions of the word "treasure." In the third section, the narrower arm of the Y, Donne almost perversely piles up financial metaphors, with great success, to describe the treasure of the godly man. The antiphonal structure of the sentences, the close association of this wealth with spiritual meaning, and the noticeable relief from irony all contribute to the effectiveness of the device:

Lay up a million one day, in taking Gods Cause to heart; and lay up ten millions next day, in taking Gods Cause in hand. Let every soul lay up a peny now, in resisting a small temptation; and a shilling anon, in resisting a greater; and it will grow to be a treasure, a treasure of Talents, of so many Talents, as that the poorest soul in the Congregation, would not change treasure with any Plate-Fleet (ll. 478–84).

This third section moves gradually into a first person account of the joys of heaven to come; and this further change in tone raises the level of the sermon again to that of a song of exultation describing the eternal treasure of joy and glory. What Donne calls the narrow beam of the Y opens into infinity.

These three patterns all demonstrate that Donne's primary concern is the moral application of the words of the text to the Christian listener. The fourth type employs immediate contemporary experience as symbolic illustration of the chosen text, and because it is the most interesting, I want to illustrate with two examples. Instead of merely applying the text to the hearer, he assumes the world and the hearer into the sermon, again, in this more compelling way, merging printed with physical symbol.

A sermon probably preached at the marriage of Margaret Washington in 1621 has as its text Hosea 2:19: "And I will mary thee unto me for ever" (III, No. 11). As is so frequently his habit, he presents a division of the text that compresses all time into one sermon:

Be pleased therefore to give me leave in this exercise, to shift the scene thrice, and to present to your religious considerations three objects, three subjects: first, a secular mariage in Paradise; secondly, a spirituall mariage in the Church; and thirdly, an eternall mariage in heaven. And in each of these three we shall present three circumstances; first the Persons, *Me* and *Tibi, I will mary thee;* And then the Action, *Sponsabo, I will mary thee;* And lastly the Term, *In aeternum, I will mary thee to mee for ever* (ll. 20–27).

This kind of pattern may be identified as development of the text according to the four senses, in three stages—literal-moral, spiritual, and anagogical. But the use of the four senses, and "allegorical" interpretation in general, were distasteful to Donne. What he means to do here (a common practice in his sermons) is to trace the history of the progress of the soul in knowledge of love. He begins with Adam and Eve, but only to make them stand for the secular life of men; his consideration of the purposes of marriage in this first part is couched in general terms with specific application to the couple to be married. The text, "I will mary thee unto me for ever" is about Adam and Eve, about all men and women, and about this couple, who are made in this sermon a visible symbol of all humanity. His discussion of each of the uses of marriage, and of the words "for ever" as applied to an earthly union, is followed by a prayer for the blessing of God upon these two people in their mutual love, in the children they are to have, in their support of one another, and in the symbolic eternity of their marriage. The second part of the sermon is a discussion of the spiritual marriage of Christ and the church; but as the first part dealt with Adam and Eve only as prelude to discussion of human marriage in general, this section actually considers Christ's marriage to the human soul. The section opens with a great period on the wonder of the union between a perfect Christ and the imperfect, sinful "I," for here Donne, as so often in the latter parts of his sermons, begins to use the first person. The three purposes of marriage are applied again, this time symbolically, and the section ends with another discussion of the words "for ever." In the third part, which is a consideration of the eternal or mystical marriage in heaven between Christ and the soul, Donne's use of the first person becomes even more dramatic, for heaven is the scene, and the congregation is made up of the Virgins, Martyrs, Confessors, and Patriarchs. These are visualized as seeming to mur-

mur among themselves against the likelihood of Christ's marriage to the soul, which stands painfully aware of its unworthiness, "and yet there and then this Lamb shall mary me, and mary me *In aeternum,* for ever" (ll. 457–77).[27] In the last paragraph of the sermon, Donne's prose, interwoven with the language of the Apocalypse, leads to a conclusion in another prayer, beginning with the first line of a collect:

Lighten our darkness, we beseech thee, ô Lord, that in thy light we may see light: Illustrate our understandings, kindle our affections, pour oyle to our zeale, that we may come to the mariage of this Lamb, and that this Lamb may come quickly to this mariage: And in the mean time bless these thy servants, with making this secular mariage a type of the spirituall, and the spirituall an earnest of that eternall, which they and we, by thy mercy, shall have in the Kingdome which thy Son our Saviour hath purchased with the inestimable price of his incorruptible blood (ll. 514–23).

With the help of the text, Donne has, in this sermon, made the occasion, the marriage of the two people before him, a symbol invested with universal spiritual meaning. By the careful and direct elaboration of the first part of the sermon, he identifies Margaret Washington and her husband with Adam and Eve and with all humanity, and establishes the value of the marriage in real and immediate terms. Its subsequent use as a type of spiritual and eternal marriage, then, adds a steadily widening meaning to it, the refinement of the human soul in its understanding of love. The sermon is an example of the genius with which Donne merges amplification with application and brings the world into the text. Because the action of real life is made the subject of the text, a specific application is unnecessary; a single symbol is both text and occasion.

A sermon of consolation, the first sermon preached at St. Dunstan's after the dispersion of the congregation on account of the plague, provides a contrasting example of the same technique. The text is Exodus 12:30: "For there was not a house where there was not one dead" (VI, No. 18), and was of course chosen for its applicability to the ordeal through which the people of London had just passed. The proem, demonstrating his intention of making the world part of the text, affirms God's mercy in providing so many copies of his meaning—here, in the printed words; in every house and family; in every Christian soul; and in the church itself, which housed so many graves. The home, the self, and the church all are the text, and in the spoken words, the people find themselves and their surroundings and so grasp the sense of the verse.

The sermon division speaks of the first four parts of the sermon as four houses, and the meaning of each of these is taken up in turn. Discussion of the historical meaning of the text is longer than usual, and makes the death of the Egyptian first-born, and of Pharaoh's armies, a symbol of the constancy of God's judgment, as well as a sign of his mercy in establishing for the edification of the rest of the world this monument of the fate of obdurate men. The second house is the household of the Christian listener, where a son or daughter (a first-born) may have suffered spiritual death as a result of the negligence of the head of the house. The third is the self, "this House of Clay" (l. 257), whose first-born, love of God and religious zeal, may have been allowed to atrophy, or that other first-born, the material results of sin, to build up a body of death. The fourth is the church, a graveyard for men whose physical deaths are the results of Adam's sin; and this too is the death of a first-born, for the body was made before the soul. The tone of these first four parts is somber, but running through them is a thread of cheer, the continual though faint suggestion of the continual possibility of mercy.

In these four parts, the house provides an emblem and a framework for discussion. But the more important symbol is the death of the Egyptian children: because the Egyptians failed to heed God's warning, the death of their first-born was followed by their own destruction. To relate this historical text to the present, Donne uses the London plague, but his real concern is the sin of Adam in which all men share, which always brings about physical death but need not result in spiritual death unless men's souls become hardened against God. In the process of generalizing the text from its historical to its more universal meaning, Donne does not suggest in any sense that the plague is punishment for specific guilt; the deaths caused by the plague are only immediate and poignant illustrations of the bodily mortality which is the lot of all the children of Adam.

The sermon now continues, to elaborate the idea of mercy suggested during the first parts. In transition, Donne summarizes what he has said of the four houses as "so many places of Infection, so many temporal or spiritual Pesthouses" (ll. 329–30):

> But now the very phrase of the Text, which is, *That in every house there was one dead, There was,* invites us to a more particular consideration of God's mercy, in that, howsoever it were, it is not so now; in which we shall look how far this beam of mercy shines out in every one of these houses, that it is not so now, There is not one dead in every house now; but the Infection, (Temporal and Spiritual Infection) is so far ceased, as that not only those that are alive, do not die, as before; but those whom we called dead, are not dead; they are alive in their spirits, in *Abrahams bosome;* and they are alive in their very bodies, in their contract and inherence in Christ Jesus in an infallible assurance of a joyful Resurrection (ll. 331–42).

The second part of the sermon again takes up the four houses in order, building upon what has already been stated. It is a symbolic shining of the beam of mercy upon the first-born in these houses, and the comprehensiveness of the symbol's meaning and significance widens steadily until the end. In the household of Egypt, as among the plunderers who tried to benefit from the plague, the beam of mercy was not allowed to shine, for those men had hardened their hearts against mercy and could receive only more and more justice. But the plague has wrought correction and mercy in the next house, the Christian family, where the "savor of death" has been the "savor of life" (l. 402), wakening the first-born, the members of the household to "a blessed resurrection from all their sinfull habits" (l. 417). In the individual soul, the first-born love of God is renewed through hardship and pain. The fourth house, the church, whose very ground is "made of the bodies of Christians, and therein hath received a second consecration" (ll. 489–91), becomes a great symbol of the resurrection of man through the sacrifice of Christ. The first-born bodies must die inheritors of Adam's sin, but they are to rise again with their souls at the last day. The dual symbol of justice and mercy that has been made of these last three houses, with their first-born, is here given overwhelming immediacy; the air that the people breathe contains the dust of Christian bodies: "Every puff of wind within these walls, may blow the father into the sons eys, or the wife into her husbands, or his into hers, or both into their childrens, or their childrens into both."[28] This graphic illustration of mortality is made a prelude to the assertion of immortality, of the timeless resurrection that will raise the bodies dead in the Christian church, with the bodies of those who now worship over their graves in a city of death, to eternal life in the Christian heaven:

. . . they whom we tread upon now, and we whom others shall tread upon hereafter, shall meet at once, where, though we were dead, dead in our several houses, dead in a sinful *Egypt,* dead in our family, dead in our selves, dead in the Grave, yet we shall be received, with that consolation, and glorious consolation, you were dead, but are alive. *Enter ye blessed into the Kingdom, prepared for you, from the beginning* (ll. 544–50).

Thus, although Donne's most comprehensive organization is not dramatic, he does follow the intention implied in proems and sermon divisions to draw the sermon out of the text, and to draw the listener into text and sermon. In many sermons whose organization I have not discussed, his method is more prosaic, but almost always, when the text provides opportunity for a literary symbolic development, he chooses one of these patterns.

In bringing his sermon to a close, Donne makes use of the devices recommended by the writers of ecclesiastical rhetorics; these are, in particular, the repetition of the main points or sermon headings, exhortation, and prayer.[29] But more important to an understanding of the part of the conclusion in the whole structure of his sermons is a point that I touched upon earlier: the sermon, beginning with the obvious historical meaning of the text, or with its most pessimistic interpretation, opens outward toward its most universal and most positive sense. In likening the winged beasts of the Apocalypse to Christian ministers, Donne says that the duty of the minister is to raise the hearer upon his wings to contemplation of spiritual truth (VIII, No. 1, ll. 258–72). The outward movement of the sermon is in effect this rising motion, and Donne's chief aim in conclusion is to leave the sermon open, not to bring the hearer back to earth by use of a too mundane or didactic style. Only rarely does he conclude with a point-by-point summary of the headings of the text. Generally such a recapitulation is entirely unnecessary, since the narrower meanings open into the larger ones without being themselves forgotten; a concrete symbol, for example, remains as a reminder of all that Donne has read into it.

The tone of the conclusion is elevated. Exhortation frequently occurs, but it is most often a specific kind of exhortation, a reminder that by the practice of the Christian virtues, the hearer can obtain inchoation of eternity in this life. The emphasis is not so much on practical advice as on awakening in the hearer a thirst for heaven. At the close of one sermon, preached probably in 1629, and so near the end of his life, he indicates his conscious and habitual employment of this practice:

But if God bring thee to that humiliation of soule and body here, hee will emprove, and advance thy sanctification *abundantiùs,* more abundantly, and when he hath brought it to the best perfection, that this life is capable of, he will provide another *abundantiùs,* another maner of abundance in the life to come; which is the last beating of the pulse of this text, the last panting of the breath thereof, our anhelation, and panting after the joyes, and glory, and eternity of the kingdome of Heaven; of which, though, for the most part, I use to dismisse you, with saying something, yet it is alwaies little that I can say thereof; at this time, but this (IX, No. 5, ll. 829–38).

He underrates his own descriptive power here, as he himself demonstrates in the following thirty lines, a series of hyperboles illustrating the joys of heaven. The devices which, in these conclusions, contribute to openness and heightened tone are extreme and hyperbolic comparisons of earth and heaven; ritual language; long, spiralling complex and periodic sentences; use of the first person to describe the soul's passage into eternity; and the almost invariable appearance of the words "grace," "joy," and "glory." The following passage from a very long conclusion illustrates the last three techniques:

But as my soule, as soone as it is out of my body, is in Heaven, and does not stay for the possession of Heaven, nor for the fruition of the sight of God, till it be ascended through ayre, and fire, and Moone, and Sun, and Planets, and Firmament, to that place which we conceive to be Heaven, but without the thousandth part of a minutes stop, as soone as it issues, is in a glorious light, which is Heaven . . . As my soule shall not goe towards Heaven, but goe by Heaven to Heaven, to the Heaven of Heavens, So the true joy of a good soule in this world is the very joy of Heaven; and we goe thither, not that being without joy, we might have joy infused into us, but that as Christ sayes, *Our joy might be full* . . . in the agonies of Death, in the anguish of that dissolution, in the sorrowes of that valediction, in the irreversiblenesse of that transmigration, I shall have a joy, which shall no more evaporate, then my soule shall evaporate, A joy, that shall passe up, and put on a more glorious garment above, and be joy super-invested in glory. *Amen* (VII, No. 1, ll. 723–49).

To conclude the sermon without breaking the mood, Donne finds two general formulae particularly useful. The first is a return to the text or to a variation of the text in the last line of the sermon, and the second includes several different kinds of closing prayers. Repetition of the text has the obvious uses of making the whole sermon into a kind of poem, with the same opening and closing lines, and of making the text the last words as well as the first to be sounded, and so more memorable. But his use of the text in conclusion is not simple repetition; it is a demonstration of what has been done with the words during the course of the hour. As the division and interpretation of the text is called its "opening," we can say metaphorically that when first read from the pulpit before the sermon began, it was not "open," but that Donne's treatment of it, making it in the proem a spacious land to walk in and in the amplification an extended symbol, has opened it fully, so that its repetition does not make the sermon close in, but indicates that it has only reached this degree of expansion and this heightened tone through the opening out of the text itself. And the identity of the text with the whole sermon is invariably emphasized by the fact that it is presented at the end as the conclusion of a final sentence, not as a thing in itself. Preaching upon the text, "Blessed be God, even the Father of our Lord Jesus Christ, the Father of Mercies, and the God of all Comfort," he comes through vision of heaven to repetition of the text as final prayer:

That great day of thy glorification will breake out even in this life, and either in the possessing of the good things of this world, thou shalt see the glory, and in possessing the comforts of this World, see the joy of Heaven, or else, (which is another of his wayes) in the want of all these, thou shalt have more comfort then others have, or perchance, then thou shouldest have in the possessing of them: for he is *the God of all comfort,* and of all the wayes of comfort; And therefore, *Blessed be God, even the Father, &c* (III, No. 12, ll. 625–33).

A final variation on the text may be employed to further emphasize the explication of its meaning, as in the following illustration, where he briefly summarizes the sermon headings. The text is "What man is he that liveth, and shall not see death?" The conformity with Christ spoken of here is also a frequent subject for sermon closings:

If God give me *mortem raptus,* a death of rapture, of extasie, of fervent Contemplation of Christ Jesus, a Transfusion, a Transplantation, a Transmigration, a Transmutation into him, (for good digestion brings alwaies assimilation, certainly, if I come to a true meditation upon Christ, I come to a conformity with Christ) this is principally that *Pretiosa mors Sanctorum, Pretious in the sight of the Lord, is the death of his Saints,* by which they are dead and buryed, and risen again in Christ Jesus: precious is that death, by which we apply that pretious blood to our selves, and grow strong enough by it, to meet *Davids* question, *Quis homo?* what man? with Christs answer, *Ego homo,* I am the man, in whom whosoever abideth, shall not see death (II, No. 9, ll. 545–55).

As I have shown in two of the three previous illustrations, Donne does not always conclude his sermons with a prayer, and only rarely is the prayer completely detached from the sermon. Very often he ends with the brief formula, "And to this glorious Son of God, &c"; or with variations of the phrases "Lighten our darkness, we beseech thee O Lord," the opening of a collect for Evening Prayer, echoing Psalm 18:28 (III, No. 11, ll. 514–23; No. 17, 1018–23); or "Come Lord Jesu, come quickly, come now" (II, No. 12, l. 685; No. 15, l. 504; IV, No. 10, l. 636), elaborated from Revelation 22:20. Sometimes, as we have seen, the prayer is the final sermon division, or, more frequently, it merges with the last division or the conclusion as it does here:

Thou shalt adde a step to the Resurrection it selfe, by having brought it so much nearer, as to have done thy part for the filling up of the number of the Saints, upon which fulnesse the Resurrection shall follow. And thou shalt adde a Voyce, to that Old, and ever-new Song, that Catholique Hymne, in which, both Churches, *Militant* and *Triumphant,* shall joyne, *Blessing, Honour, Glory, and Power, bee unto him, that sitteth upon the Throne, and to the Lambe, for ever, and ever.* Amen (VIII, No. 12, ll. 787–94).

Here the prayer is so far from breaking the mood of the conclusion that it is itself part of the description of heaven. In other instances it may be joined with the rest of the sermon by its continuation of a major symbol or metaphor, as in the concluding prayer to the sermon on the text, "For, where your treasure is, there will your heart be also" (IX, No. 7):

There I shall have all joys, altogether, always. There *Abraham* shall not be gladder of his own Salvation, then of mine; nor I surer of the Everlastingness of my God, then of my Everlastingness in Him. This is that Treasure, of which the God of this Treasure, give us those Spangles; and that single Money, which this Mint can coin, this World can receive, that is, Prosperity, and a good use thereof, in worldly things; and Grace, and Peace, and Faith, in spiritual. And then reserve for us the Exaltation of this Treasure, in the Joy and Glory of Heaven, in the Mediation of his Son Christ Jesus, and by the Operation of his Blessed Spirit. AMEN (ll. 561–71).

Donne builds his sermons in accordance with his belief that preaching is sacramental, as if it were itself the kind of symbol that links spiritual with physical things. Thus, the proem and the division, particularly by means of figures of time and space, indicate that the text is a thing that may be entered and walked through; while the emphasis on music and style calls attention to the importance of the letter of the Scripture as the outward sign of truth. Symbol and sermon are developed in the body of the discourse in such a way that, whenever possible, the occasion becomes part of the text, part of the metaphor; and the symbol grows throughout the sermon in scope, in spiritual meaning and in intensity. The heightened tone of the closing exhortation, summary, scene, or prayer emphasizes the fact that climax and conclusion are simultaneous. The openness of the sermon at its end implies that insofar as is possible it has imitated the whole action of a symbol, whose most important and visible portion is narrow, wholly dependent for expression upon space and time (as indicated in the proems), while the intangible or spiritual meaning behind it (to which Donne again and again claims that he does poor justice in the conclusions) is infinite, only barely touched at the end of the sermon, whose prayers suggest the means to its possession.

W. Y. Tindall has pointed out that when a whole work of art becomes a symbol it must differ from symbolic elements within it because these internal figures gain much of their strength from interaction with their context, while a novel or poem that is a symbol has no setting.[30] The sermon, whose symbolic character is sacramental, has, however, a specific environmental context which must be considered. Its original auditory was part of its immediate surrounding; its effectiveness as symbol was, then, for that auditory, dependent upon the success of its mediatory function as it represented a threshold between the physical and the metaphysical worlds. For the modern reader, the context can be both the sermon's symbol and as much of the original scene of delivery as he can imaginatively reconstruct, together with a very real and present heaven, which is as important to the scene as are the painted heavens in baroque vaults, because part of the sermon's function is to bring it near. Certainly much of the dramatic power of these sermons for a twentieth-century reader is contingent upon his willingness to recreate this panorama.

And contingent too upon our understanding of Donne. For, preaching himself, he was bone and sinew, rhythm and texture of his work. In his *Devotions,* he says, "I need thy *thunder,* O my God; thy musicke will not serve me," but the sermon as he conceived it is both thunder and music, as it simultaneously expresses both power and order. The sentences are copious, nervous, meditative, and rhythmic. The metaphors are insistent, overzealous, strongly controlled. The texture is tremulous, legalistic, macabre, witty, exalted, and above all, literary. Things became words, and words came alive, when Donne erected for his congregation a gorgeous palace that would subside into print after the hour's end.

VII

Contrary Music

Donne preached to himself always, and during a long illness in 1623 he wrote a whole book to himself, since he could not then preach from the pulpit. He once said in a sermon that "in a heart absolutely surrendred to God, vehement expostulation with God, and yet full submission to God, and a quiet acquiescence in God; A storme of affections in nature, and yet a setled calme, and a fast anchorage in grace, a suspition, and a jealousie, and yet an assurance, and a confidence in God, may well consist together" (VII, No. 15, ll. 462–67). If he thought this of a rectified conscience, it is no wonder that his writing is so full of contrasting moods and conflicting harmonies. And it is no wonder that in his *Devotions Upon Emergent Occasions,* physical illness having intensified these moods, the contrasts are unusually sharp and clear.

He writes of himself. The changes which the "I" undergoes reflect different spiritual states implicitly expressed in the changing style. The sentences and separate meditations are held together by repetition of single words, a technique which I have already discussed in relation to sentence structure and sermon organization. Used to emphasize and elaborate images, it also has rhythmic value; in a passage on the heart, for example, the word becomes a persistent poetic beat (*Devotions,* pp. 63–66). And it shows the symbolic importance which Donne gives to language, as well as the associative manner of his thinking. Whole sections of the *Devotions* are written around single words, whose repetition is a continual reminder of the central theme.

The *Devotions* are divided into twenty-three units, each of which contains a "meditation upon our humane condition," and "expostulation, and debatement with God," and a prayer. Each unit progresses from negation and despair in the meditations, through questioning, rebellious love in the expostulations, to affirmation and calm submission in the prayers. The style changes accordingly. To some extent this movement may represent Donne's own progress toward faith. However, the cyclic character of the arrangement suggests that he does not really put the first two attitudes out of his mind; although they may be subordinated to prayer "in a heart absolutely surrendred to God," they do "consist together." The pattern has some connection with meditational organization, although it is bolder and more daring than the ordinary spiritual exercise, more expostulatory than the meditational elements in his sermons. Finally, its subject matter is an exploration of the possibilities for knowledge inherent in the three traditional instruments of revelation: the Book of the Creatures, the Scriptures, and the Church.

The meditation, as developed in English devotional literature, was an extraordinarily minute and vivid examination of some subject intended to awaken the Christian to "the love and exercise of vertue, and the hatred and avoiding of sinne."[1] Designed to be carried out over a period of time, these spiritual exercises were usually arranged in a sequence, beginning with knowledge of the self and the world, and progressing through consideration of death and judgment to meditations upon hell and heaven. Donne confines his meditations (the first section of each unit) to "our humane condition"; thus we can expect to find their nearest counterparts in the opening sections of earlier exercises.

The purpose of considering the nature of man is set forth in a sixteenth-century manual written by Thomas Becon:

When he hath on this manner considered of God, then must he ponder what he himself is, even a very miserable sinner, destitute of all goodness, void of all godliness, and unworthy to approach unto the throne of the divine majesty. For this humiliation of ourselves helpeth greatly to the advancement of our prayer. For the more that any man dejecteth and throweth down himself, the nearer is he made unto God.[2]

Such self-consideration was generally held in check by the form of the meditation, the didactic tone of the treatise, and the Christian vocabulary of the writer, who was more apt than not to take the long view throughout, to make clear that the misery of man is a result of sin and that through penitence he can be cured of sin and misery by the mercy of God.

Donne limits his meditations to man and the creatures. His diction almost entirely excludes any Christian implications, and is further removed from the ordinary meditation by its ironic tone. His imagery, based on physical comparisons, avoids any links with the spiritual world. Thus his vocabulary is more limited than that of the natural man, who is able to construct a philosophy within which to order the matter of existence; Donne brings to his meditations an overwhelming sense of the wretched condition of a man who is aware of himself, but is able to compare himself only to other animals and to the world, and with few exceptions, only by noting the deficiencies that they share and the advantages possessed by non-human or insensate things. It is almost a parody of the enthusiastic approach to self-knowledge of men like Montaigne.

The dominant symbol for portrayal of man's condition is the microcosm-macrocosm analogy. Often in his sermons Donne uses this concept as an explanation of the ways in which man can see God through the Book of the Creatures. Contemplation of himself naturally leads to contemplation of that larger world which is also the handiwork of God; and man is thought of as a reflection not only of the world but of God as well, since he is made in God's image and bears within himself the trinity of memory, will, and understanding. Donne's use of the image in these meditations is very different; as the way in which he regards it is skewed by his physical condition, so the body is always the center of his concern, not the soul, and not the larger truth which might be observed by consideration of man as matter informed by soul.

Beneath all his ironic and symbolic uses of the microcosm is a firm conviction that nature represents order (*Devotions* p. 11, l. 10), that it is indeed a half-atheism to rebel against nature, God's im-

mediate commissioner (p. 68, l. 5). Yet the fever (a natural unnatural condition) brings this half-atheism upon him, and so his
use of the microcosm always involves some degree of tension. Man
is never a clear reflection of the world here. One of the first and
most spectacular uses of the image relies for its effect upon the
exaggerated role of the body in illness, and the rapidity with which
a certainty of such exaggeration can come and go when the sick body
plays tricks upon the mind. "It is too little to call *Man* a *little
world*," he says, and immediately sees himself infinitely extended:
his veins are rivers, his muscles hills, his bones stone quarries; he
himself is an orb. But with this bodily extension, the sickness too is
horribly enlarged, and at the very instant of its greatness overcomes
that orb, and reduces the helpless man to a handful of dust (pp.
15–17).

Man may also present such a distorted reflection of reality that
he who tries to know himself must be struck by the apparent disorders in nature, and mock at those who think it good that man
bears any likeness to his environment: "Is this the honour which
Man hath by being a *little world,* That he hath these *earthquakes*
in him selfe, sodaine shakings; these *lightnings,* sodaine flashes;
these *thunders,* sodaine noises . . . these *Eclypses* . . . these *Blazing
stars* . . . these *Rivers of blood* . . . ?" (p. 2, ll. 3–9). Any view of
the world which detracts from its order and stability is seized upon;
the new philosophy, like the problem of natural evil, is easily bent
to irony:

I am *up,* and I seeme to *stand,* and I goe *round;* and I am a new *Argument*
of the *new Philosophie,* That the *Earth* moves round; why may I not beleeve,
that the *whole earth* moves in a *round motion,* though that seeme to mee to
stand, when as I seeme to *stand* to my *Company,* and yet am carried, in a
giddy, and *circular motion,* as I *stand?* (p. 128, ll. 4–9).

The little world becomes a summary of the evils of the universe,
and the wasting action of the fever is compared to the earth's
progress toward annihilation. In nature Donne finds a parallel of
his own fear of non-existence, for nature too abhors and fights
against a vaccuum (p. 127, ll. 21–22); yet both man and nature are

bound toward annihilation, which is their center and their end.

The parallels between man and nature lead Donne to postulate briefly a causative and untheological connection. Man is the innocent plaything of a malevolent world, which, far from being a reflection of man, wrests him into its pattern of destruction (p. 68, ll. 4–10). But this again is half-atheism; and Donne's most consistent, though no more comforting, viewpoint in the meditations is that man, like nature, is an independent world, breeding his own fever, serving as his own executioner, forced by internal revolution to be an active participant in his own extinction. But man is a poorer world than nature, for even animals can cure their own sicknesses; only man requires the assistance of a physician (p. 17, ll. 19–22). Like the idea of the malevolent universe, this viewpoint excludes any Christian explanation of evil, nor is any other solution suggested; the metaphors remain extravagantly pessimistic.

When the microcosm analogy draws its material from the state rather than from nature, Donne at least shows some possibility of hope. The state is one governed by intelligent self-interest; as counselors, because it is to their advantage, combine to form a stable body politic, and as the other parts of the body serve the heart, so the physicians try to restore the body of the patient to health. One thing that disturbed Donne in the nature analogies was that man, unlike other animals, was powerless to cure his own sickness. The counselor has his place in the body politic, and the physician may minister to the physical body. But as Donne's view of the state is realistic, he admits that it too may fall into disorder. Diseases "hold *Consultations,* and conspire how they may multiply" (p. 35, ll. 22–23); the captive is made prisoner in his own bed (p. 10, l. 24); the spots which appear during the course of the sickness are like confessions upon the rack, involuntary, and indicative of nothing (p. 74, l. 26—p. 75, l. 9).

Donne does not lift up his head very often during the meditations. Almost no use is made of the third microcosm analogy, the evidence of God in man. And when he does use it, it is rather defiantly. He rebels, for example, against the solitude imposed upon him in his sickness and declares that even God himself is three persons in one, "and all his externall actions testifie a love of *Societie and communion*" (p. 23, l. 7). He flouts tradition here, as, indeed, he does throughout the meditations; and also, as with nature and the state, he is not looking in man for evidence of God, but in God for evidence to support his own feelings. Taken as a whole, Donne's use of the microcosm-macrocosm analogies would probably have been seen, against the background of contemporary ideas, as a purposeful distortion of traditions, and a purposeful singling out for ironic symbol of aspects of tradition which could only be seen properly when viewed as parts of a whole great design.

After the dominant symbol, the most important tonal factor in the meditations is their key word—misery—, which is implicitly the subject of almost every meditation, and explicitly of at least two. As he inverted traditional uses of the microcosm, here he parodies a standard theological concept, and proclaims that misery is the form of man (p. 42, ll. 10–11). The substitution of misery for the soul effectively does away with spiritual being, and leaves man no alternative to annihilation. And as other men had reveled in contemplation of the resources of the soul, Donne revels in its replacement; his misery attracts metaphors that enlarge it until it entirely overcomes the little world:

His misery (for misery is his, his own; of the happinesses of this world hee is but *Tenant,* but of misery the *Free-holder;* of happines he is but the *farmer,* but the *usufructuary,* but of misery, the *Lord,* the *proprietary*) his misery, as the *sea,* swells above all the hilles, and reaches to the remotest parts of this *earth, Man* (p. 42, ll. 3–9).

"Every thing," he says, "serves to *exemplifie,* to *illustrate* mans *misery*" (p. 128, ll. 20–21). The repetition that this involves is, of course, one illustration of the pattern of repetition that is basic to the *Devotions.* The somber tone effected by constant use of the word "misery" is supported by his habitual selection, for figures of diction, of words describing time (in connection with the swiftness of its passage) and destruction. The meaning does not vary with the repetition. To cite only a few of these figures, all taken from the first meditation, is to give a fairly clear idea of the result. Here the word "die" involves both anadiplosis (final-initial repetition) and anaphora: "So that now, we doe not onely die, but die upon the Rack, die by the torment of sicknesse" (p. 1, ll. 19–20). An intricate interweaving of several figures produces the following passage, whose emphases are on the words "torment," "die," "death," "sicknes," and "come": "we die, and cannot enjoy death, because wee die in this torment of sicknes; we are tormented with sicknes, and cannot stay till the torment come, but preapprehensions and presages, prophecy those torments, which induce that *death* before either come" (p. 1, ll. 26–30). The regularity with which Donne finds that all things symbolize misery and are bound to swift annihilation creates despair on the one hand, and on the other a sense of tension that nears the breaking point, in the urgency with which he conducts his search.

The only real release that he finds seems at first cold comfort, for it is the way of the natural man—to reflect upon the miseries of others, to realize how much more fortunate he is than those who have no home, no bed, and no physician. Yet this consideration of others also has its analogies in meditative literature, for it leads him to sympathy and identification with all men in the passage on the bells, and this in turn brings him, as it had brought St. Bernard before him,[3] to realization of his own faults in those of others, a realization that will in the expostulations and prayers allow him to make a connection between misery and sin, and to establish the worth of the symbols of this world in a Christian context.

The sentence structure of the meditations is often the more striking form of Senecanism—the *stile coupé*—and although this style was adopted by Anglican writers like Joseph Hall and Thomas Browne, Donne's use of it in this context recalls its Stoic and skeptic associations and its later identification with the often materialistic viewpoints of the Royal Society. The members of the periods are short, independent, asyndetic clauses, and there is frequent imbalance in parallelism. The parallel members of the periods are developed by antithesis (point and counterpoint on the miseries of life), amplification (hammering in the point),[4] and temporal sequence. This last type is particularly interesting, because it illustrates a major subject of the meditations and of the *Devotions* as a whole. "Tyme," Donne says, "is a short *parenthesis* in a longe *period;* and Eternity had been the same, as it is, though time had never been" (*Devotions,* p. 79, ll. 18–19).[5] It is impossible to measure time or to distinguish the difference between past, present, and future: "before you sound that word, *present,* or that *Monosyllable, now,* the present, and the *Now* is past" (p. 79, ll. 10–12). Lacking a Christian framework, the brevity of life is a paralyzing concept; the fever increases his view of the rapidity of occurrences until in his mind all sequential events are simultaneous, and it is impossible to do anything, because at the instant in which one begins to do it, the time for action is already past. The parallelism illustrating this is characterized by emphasis on words describing time, which may both open and close the period, and by the accelerating force of an almost complete absence of conjunctions:

In the same instant that I feele the first attempt of the disease, I feele the victory; In the twinckling of an eye, I can scarse see, instantly the tast is insipid, and fatuous; instantly the appetite is dull and desirelesse: instantly the knees are sinking and strengthlesse; and in an instant, sleepe, which is the *picture,* the *copie* of *death,* is taken away, that the *Originall, Death* it selfe may succeed, and that so I might have death to the life (p. 6, ll. 17–24).

There is a particularly good instance of the effect of this in the first meditation, where a purposely slow, laboriously wrought image is followed by one in which time is so telescoped:

We study *Health,* and we deliberate upon our *meats,* and *drink,* and *ayre,* and *exercises,* and we hew, and wee polish every stone, that goes to that building; and so our *Health* is a long and a regular work; But in a minute a Cannon batters all, overthrowes all, demolishes all; a *Sicknes* unprevented for all our diligence, unsuspected for all our curiositie; nay, undeserved, if we consider only *disorder,* summons us, seizes us, possesses us, destroyes us in an instant (p. 1, ll. 5–13).

The whole idea of the first part of the period is contained in the first three words, while the following clauses are amplifications of it; the polysyndeton, together with repetition of the pronoun "we," further slows the leisurely expansion of the idea. The second section omits both conjunctions and subject repetition; it begins and ends with a reminder that all this occurs in an instant; the resulting change in tempo is a tremendously effective device for conveying the thought.

Very little resolution of difficulties is implied or expressed. The final sentences sometimes give indication of what is to follow, but Donne's view of life in the meditations is really too one-dimensional to allow much opportunity for release from tension. His Senecan style is here overlaid with rhetorical devices that are both an emotional declaration of man's misery and an intellectual statement of the futility of intellect in an unthinking, physical world. The image of the microcosm and the repetition of the word "misery" are used negatively, to give an ironic denial to traditional expressions of spiritual value. The meditations are a purposeful reduction of the Book of the Creatures to a world so dimmed by original sin that its inhabitants, unaware of the meaning of atonement and burdened by a misery that they cannot understand, are tempted almost beyond their endurance to the final sin of despair.

With the sections entitled "Expostulations, and Debatements with God," we enter a radically different framework of reference from that of the meditations. The form corresponds roughly to what the writers of traditional meditations called colloquies, the soul's conversations with God. Donne's use of the word "expostulations" implies a conversation of unusual intensity, a search for truth and reassurance of the sort that Christ suffered on the cross[6] and that is suffered here by a man who is to be distinguished from the unquestioning observer of the meditations, and whose vision is being clarified by his admission into the Judaeo-Christian world of the Scriptures. Nor is "suffering" a completely adequate word; Donne enters this world with a fearful joy, and his emotions shift and vary as he contemplates the God who is both the giver of laws, whose judgments are foreshadowed in thunder and lightning, and the New Testament God of mercy and peace. The searching interest in prob-

lems of theology is somewhat reminiscent of the Donne of the
Essays, but there is a much more urgent and immediate emotional
involvement here, and much less scholarship.

That the center of man in this new context is not misery but God,
is exemplified in Donne's use of the compass figure: God is the fixed
foot that makes man's circle just (p. 123, l. 30—p. 124, l. 5). And
although Donne wanders a wide circle in the expostulations, he always returns to that center where God, the great physician and
judge, makes all man's actions and the world which seemed so
wretched before, the temporal point in an eternal meaning which
comprehends and explains it.

In this section, Donne begins for the first time to make Christian
parables of his sickness and to suggest in imagery that man's life in
a material world can have eternal significance. Thus an important
group of metaphors has to do with the parallels between physical
and spiritual disease: he talks of the "fever of lust" (p. 3, l. 19),
the *"leprosie* in my *soule"* (p. 26, l. 2), the "evacuation of my *soule*
by *confession"* (p. 124, ll. 8–9). He plays constantly upon the word
"bed": he lies in a bed of sin, a bed of death:

As my bed is my *affections,* when shall I beare them so as to *subdue* them?
As my *bed* is my *afflictions,* when shall I beare them so, as not to *murmure*
at them? When shall I *take up my bed and walke?* not *lie downe* upon it, as
it is my *pleasure,* not *sinke under* it, as it is my *correction?* (p. 131, ll. 18–23).

The world is now seen to have been made wretched by original
sin, which is "the *root,* and the *fuell* of all *sicknesse"* (p. 136, l. 16).
The microcosm-macrocosm analogies make the traditional comparison of man's spiritual and physical illness to what was also caused
by Adam's fall—the sickness of the world:

But yet as long as I remaine in this great *Hospitall,* this sicke, this diseasefull
world, as long as I remaine in this leprous house, this flesh of mine, this
Heart, though thus prepared *for* thee, prepared *by* thee, will still be subject
to the invasion of maligne and pestilent vapours (p. 65, ll. 26–30).

Thus man's misery and that of the world are given a cause, their
falling away from God, and a cure, in returning to God the physi-

cian. Donne's rising from bed (a bodily resurrection) is a type of the resurrection of his soul.

The Physician is also the Old Testament Judge; the second important group of images here are legal. The "God of Order" (p. 122, l. 4) will *"bring every worke to Judgement, with every secret thing, and, there is nothing covered, that shall not bee revealed"* (p. 58, ll. 10–12). But he is a good God, who gives his sons his inheritance (p. 63, ll. 17–18) and whose mercy is man's pardon (p. 59, l. 1). The help of the earthly physician is an earnest of spiritual aid. And Donne quotes the law from the book of Exodus "that *if a man bee smitten so by another, as that hee keepe his bed, though he dye not, hee that hurt him, must take care of his healing, and recompense him.* Thy hand strikes mee into this bed; and therefore if I rise againe, thou wilt bee my recompence, all the dayes of my life, in making the memory of this sicknes beneficiall to me" (p. 14, ll. 1–6). The law of church government adds to the Old Testament metaphor its Christian equivalents. He for whom the bell tolls is made a Bishop "to as many as heare his *voice,* in this *bell* . . . to give us a *confirmation* in this action" (p. 99, ll. 1–3). God's anger at Donne's inability to come to church makes his fever "not a *Recusancie,* for I would come, but . . . an *Excommunication,* I must not" (p. 13, ll. 7–8).

The contrast established in imagery between intuitive acceptance of the parallels between physical and spiritual sin and the purgative value of the fever, and a rather anxious quibbling over interpretation of laws is basic to the temper of the expostulations. Further tensions are set up by the sentence structure, which is built around a question form. The tone of these questions ranges from fear and "murmuring" to believing sincerity as Donne explores the world of the Scriptures. "Murmuring" is, in fact, the key word of the expostulations, corresponding to "misery" in the meditations. The murmuring of the people in the Bible is something which he has observed to have unfortunate consequences (p. 142, ll. 17–18), and when his own questions begin to seem too bold to him, he checks himself: "But comes not this *Expostulation* too neere a *murmuring?*" (p. 26, ll. 5–6). Yet he is disturbed by so many things—by the fear of God's judgment, by apparent theological contradictions, by his own illness—that he does come near a murmuring many times in the course of the expostulations, and the question which he asks are not rhetorical:

When thou bidst me *to put off the old Man,* doest thou meane, not onely my old *habits* of *actuall sin,* but the *oldest of all, originall sinne?* When thou biddest me *purge out the leven,* dost thou meane not only the sowrenesse of mine owne ill contracted *customes,* but the innate *tincture* of sin, imprinted by *Nature?* How shall I doe that which thou requirest, and not *falsifie* that which thou hast *said, that sin is gone over all?* (p. 137, l. 29—p. 138, l. 4)

In other kinds of questions, the murmuring is less evident. He may consider rival interpretations of a Bible text, or, while accepting God's justice, examine his sins or voice his own fear of unworthiness:

And would not the *Angels,* that *fell,* have *fixed* themselves upon thee, if thou hadst once *readmitted* them to thy *sight?* They never *relapsed;* If I doe, must not my case be as desperate? (p. 145, l. 30—p. 146, l. 1)

All these questions show an urgent need for replies, which are often forthcoming in his own words or in those of the Bible. Only when the query seems to Donne to be insoluble does he leave it hanging.

The intensity provided by the question form is increased by several minor devices. First, the expostulations almost invariably begin abruptly, "My God, my God," and with no other preliminaries burst upon the subject he has been considering. The impression of haste is increased by the numerous incomplete sentences in this section—answers given in a phrase, objections voiced in a word: "So well hast thou provided, that we should . . . fear no person but thee, nothing but thee; no men? No. Whom? *The Lord is my helpe, and my salvation, whome shall I fear? Great enemies?* not *great enemies;* for no enemies are great to them that feare thee" (p. 30, ll. 19–24). Yet he checks himself in his haste, as he does in his murmurings; and invocations and parenthetical expressions within the expostulations help to give them their peculiar blend of fear and love: "But thou art also (*Lord* I intend to thy *glory*, and let no *prophane mis-interpreter* abuse it to thy *diminution*) thou art a *figurative*, a *meta-phoricall God too*" (p. 113, ll. 4–6).

The Bible is the subject matter here. The telescoping of time which so frightened him in the meditations now enables him to use Scripture as personal experience, since all ages are one: "I heare thy *Prophet* saying to *Ezechias, Set thy house in order, for thou shalt die, and not live;* Hee makes us of his *familie,* and calls this a setting of *his* house in order, to compose *us* to the *meditation* of *death*" (p. 99, ll. 18–22). And he uses the words of the Bible to voice his own thoughts:

I lye here, and say, *Blessed are they, that dwell in thy house;* but I cannot say, *I will come into thy house;* I may say, *In thy feare will I worship towards thy holy Temple;* but, I cannot say, *in thy holy Temple:* and, *Lord, the zeale of thy House, eats me up,* as fast as my fever (p. 13, ll. 2–7).

In his searching consideration of man and God in the expostulations, particularly in such passages as those on hearts and on the metaphorical nature of God, Donne comes close to the style of Augustine's *Confessions.* But in Donne there is always an inability or refusal to surrender himself wholly to abstract metaphysical thought, so that we cannot quite call Donne's, like Augustine's, a passionate mind. Augustine might be called a mystic; Donne could not. He can imaginatively identify himself with people in the Bible, but he cannot safely range beyond this pre-established framework, although often, in the expostulations, he finds the framework too confined. He breaks from it in the direction of human weaknesses—desires, and failures in belief, and self-interest—which express themselves in questions not completely answered and in images which are sometimes brilliant, sometimes not entirely convincing (he does not really establish the exact relationship between sin and misery until he comes to the prayers). Incapable of free surrender, although he cries out in terror against God's anger, it is the physical force of that anger which he requires: "I need thy *thunder*, O my *God;* thy *musicke* will not serve me" (p. 129, ll. 16–17). He eventually finds this thunder, not in the imagined mystical experience of "Batter my heart, three person'd God," but in the ordered and immediate discipline of the Anglican church.

After the feverish pace of the meditations and expostulations, it is a relief to come to the prayers, which represent in part the stability of that church in which Donne found as much relief and rest as was possible for him. The difficulties set forth in the curt Senecan style of the meditations, and questioned and wrestled with in the expostulations, are brought here to resolved paradoxes whose finality is emphasized by a modified Ciceronian style, somewhat more periodic than that of the sermons.

Insistence upon the authority of the church in an increasingly non-authoritarian atmosphere generally manifested itself in esthetic as well as moral discipline, creating a distrust for personal devotions and a feeling that one should adhere at all times to the established forms of worship. The Anglican church rarely produced the effusively personal, sometimes mystical meditations that were being written on the continent, and even in England, by Roman Catholics. The Right Reverend John Cosin, a younger contemporary of Donne's, published in 1627 a volume of "private devotions" made up of excerpts from the Book of Common Prayer, ancient breviaries, and the writings of the Fathers. The avowed purposes of this publication were "to avoid, as near as might be, all extemporall effusions of irksome and indigested prayers," to assure a "grave and pious language" in prayer, that we might not "lose ourselves with confusion in any sudden, abrupt, or rude dictates, which are framed by private spirits and ghosts of our own," to make it plain to all that the English church is not a new one, and to interest others in the Catholic faith.[7] Cosin insisted that even bishops and priests were to use these prayers, nor should any man, without recourse to authority, employ in worship prayers of his own devising. To others, his words of course would have been suggestion and not law, but they are quite typical of Anglican opinion at the time.

Donne's attitude toward the church is set forth in numerous passages in the sermons. Preaching on the text, "I am come that they might have life, and that they might have it more abundantly," he says that Christ gave this abundant life to men through the establishment of the church (*Sermons,* IX, No. 5, ll. 644–47), and speaking for himself in another sermon, he explains what the church means to him:

> . . . let thy Spirit beare witnesse with my spirit, that I am of the number of thine elect, because I love the beauty of thy house, because I captivate mine understanding to thine Ordinances, because I subdue my will to obey thine, because I find thy Son Christ Jesus made mine, in the preaching of thy word, and my selfe made his, in the administration of his Sacraments (VIII, No. 13, ll. 699–704).

And in other sermons he speaks of the importance of set prayers, using Cosin's arguments, together with examples of his own failures at private devotions (IX, No. 9, ll. 200–240).

I can best illustrate the effect of this discipline upon Donne's style by citing for comparison one of Cranmer's opening periods from the Book of Common Prayer:

> O MOSTE mighty God, and mercyfull father which haste compassion of all men, and hatest nothing that thou haste made: which wouldest not the deathe of a synner, but that he should rather turn from synne, and be saved: mercifully forgeve us our trespasses, and comforte us, whiche be grived and weryed with the burden of oure synne.[8]

These prayers begin with a direct invocation, including one or two epithets, followed by several clauses reminding Divinity of its own nature, generally in terms which have some direct application to the sort of request that is to be made. The indirection of such an opening gives it a slow and stately movement that is reinforced by parallelism and by skillful use of prose rhythms. The main thought is held in suspense until the end of the sentence. Donne's opening periods, although the differences in diction will be immediately apparent, work basically on the same principles, as in the following illustration from the Devotions:

> O Eternall, and most gracious God, who, considered in thy selfe, art a Circle first and last, and altogether; but considered in thy working upon us art a direct line, and leadest us from our beginning, through all our wayes, to our

end, *enable me by thy grace,*[9] to looke forward to mine end, and to looke backward to, to the considerations of thy mercies afforded mee from my beginning; *that so* by that practice of considering thy mercy, in my beginning in this world, when thou plantedst me in the Christian church, and thy mercy in the beginning in the other world, when thou writest me in the Booke of life in my Election, *I may come to a holy consideration* of thy mercy, in the beginning of all my actions here: *that* in all the beginnings, in all the accesses, and approches of spirituall sicknesses of Sinn, *I may heare* and *hearken* to that voice, O thou Man of God, there is death in the pot, *and* so *refraine* from that, which I was so hungerly, so greedily flying to (p. 4, ll. 14–30).

The style slows the thought. The invocation, with its many parallel modifiers, allows time for the metaphor (a thought figure, and so unlike Cranmer's, but still traditional) to be developed. Because the parallelism is not in itself the structure of the sentence, as it often is in the meditations, but only elaborates the meaning, the movement is slower. In the second part of the period, the purpose clauses permit a temporal cause and effect progression that was seldom allowed in the meditations and expostulations. The point of this is, surely, to promote the idea that men can only have time when they have given it up, that a consideration of one's end and one's beginning is in a Christian world only possible when the end and the beginning are rooted in eternity.

After the opening period, most of the sentences proceed in a leisurely fashion, with subordinate clauses coming before the main thought. Extensive use is made of noun or purpose clauses beginning with the word "that," which obviously contribute to the integrity of the sentence, to the smoother progress of the thought. Most of the sentences are longer than those in the meditations and expostulations, and there are few incomplete sentences. Those which are short or fragmentary are not ragged; they do not have the interrupting effect of the brief question, nor do they have the sharp aphoristic independence of the curt period. Rather they are interwoven, by use of repetition, with sentences before and after; they are apt to be long, rolling, parallel clauses whose sweep increases with the progress of the paragraph. The following period, which uses "that" clauses in this way, is an example:

That therefore this *soule*, now newly departed to thy *Kingdome*, may quickly returne to a joifull *reunion* to that *body* which it hath left, and that *wee* with *it*, may soone enjoy the full *consummation* of all, in body and soule, I humbly beg at thy hand, O our most mercifull *God*, for thy *Sonne Christ Jesus sake*. That that blessed *Sonne* of thine, may have the *consummation* of his *dignitie*, by entring into his *last office*, the office of a *Judge*, and may have *societie* of humane *bodies* in *heaven*, as well as he hath had ever of *soules;* And that as thou hatest *sinne* it self, thy *hate* to *sinne* may bee expressed in the abolishing of all *instruments of sin*, The *allurements* of this *world*, and the *world* it selfe; and all the temporarie *revenges* of sinne, the *stings* of *sicknesse* and of *death;* and all the *castles*, and *prisons*, and *monuments* of *sinne*, in the *grave*. That *time* may bee swallowed up in *Eternitie*, and *hope* swallowed in *possession*, and *ends* swallowed in *infinitenesse*, and *all men* ordained to *salvation*, in *body* and *soule* be *one intire* and *everlasting sacrifice* to thee, where thou mayest receive *delight* from them, and they *glorie* from thee, for evermore (p. 110, ll. 2–21).

Donne's concept of the relationship between time and eternity comes to its fullest expression here as the same theme that runs through his sermons. The idea that time will be swallowed up (the idea of time's nothingness) is linked with the belief that God's mercy can explode time into eternity, a minute can become forever, and "*Heaven* it selfe is but an *extention* of the same *joy*" (p. 119, l. 9) that the Christian receives on earth from God, through the church. So time—the parenthesis—becomes meaningful; it is in a sense the seed of eternal life. The spaciousness of these loose periods is an expression of the freedom Donne finds in this idea, as their ordered movement is an expression of the church in which he finds it.

The tone of the prayers is set by the words "eternal" and "merciful," beginning with the invocations to an eternal, gracious, or merciful God. The differences between the eternal and temporal set up by the sentence structure are also essential to the conception of a merciful God, since to regard man's life as ruled by time is to see it as miserable and unjust; to behold it with somewhat less limited vision is to see it as God's correction of man's sinful nature; to view it *sub specie eternitatis* is to entirely reverse one's first impressions: "Let me think no degree of this thy correction, *casuall*, or without *signification*; but yet when I have read it in that language, as it is a *correction*, let me translate it into another, and read it as a *mercy*" (p. 41, ll. 20–23).

Many of the metaphors of the prayers are far more traditional than those in the earlier sections. This increases the smoothness of the sentence structure, since often they are, like Cranmer's and Hooker's, contributive to the emotional and ethical tone of the sentence, and further its progress without focusing the reader's attention upon them. Such metaphors are "thy right hand, thy powerfull hand set over us" (p. 47, ll. 23–24), "no prison of death" (p. 41, l. 17), "the *light* of thy *spirit*" (p. 85, l. 27). Of the more fully developed thought figures, the most significant are concerned with transplanting, transmigrating, and translating, processes which reveal the mechanics of giving spiritual meaning to physical fact. We have seen Donne's use of antithesis in the meditations and expostulations. The metaphors of translation are based on resolved paradox, which is, in the idea of the fortunate fall, at the center of the Christian religion. The figures of prison and torture, for example, which were so frequent in the meditations, are here given spiritual point in the translation of correction into mercy. In this connection, his mention of the two qualities implanted by God in every element is important: "as thy fire *dries*, so it *heats* too; and as thy water *moysts*, so it *cooles* too, so *O Lord*, in these corrections, which are the *elements of our regeneration*, by which our *soules* are made thine, imprint thy two qualities, those two operations, that as they *scourge* us, they may scourge us into the way to thee" (p. 41, ll. 2–7). These paradoxes, in contrast to the antitheses of earlier sections, are often used so affirmatively that the major stress of the sentence is not upon the paradoxes at all:

O Most gracious *God,* who pursuest and perfitest thine own purposes, and dost not only remember mee by the first accesses of this sicknes, that I must die, but informe me by this further proceeding therin, that I may die now, who hast not only waked me with the first, but cald me up, by casting me further downe, and clothd me with thy selfe, by stripping me of my selfe, and by dulling my bodily senses, to the meats, and eases of this world; hast whet, and sharpned my spiritual senses, to the apprehension of thee, by what steps and degrees soever it shall please thee to go, in the dissolution of this body, hasten *O Lord,* that pace, and multiply, *O my God,* those degrees, in the exaltation of my *Soule,* toward thee now, and to thee then (p. 9, ll. 1–14).

Donne's mind works associatively, and the prayers move through climax and anticlimax rather than steadily building to a single cumulative point. His periods are affectively rather than syntactically ordered. But there is direction in his purposeful connection of clauses and periods with one another, and he pays much more attention to rhythm than in the other sections. Qualifying clauses, which are exploratory and digressive in the meditations and expostulations, are more apt to be explanatory here. The only real tension in the style is set up, not by any conflict in ideas, but by the smooth and flowing movement of the periods around the thought figures, and this is less a tension than a coming at the same end in two different ways, a kind of complexity that enriches the resolution of sentences.

None of the styles that form the *Devotions* is the exact equivalent of Donne's sermon style, although his sermon style is certainly more various than I have been able to demonstrate in five chapters. He has presented here, in exaggerated form, three strands of his thought, comprising a fuller spiritual biography, with more concentrated doubts and fears than he could have permitted himself to voice in public. Yet he intended this too as a work of edification, and it is the only writing, aside from some of the sermons, to which he allowed publication during his lifetime. Suspicion and expostulation and a storm of affections, he said, may well consist together in a heart absolutely surrendered to God. The curt Senecan style used in his approach to the Book of the Creatures, the restless Augustinian sentences employed in his handling of the Scriptures, and the Anglican periods that shape his prayers consist together in his sermons, in a richer, more contrapuntal style that combines and transmutes these elements of his thought and expression into his public, and contrary, music.

> When thou hast done, thou has not done
> For I have more.
>
> JOHN DONNE, "A Hymne to God the Father"

NOTES
INDEX

Notes

I. THE MAKING OF A PROSE STYLE

1   The reference is to Milton's "Elegia Sexta ad Carolum Diodatum," *The Works of John Milton,* ed. Francis A. Patterson (New York, 1931–38), I, 210–12. Here the young Milton explains his concept of the responsibilities of the serious poet.

2   See "The Progresse of the Soule," *The Poems of John Donne,* ed. H. J. C. Grierson (Oxford, 1912), I, 294: "I will have no such Readers as I can teach"; and p. 315: "Who ere thou beest that read'st this sullen Writ,/Which just so much courts thee, as thou dost it,/Let me arrest thy thoughts. . . . See also A. Alvarez, *The School of Donne* (London, 1961), pp. 20–27.

3   Jonas A. Barish, "The Prose Style of John Lyly," *Journal of English Literary History,* XXIII (March, 1956), 14–35.

4   See Gilbert Phelps, "The Prose of Donne and Browne," *From Donne to Marvell,* ed. Boris Ford (London, Pelican Books, 1956).

5   W. Frazer Mitchell, *English Pulpit Oratory from Andrewes to Tillotson* (London, 1932), p. 180.

6   On this point, see "The Preacher of Paradox," *Times Literary Supplement* (August 28, 1953), p. 548.

7   His letters show good control of language from the beginning. But, besides being personal and brief, they have a stylistic tradition of their own, and for these reasons I have chosen not to discuss them here.

8   Edmund Gosse, *Life and Letters of John Donne* (London, 1899), I, 196; II, 124–25.

9   See George Williamson, "Libertine Donne: Comments on *Biathanatos,*" *Philological Quarterly,* XIII (July, 1934), 276–91.

10 For casuistical background, see Thomas Wood, *English Casuistical Divinity During the Seventeenth Century* (London, 1952); George L. Mosse, *The Holy Pretence* (Oxford, 1957); and H. R. McAdoo, *The Structure of Caroline Moral Theology* (London, 1949). In "John Donne and the Casuists," *Studies in English Literature,* II (Winter, 1961),

57–76, A. E. Malloch explains the character of Donne's sources in this field and suggests that his ambiguous attitude toward casuistry reflects his simultaneous interest in subjective and in objectified experience. "He insists that moral action must proceed from an assent of the self and yet he toys constantly with a literature of casuistry which sets moral action within a legal arena and allows little room for the self" (p. 75).

11 Thomas Wilson, *The Rule of Reason* (London, 1568), p. 34ᵛ. Wilson goes on to say that a skillful logician can turn the horns of this argument back against its maker.

12 Such is the question considered here, in regard to suicide and lying: "Whereupon our country-man *Sayr* confesseth, that this SELF-HOMI-CIDE is not so intrinsically ill, as to Ly. Which is also evident by *Cajetan* where he affirmes, that I may not to save my life, accuse my self upon the Racke" (*Biathanatos,* p. 36).

13 Charles Moore, *A Full Inquiry into the Subject of Suicide* (London, 1790), II, 8. For Beza's account of the incident, see Theodorus Beza, "Epistola ad M. Volmarium Rufo," *Volumen Primum Tractationum Theologicarum,* 2nd ed. (Geneva, 1582), fol. B1ᵛ.

14 Robert Ornstein, "Donne, Montaigne, and Natural Law," *Journal of English and Germanic Philology,* LV (1956), 213–29. For a view some-what closer to my own, see A. E. Malloch, "The Techniques and Func-tion of the Renaissance Paradox," *Studies in Philology,* LIII (April, 1956), 191–203. Although I do not fully agree with the conclusions of this article, I think that Malloch's designation of *Biathanatos* as paradox is correct.

15 His position is quite clear in *Biathanatos,* p. 37. For an account of an Anglican voluntarist, see Robert Hoopes, "Voluntarism in Jeremy Taylor and the Platonic Tradition," *Huntington Library Quarterly,* XIII (August, 1950), 341–54.

16 Sister Thomas Marion, "Donne's Casuistry: A Study of *Biathanatos* and *Pseudo-Martyr*" (Unpublished essay written for Professor David Novarr, Cornell, 1956). It is a cross between a problem and a casuistical case because "it partakes of the ingenuity of the one, and the complexity of the other" (p. 24). The technique of excessive citation particularly sug-gests to her that he is mocking the casuistical tradition (p. 21). For Donne's own unclear comments about *Biathanatos,* see Gosse, *Life and Letters,* I, 196; II, 124–25.

17 The changes in the kinds of things Donne says about Augustine are interesting, and to some extent correspond with the changes in Donne's style of writing. In *Biathanatos,* he opposes him vigorously, and rather unkindly, on several issues. His remark in the *Essays* shows an unwilling

acknowledgment of Augustine's superiority. In the sermons, it becomes overwhelmingly clear that he has taken Augustine for his particular guide. But he never shares Augustine's joy in that pure intellectual speculation that reaches toward mysticism. His style is freest when he acquires an imaginative understanding of the paradoxes of faith, an understanding grounded on what he takes to be concrete realities; and a major difference between his mature style and that of Augustine is seen in Donne's far greater use of concrete words and images.

18 Gosse, *Life and Letters,* II, 63. See also Milton A. Rugoff, *Donne's Imagery: A Study in Creative Sources* (New York, 1939), p. 134 ("uninspired pages") and Evelyn Hardy, *Donne: A Spirit in Conflict* (London, 1942), p. 160 ("awkward and ingenious as a whole"). Evelyn Simpson is apparently the first modern critic to have read the *Essays* with care and appreciation.

19 There is continual similarity in content, particularly through the section on Genesis. Much later in his career, Donne specifically commented on this stylistic aspect of the *Confessions:* "Hee passes from prayer, and protestation, to counsell, and direction" (*Sermons,* IX, No. 3, ll. 95–96).

20 Samuel Hieron, *Truths Purchase* (London, 1632), p. 45.

21 Donne normally speaks of Scripture in this way. See also the official *Certain Sermons or Homilies Appointed to be read in Churches in the Time of Queen Elizabeth* (London, 1754), pp. 15, 284, 343, for the same practice.

22 Dennis Quinn, "Donne's Christian Eloquence," *Journal of English Literary History,* XXVII (December, 1960).

23 *Ibid.,* p. 279. See also Donne's comments, such as the following: "that's a difference betweene *Sermons* and *Lectures,* that a Sermon intends *Exhortation* principally and *Edification,* and a holy stirring of religious affections, and then *matters of Doctrine,* and points of *Divinity,* occasionally, secondarily, as the words of the text may invite them; But *Lectures* intend principally *Doctrinall points,* and matter of *Divinity,* and matter of *Exhortation* but *occasionally,* and as in a *second* place" (*Sermons,* VIII, No. 3, ll. 9–16).

24 Quinn in *ELH,* XXVII, 278.

25 For secular rhetoric, see, in particular, the following by Morris Croll: "Attic Prose: Lipsius, Montaigne and Bacon," *Schelling Anniversary Papers* (New York, 1923), pp. 117–50; "Attic Prose in the Seventeenth Century," *Studies in Philology,* XVIII (April, 1921), 78–128; "The Baroque Style in Prose," in *Studies in English Philology,* ed. Kemp Malone and Martin B. Ruud (Minneapolis, 1929). See also George Williamson, *The Senecan Amble* (Chicago, 1951); Izora Scott, *Con-*

troversies over Cicero (New York, 1910); and Wilbur S. Howell, *Logic and Rhetoric in England, 1500–1700* (Princeton, 1956).

26 This is an extreme oversimplification, of course. There is no such thing as a really Ciceronian style in English, and some varieties of Senecanism were more studied and polished than what their authors claimed to be trying to avoid. Nevertheless, there is a great difference between the writing of men like Hooker and Ascham (and non-Ciceronian, but ornate writers like Sidney) and that of men like Donne, Browne, Bacon, and Jonson, and much of the difference is explainable in terms of the controversy. See the works cited in note 25 for the full background.

27 For one source of Donne's theory, see Augustine, *De Magistro*, in *The Greatness of the Soul* [and] *The Teacher*, trans. Joseph M. Colleran (Westminster, Md., 1950). The book is a dialogue with his son Adeodatus on the function of the teacher. The ultimate derivation of the theory, and its significance, are explained in a very important passage in one of Donne's early sermons: "Of our perversenesse in both faculties, *understanding*, and *will*, God may complain, but as much of our *memory;* for, for the rectifying of the *will*, the *understanding* must be rectified; and that implies great difficulty: But the *memory* is so familiar, and so present, and so ready a faculty, as will always answer, if we will but speak to it, and aske it, *what God hath done for us, or for others*. The art of *salvation*, is but the art of *memory*. . . . *Plato* plac'd *all learning* in the memory; wee may place *all Religion* in the memory too: All knowledge, that seems new to day, says *Plato*, is but a remembring of *that*, which your soul knew before. All instruction, which we can give you to day, is but the remembring you of the mercies of God, which have been *new every morning*. Nay, he that hears no Sermons, he that reads no Scriptures, hath the Bible without book; He hath a *Genesis* in his *memory;* he cannot forget his *Creation;* . . . He hath *all* in his memory, even to the *Revelation;* God hath *revealed* to him, *even at midnight alone*, what shall be his portion, in the next world; And if he dare but remember that nights communication between God and him, he is well-near learned enough. There may be enough in *remembring our selves;* but sometimes, that's the hardest of all; many times we are farthest off from our selves; most forgetfull of our selves" (II, No. 2, ll. 46–52; 67–84).

28 *Sermons*, II, No. 11, ll. 47–48. Donne wrongly ascribes the phrase to Bernard. Augustine's discussion of the memory is in Book X of the *Confessions*. See also *St. Gregory of Nyssa: The Lord's Prayer / The Beatitudes*, ed. and trans. Hilda C. Graef (Westminister, Md., 1954),

p. 148; and *Saint Bernard on the Song of Songs,* trans. and ed. A Religious of C.S.M.V. (London, 1952), pp. 253 ff.

29 *Sermons,* VIII, No. 11, ll. 14–16: "we shall not be subject to new Doctrines, but taught by remembring, by establishing us in things formerly Fundamentally laid."

30 Croll, in *Studies in English Philology,* p. 452.

31 Roger Ascham, *English Works,* ed. William A. Wright (Cambridge, 1904), pp. 265–66. Compare the following statement by Donne: "He that undervalues *outward things,* in the religious service of God, though he begin at *ceremoniall* and *rituall* things, will come quickly to call *Sacraments* but outward things, and *Sermons,* and *publique prayers* but outward things, in contempt. As some *Platonique* Philosophers, did so over-refine Religion, and devotion, as to say, that nothing but the *first thoughts* and *ebullitions* of a devout heart, were fit to serve God in. If it came to any *outward action* of the body, *kneeling,* or lifting up of *hands,* if it came to be but invested in our *words,* and so made a *Prayer,* nay if it passed but a revolving, a turning in our inward thoughts, and thereby were mingled with our *affections,* though *pious affections,* yet, say they, it is not pure enough for a service to God; nothing but the *first motions* of the heart is for him. Beloved, outward things apparell God; and since God was content to take *a body,* let us not leave him naked, nor ragged" (*Sermons,* III, 17, 741–55).

32 See Don Cameron Allen, "Dean Donne Sets His Text," *Journal of English Literary History,* X (September, 1943), 208–29. See also Evelyn Simpson's chapter on Donne's sources, in *Sermons,* X, pp. 306–28.

33 See, for example, Richard Bernard, *The Faithfull Shepheard* (London, 1607), p. 66; Donne, *Sermons,* II, No. 7, ll. 127–31.

34 *Sermons,* IV, No. 15, ll. 86–89. Ruth Wallerstein also cites this passage, in "Studies in Donne," pp. 193–94. The reference is to a book on Renaissance Neoplatonism which Miss Wallerstein was writing at the time of her death in 1958. Only the chapters on Donne had been undertaken, and remain at varying stages of completion. The material was edited as a doctoral dissertation by Barbara Davis at the University of Wisconsin in 1961, under the title given above.

35 Donne notes this especially in connection with St. Bernard, although he also says that most of the Fathers were poets (*Sermons,* IX, No. 1, ll. 499–500). See X, No. 10, ll. 466–67: "In rejoycing in another thing Saint *Bernards* harmonious charme will strike upon us, *Rara hora, brevis mora.*" See also V, No. 15, ll. 454–59.

36 Pierre Dumontier, *Saint Bernard et la Bible* (Paris, 1953), p. 157.

37 Jonas Barish, *Ben Jonson and the Language of Prose Comedy* (Cambridge, Mass., 1960), p. 86.

38 Morris Croll, "The Baroque Style in Prose" in *Studies in English Philology;* Jean Rousset, *La Littérature de L'Age Baroque en France* (Paris, 1953); Marcel Raymond, *Baroque et Renaissance Poétique* (Paris, 1955); Odette de Mourgues, *Metaphysical, Baroque and Précieux Poetry* (Oxford, 1953). See also Imbrie Buffum, *Studies in the Baroque from Montaigne to Rotrou* (New Haven, 1957); Wylie Sypher, *Four Stages of Renaissance Style* (Garden City, 1956); Giuliano Pellegrini, *Barocco Inglese* (Florence, 1953). René Wellek's "The Concept of Baroque in Literary Scholarship," *Journal of Aesthetics and Art Criticism,* V (December, 1946), 77–109, is a thorough survey of the scholarship and the difficulties involved in it, and includes a lengthy bibliography. For analyses of baroque art, see T. H. Fokker, *Roman Baroque Art: The History of a Style* (2 vols.; New York, 1938); Giulio Carlo Argan, *L'Architettura Barocca in Italia* (Milan, 1957); Heinrich Wolfflin, *Principles of Art History* (New York, 1932).

39 Much of the above follows Odette de Mourgues. But I think that in her essay she overemphasizes the extravagance of the baroque.

40 Walter J. Ong, S.J., "Wit and Mystery: A Revaluation in Medieval Latin Hymnody," *Speculum,* XXII (July, 1947), 310–41.

41 Leo Spitzer, *Linguistics and Literary History* (Princeton, 1948), p. 52. A more specific reference is given in Wellek's article (*JAAC,* V, 77–109) to Spitzer's *Die Literarisierung des Lebens in Lope's Dorotea* (Bonn, 1932), pp. 11–12. But I have been unable to find this publication, and I rely here on Wellek's summary.

42 On this see, for example, Spitzer's analysis of *Don Quixote* in *Linguistics and Literary History.*

II. THE BAROQUE REFLECTION

1 Jean Rousset, *La Littérature de L'Age Baroque en France* (Paris, 1953), p. 157.

2 Morris Croll, "The Baroque Style in Prose," in *Studies in English Philology,* ed. Kemp Malone and Martin B. Ruud (Minneapolis, 1929), p. 453.

3 George Williamson, *The Senecan Amble* (Chicago, 1951), *passim.*

4 Owen Felltham, *Resolves: A Duple Century,* 3rd. ed. (London, 1628). See in particular No. 20, "Of Preaching," pp. 69–70: "Long and distended clauses are both tedious to the eare, and difficult for their retaining. A *Sentence* well couch'd, takes both the *sense* and the *understanding.*

I love not those cartrope speeches, that are longer than the memorie of man can fathome."

5 Croll, in *Studies in English Philology*, p. 447.

6 *Ibid.*, p. 448.

7 Williamson (*Senecan Amble*, p. 145; p. 156, note 1) contests Croll's designation of asymmetry as necessarily a Senecan characteristic. But see also Jonas A. Barish, *Ben Jonson and the Language of Prose Comedy* (Cambridge, Mass., 1960), pp. 56–57. Barish agrees that asymmetry is "tangential" in Bacon, but considers it essential in Jonson's "baroque" prose.

8 Barish, "Baroque Prose in the Theater: Ben Jonson," *PMLA*, LXXIII (June, 1958), 195.

9 Croll, in *Studies in English Philology*, p. 454.

10 *Ibid.*, p. 435.

11 One of Donne's most frequent terms for the sermon is "meditation." See *Sermons*, II, No. 1, ll. 9–13; II, No. 14, ll. 38–41.

12 Barish, *Ben Jonson and the Language of Prose Comedy*, p. 70.

13 Croll, in *Studies in English Philology*, p. 445.

14 *Essays in Divinity*, p. xxv.

15 Erasmus suggests that Ecclesiastes (his name for the preacher) should in delivering his sermon differentiate parentheses from the rest of the sentence by slightly lowering his voice.—*Ecclesiastes*, in *Opera Omnia* (Leiden, 1703–6), V, col. 962C–D.

16 Dennis Quinn, "Donne's Christian Eloquence," *Journal of English Literary History*, XXVII (December, 1960), 292.

17 For a comprehensive review of specific Elizabethan devices of logic and rhetoric, see Sister Miriam Joseph, *Shakespeare's Use of the Arts of Language* (New York, 1947).

18 Technically, brachylogia is a figure in which "we . . . proceede all by single words, without any close or coupling, saving that a little pause or comma is given to every word."—George Puttenham, *The Arte of English Poesie*, ed. Gladys Willcock and Alice Walker (Cambridge, 1936), p. 213. Donne prefers his more musical variations.

19 See Bartholomew Keckermann, *Rhetoricae Ecclesiasticae Sive Artis Formandi et Habendi Conciones Sacras*, 3rd ed. (Hanau, 1606), p. 99; and Erasmus, *Ecclesiastes*, cols. 970C and 975E–F.

20 Sister Miriam Joseph, *Shakespeare's Use of the Arts of Language*, p. 59.

21 Williamson, *Senecan Amble*, p. 264.

22 Lipsius' comment (from his Letter 49 to Albert Le Mire) is quoted by Dom. John Mabillon, *Life and Works of Saint Bernard*, trans. Samuel J. Eales (London, 1896), III, 2. Mabillon adds that Lipsius, "after

having sought out carefully from among the Fathers the perfect model of the sacred orator, whom he could put forward to be imitated . . . is of opinion that there is no one who has realized more fully this ideal than Bernard, whom he therefore prefers to all the Latin Fathers."

23   T. S. Eliot, *Selected Essays: 1917–1932* (New York, 1932), p. 292.

24   *Sancti Gregorii Magni Regulae Pastoralis Liber,* in *Patrologia Latina,* ed. J. P. Migne, LXXVII (Paris, 1849), col. 49. John Hollander writes at length of the Renaissance uses of the concept of the tuning of the soul, in *The Untuning of the Sky* (Princeton, 1961), pp. 204–6, and 266 ff.

25   Sister Miriam Joseph, *Shakespeare's Use of the Arts of Language,* p. 297.

26   W. Frazer Mitchell, *English Pulpit Oratory from Andrewes to Tillotson* (London, 1932), p. 361.

27   Croll, in *Studies in English Philology,* p. 451.

28   *Ibid.,* p. 435.

29   Sir Thomas Browne, *Religio Medici,* Bk. I, sec. lix, in *The Works of Sir Thomas Browne,* ed. Geoffrey Keynes (London, 1928), Vol. I.

30   See Quinn, in *ELH,* XXVII, p. 295.

31   See the disagreement between J. B. Leishman and Evelyn Simpson on this point. Leishman finds fewer differences among sermons preached to different audiences than Mrs. Simpson does.—J. B. Leishman, "The Sermons of John Donne," *Review of English Studies,* N.S. VIII (November, 1957), 434–43; Evelyn Simpson, "To the Editor," *RES,* N.S. IX (August, 1958), 292–93; J. B. Leishman, "Reply to Mrs. Simpson's Letter," *RES,* N.S. IX (August, 1958), 293–94.

32   Croll, in *Studies in English Philology,* p. 443.

33   Augustine, *Sermons for Christmas and Epiphany,* trans. Thomas C. Lawler (London, 1952), p. 85. The Latin is in *Sermo CLXXXVII (de Tempore* 27), Migne, *PL,* XXXVIII (Paris, 1845), col. 1001.

34   The original in Bernard is in Sermon II on the *Missus Est,* Migne, *PL,* CLXXXIII (Paris, 1854), col. 65.

35   *S. Aureli Augustini De Doctrina Christiana Liber IV,* ed. and trans. Sister Therese Sullivan (Washington, D.C., 1930), ch. vi.

III. THE MANACLED ABSTRACTION

1   *Moralium Libri Sive Expositis Librum B. Job,* Migne, *PL,* LXXV (Paris, 1862), Bk. IV, ch. lv, 70.

2   Lancelot Andrewes, *XCVI Sermons,* 4th ed. (London, 1641), Sermon II, p. 398.

3.   See Josephine Miles, "The Primary Language of Poetry in the 1640's," in *The Continuity of Poetic Language* (Berkeley, 1951), and her *Eras and Modes in English Poetry* (Berkeley, 1957) for discussion of paucity of

adjectives in Donne's poetry. There is a brief comment on his prose, in "The Primary Language of Poetry," pp. 116–17.

4 Walter J. Ong, S.J., "Wit and Mystery: A Revaluation in Medieval Latin Hymnody," *Speculum,* XXII (July, 1947), 337.

5 Compare John D. Russell, "Donne's 'A Lecture Upon the Shadow,'" *The Explicator,* XVII (November, 1958), No. 9.

6 See the development of this theme in Gregory the Great, who believed that at the Fall man lost the four chief marks of his original status: immortality, stability, spiritual vision, and righteousness. His theory is summarized by F. Homes Dudden, *Gregory the Great* (London, 1905), II, 380–83.

7 For other contemporary use of figures dealing with glasses, and for possible scientific influences, see Marjorie Nicolson, *Science and Imagination* (Ithaca, 1956).

8 Erasmus, *Ecclesiastes,* in *Opera Omnia* (Leiden, 1703–6), V, col. 969B.

9 See, for example, Francis Quarles, *Emblemes* (London, [1710?]), Bk. I, Emblem 4. The emblem books frequently helped to popularize old traditions.

10 For further background to these particular images, see the tradition of Christ as weight, for example, in the Good Friday adoration of the Cross, *Sarum Missal* (Oxford, 1916), p. 113; and as balance, in Francis Wormald, "The Crucifix and the Balance," *Journal of the Warburg Institute,* I (1937–38), 276–80.

11 In iconography of the Triumph of the Cross, the cross reaches from earth to heaven; the prescribed arrangement is described by Adolphe Didron, *Christian Iconography* (London, 1886), I, 414.

12 Even Evelyn Simpson, who elsewhere defends Donne against such charges, writes, in *Sermons,* VIII, p. 10, "This is one of the few sermons of Donne's which can justly be described as morbid." For further discussion of this issue, see my Chapter IV.

13 *Richard III,* V, iii, 194. Donne's idea springs from St. Paul's "who shall deliver me from the body of this death?" (Romans 7: 24)

14 *Sermones in Cantica,* Migne, *PL,* CLXXXIII (Paris, 1854), Sermon XXVI, ii, and Sermon XXXVII, iv.

15 Bartholomew Keckermann, *Rhetoricae Ecclesiasticae Sive Artis Formandi et Habendi Conciones Sacras,* 3rd ed. (Hanau, 1606), p. 47.

16 Erasmus, *Ecclesiastes,* col. 777B.

17 *Sermones in Cantica,* Sermon VII, v.

18 Leo Spitzer, "Marvell's 'Nymph Complaining for the Death of Her Fawn': Sources Versus Meaning," *Modern Language Quarterly,* XIX (September 1958), 237–40.

19   See also VI, No. 10, ll. 169 ff for a similar figure, which is based on a passage from Chrysostom.

IV. THE PREACHER'S VOICE

1   The adjective is his own, in a letter to the Countess of Montgomery, sending her a sermon: "In one circumstance, my preaching and my writing this Sermon is too equall: that that your Ladiship heard in a hoarse voice then, you read in a course hand now."—*Letters to Severall Persons of Honour,* ed. Charles E. Merrill, Jr. (New York, 1910), p. 22.

2   Dylan Thomas, "A Few Words of a Kind," *Readings,* III (Caedmon Records, New York, n.d.).

3   J. B. Leishman, "The Sermons of John Donne," *Review of English Studies,* VIII (August, 1957), 441. Review of Simpson and Potter, Vols. II and VII.

4   Richard Bernard, *The Faithfull Shepheard* (London, 1607), p. 79: "it is not fit, yea it is verie hurtfull, to make the Pulpit a place for a continuall and full handling of controversies in a common auditorie." See also Bartholomew Keckermann, *Rhetoricae Ecclesiasticae Sive Artis Formandi et Habendi Conciones Sacras,* 3rd ed. (Hanau, 1606), p. 102; George Herbert, *The Country Parson and Selected Poems,* ed. Hugh Martin (London, 1956), p. 23.

5   For James's "Directions Concerning Preachers" (1622), see Arthur Wilson, *The History of Great Britain, Being the Life and Reign of King James the First* (London, 1603), pp. 199–200. Donne preached a sermon on these directions (*Sermons,* IV, No. 7). And in a polemical sermon preached in 1626, he observes that polemics is again permitted: "Things being now, I say, in this state, with these men, since wee heare that Drums beat in every field abroad, it becomes us also to returne to the brasing and beating of our Drums in the Pulpit too" (VII, No. 6, ll. 94–97).

6   Leishman, in *RES,* VIII (1957), 439.

7   *Ibid.,* p. 441.

8   Milton, Preface to *Animadversions, Complete Prose,* I, ed. Don M. Wolfe (New Haven, 1953), 663.

9   For anthology passages, see, for example, *Donne's Sermons: Selected Passages,* ed. Logan Pearsall Smith (Oxford, 1920). In his introduction, Smith says of the passages dealing with death and the macabre: "Unpleasant in their details as are most of these great passages, there is a kind of splendid horror about them which has made me include many— I hope not too many—of them in this selection" (p. xxvi). Evelyn Simpson comments on the undue influence of such passages upon

opinions of Donne's sermons, in *A Study of the Prose Works of John Donne,* 2nd ed. (Oxford, 1948), pp. 64–65. But see Evelyn Simpson herself on Donne's morbidity, in *Sermons,* III, p. 7.

10 Clay Hunt, *Donne's Poetry* (New Haven, 1954), pp. 138–48.

11 On this, see the count made by Adolph Wasilifsky, in "John Donne the Rhetor: A Study of the Tropes and Figures in the St. Paul Sermons" (Unpublished Ph.D. dissertation, Cornell, 1935).

12 New Haven, 1954.

13 Luis de Granada, *Spiritual and Heavenly Exercises,* trans. F. Meres (Edinburgh, 1600), pp. 24–40 and *passim.* See Ruth Wallerstein's chapter "The Pattern of Christianity: Donne and Bernard of Clairvaux" in her "Studies in Donne," edited by Barbara Davis (Unpublished Ph.D. dissertation, Wisconsin, 1961), for comment on the similar use of such description in Donne and Bernard.

14 *King Alfred's Old English Version of St. Augustine's Soliloquies,* ed. and trans., with Alfred's additions in italics, by Harry Lee Hargrove (New York, 1904).

15 See, for example, *Gregorii Magni Dialogi,* ed. Umberto Moricca (Rome, 1924). See also Thomas Taylor, *Works* (London, 1653). Taylor wrote catechisms and used the technique in his sermons.

16 Keckermann, *Rhetoricae Ecclesiasticae,* p. 84; Andreas Gerardus Hyperius, *The Practice of Preaching* (London, 1577), p. 49^r.

17 See, for the prototypes, *The Spiritual Exercises of St. Ignatius of Loyola,* ed. W. H. Longridge (London, 1950) ; and St. Francis de Sales, *Introduction to the Devout Life,* ed. Allan Ross (Westminster, Md., 1948).

18 See Mrs. Simpson's comment on *Sermons,* VII, No. 16, ll. 742–50, in VII, No. 37, note 81. See also Milton Rugoff, *Donne's Imagery: A Study in Creative Sources* (New York, 1939), p. 107; and M. M. Mahood, *Poetry and Humanism* (London, 1950), pp. 89–90.

19 Leishman, in *RES,* VIII (1957), p. 435, opposes Evelyn Simpson's characterization of the Lincoln's Inn sermons (II, Nos. 11 and 12) on the grounds that legal images are equally frequent in other sermons. I would say that legal images are more characteristic of the early sermons than of the later ones, and that his congregation of lawyers at Lincoln's Inn was probably responsible for a slightly more frequent use of such images there than elsewhere. See my Chapter VII for analysis of a use of legal imagery that helps to substantiate what I have said here of his reasons for introducing it.

20 Compare Chrysostom, *The Priesthood,* trans. W. A. Jurgens (New York, 1955), Bk. IV, ch. iii, for discussion of application of the Word as medicine for the inflamed and sickly soul. The tradition of Christ as

physician is of course in the background, and figures of healing were very common.

21 See Frances M. Comper, *The Book of the Craft of Dying, and other Early English Tracts Concerning Death* (London, 1917); and Sister Mary Catherine O'Connor, *The Art of Dying Well* (New York, 1942).

22 Granada, *Spiritual and Heavenly Exercises,* p. 144.

23 I think of Ovid's description of his own departure, *Tristia,* Bk. I, sec. iii, ed. and trans. Arthur Leslie Wheeler (London, 1924), of the Regulus story, and of Politian's Renaissance poem, inspired by Ovid, "De Ovidii Exsilio et Morte," in W. Parr Greswell, *Memoirs of Angelus Politianus and Others,* 2nd ed. (Manchester, 1805), pp. 54–55.

24 Bernard, *Faithfull Shepheard,* p. 70.

25 For other stage figures, see III, No. 3, 56–57; III, No. 9, ll. 429–33; IV, No. 10, ll. 1–7; IX, No. 13, ll. 478–83.

26 One may choose to carry all this one step farther, and say that from the viewpoint of the living person who stands at the chapel rail, the whole thing, including the heavens, is artificial; but then it would be necessary to go the whole way, and refer to the real heaven over the chapel and the church. The baroque lends itself to this mirrors-within-mirrors concept of reality.

V. WORD AND WORLD

1 The source of the phrase is St. Paul's, "For Christ sent me not to baptize, but to preach the gospel: not with wisdom of words, lest the cross of Christ should be made of none effect" (I Cor. 1: 17). Christian rhetoricians from Augustine on cited this verse, and in Donne's time it became almost a battle cry in the attack of the Puritans on Anglican preaching. On this use of the phrase, see William Haller, *The Rise of Puritanism* (New York, 1938), p. 23. But see also Donne himself, who obviously uses it sincerely: "I take it for one of God's great blessings to me, if he have given me now an auditory . . . of such spiritual and circumcised Ears, as come not to hear that Wisdom of Words, which make the Cross of Christ of none effect" (IV, No. 3, ll. 376–79). The ambiguity inherent in the concept of Christian rhetoric is illustrated by this whole conflict between Puritan and Anglican. By careful selection of Donne's comments on preaching, it is possible to prove that he was in favor of a plain style, and one passage in particular is often misquoted, as follows: "with such succinctness and brevity, as may consist with clearness, and perspicuity, in such manner, and method, as may best enlighten your understandings, and least encumber your memories, I shall

open unto you the meaning of the text."—W. Frazer Mitchell, *English Pulpit Oratory from Andrewes to Tillotson* (London, 1932), p. 191; George Williamson, *The Senecan Amble* (Chicago, 1951), p. 243. The passage actually ends, "I shall open unto you that light, which God commanded out of darkness, and that light by which he hath shin'd in our hearts; and this light, by which we shall have the knowledge of the glory of God, in the face of Christ Jesus" (IV, No. 3, ll. 119–25). With the direct reference to the symbol that he means to unfold, the passage takes on a rather different implication from that of the succinctness and brevity which critics have made it seem to emphasize. The Puritan objection to the wisdom of words was an objection to Anglo-Catholic preaching, while Donne's is an objection to the misuse of a style that he considered as important as ritual and ceremony. Donne's idea of succinctness and brevity was not that of the Puritan preachers; nor was it that which is ordinarily thought of in connection with Senecanism.

2 Donne could not have read Gregory of Nyssa in the original, and much of the latter's work is technical philosophy. In his popular writing, however, I find some similarity to Donne. Gregory is noticeably conscious of the reality of the words of Scripture and thinks of Scripture itself as a landscape. Abstractions are vividly imaged, and he employs forceful and startling analogies; he likes to pile up metaphors. Like Donne and Bernard, he stresses the concept of the need for humility and self-knowledge through the familiar concept of the image of God in man. Gabriel Horn writes of his handling of the sort of mirror imagery that I have examined in Chapter III, in "Le 'Miroir,' 'La Nuée': Deux Manières de voir Dieu d'Apres S. Grégoire de Nysse," *Revue d'Ascetique et de Mystique*, VIII (1927), 113–31. All these points are well illustrated in the most readily available edition, a translation by Hilda C. Graef of *The Lord's Prayer; The Beatitudes* (Westminster, Md., 1954).

3 For Renaissance use of the terms, see A. C. Howell, " 'Res et Verba': Words and Things," *Journal of English Literary History*, XIII (June, 1946), 131–42.

4 For Bernard's position, see Sermon I on the *Missus Est,* in Migne, *PL,* CLXXXIII, cols. 55–61.

5 Compare Augustine's analogy between the Incarnation and thought made into speech, *De Doctrina Christiana*, Bk. I, sec. xiii, and *Sermons for Christmas and Epiphany*, trans. Thomas C. Lawler (London, 1952), pp. 87–88.

6 For examples in a wide range of contexts, though all significantly Angli-

can, see George Herbert, "Longing," *The Works of George Herbert,* ed. F. E. Hutchinson (Oxford, 1941), p. 149; Sir Thomas Browne, *Religio Medici,* Bk. I, sec. xvi, in *Works,* ed. Geoffrey Keynes (London, 1928), Vol. I; Henry King, *A Sermon of Deliverance* (London, 1626), p. 4. For background, see Mario Praz, *Studies in Seventeenth-Century Imagery* (London, 1939); and Ruth Wallerstein, *Seventeenth-Century Poetic* (Wisconsin, 1950).

7   Milton, "An Apology Against a Pamphlet," *Complete Prose,* I (New Haven, 1953), p. 890. Herbert too said that the preacher must be his own sermon, *Country Parson* (London, 1956), pp. 83–84. Behind this of course is the traditional idea that the orator must be a good man; cf. Quintilian, *Institutio Oratoria* (London, 1920), I, Bk. I, p. 9.

8   See, for example, Richard Bernard, *The Faithfull Shepheard* (London, 1607), pp. 48–50. The Elizabethans in general were very conscious of the figures of speech, and thought of them as things with individual character, as Puttenham did, for example in christening his figures with such names as "the Ringleader," "the Middlemarcher," and "the Trespasser."—George Puttenham, *The Arte of English Poesie,* ed. Gladys Willcock and Alice Walker (Cambridge, 1936), pp. 164 and 168.

9   Don Cameron Allen, "Dean Donne Sets His Text," *Journal of English Literary History,* X (September, 1943), pp. 212–19.

10 Mario Praz, *Studies,* pp. 195–96.

11 See, for example, Jean David, *Occasio Arrepta, neglecta, huius commoda, illius incommoda,* 2nd ed. (Antwerp, 1605).

12 Francis Quarles, *Emblemes* (London, [1710?]), "To the Reader."

13 For analysis of emblematic elements in this poem, see Eleanor James, "The Emblem as an Image-pattern in Some Metaphysical Poets," (Unpublished Ph.D. dissertation, Wisconsin, 1942), pp. 97–99. See also, for a source that she overlooks, Adolphe Didron, *Christian Iconography* (London, 1886), I, 373, quoting a passage from Jerome's *Commentary on Mark,* of which part of Donne's poem seems to be a direct paraphrase.

14 Rosemary Freeman, *The English Emblem Books* (London, 1948), pp. 23–29.

15 *Ibid.,* p. 163.

16 Mitchell, *English Pulpit Oratory,* pp. 184–85.

17 *Ibid.,* p. 147.

18 For a detailed and very illuminating definition of Laud's position, see H. R. Trevor-Roper, *Archbishop Laud* (London, 1940).

19 See "Of Ceremonies," in the 1559 Book of Common Prayer, for a statement of the importance of traditional ceremony to order and discipline;

and the two homilies "Of the Place and Time of Prayer," in *Certain Sermons or Homilies Appointed to be read in Churches in the Time of Queen Elizabeth* (London, 1754), pp. 295–306. Stress on order and discipline here begins to replace stress on the importance of sacraments, and, in the early seventeenth century particularly, the Anglicans made much use of the church Fathers to emphasize the conservative and ancient dignity of their church. For Puritan opinion of this tradition, see Milton, "Of Reformation in England," *Complete Prose* (New Haven, 1953), I, 549–56.

20 As Mitchell points out, however, Donne is unusually critical of the Fathers (*English Pulpit Oratory*, pp. 183–84) ; the attitude expressed in *Biathanatos* (pp. 32–33) against formulation of doctrines out of some one Father is also his attitude as a preacher; he also remarks more than once that sometimes the Fathers, eager to make an impression on their auditories, were more eloquent than precise (*Sermons*, VII, No. 7, ll. 469–90). Donne always begins with the text itself, and brings in the Fathers to support what he thinks is the correct reading, or to assist a symbolic extension of the text.

21 Specific references are indexed in the *LXXX Sermons* (London, 1640) and in Simpson and Potter, Volume X. See also, in Volume X, Evelyn Simpson's chapters on Donne's sources. By far the most frequent references are to Augustine; then come Jerome, Bernard, and Tertullian. Tertullian's style is characterized by the short, abrupt, vigorous sentence, by wordplay and irony, and, to a lesser extent, by vivid and arresting analogies, used to depict spiritual states. One figure which Donne uses several times, for example, that of gold beaten out to airy thinness, is Tertullian's description of the growth of the soul (Wallerstein, *Seventeenth Century Poetic*, pp. 30–34). Jerome's style is more fluid than Tertullian's, since his rhetorical allegiance was to Ciceronianism, and it also has a robustness about it that Donne must have admired; like Donne, Jerome can vividly evoke a scene by supplying a few concrete details. Of Gregory of Nyssa, I have spoken before (see note 2 of this chapter). The metaphor of Gregory the Great is perhaps the most homely, the most like the figures of the medieval English vernacular preachers, of all the imagery in the Latin Fathers; and some of his particular interests, like the problem of the resurrection of the body (for which see my Chapter III), are expressed in figures which Donne admired and incorporated into his own prose. Miss Wallerstein considers Bernard the most important single influence upon Donne's sermon style, and in her "Studies in Donne," ed. Barbara Davis (Unpublished Ph.D. dissertation, Wisconsin, 1961), makes the point that quotations from

other writers are ordinarily simply incorporated into Donne's sermons, while quotations from Bernard help to determine the nature of the passages in which they occur. The Bernardine meditational pattern, in its movement from self-knowledge and humility to knowledge of God and to joy is basic to Donne's prose.

22   Ruth Wallerstein, "Studies in Donne," p. 171. The passage is V, No. 17, ll. 428 ff.

23   See Dennis Quinn, "Donne's Christian Eloquence," *Journal of English Literary History,* XXVII (December, 1960), 284–85.

24   On this passage, see Doniphan Louthan, *The Poetry of John Donne* (New York, 1951), pp. 38–39.

25   See, for example, Jerome's *Book of Hebrew Names,* Migne, *PL,* XXIII (Paris, 1845), cols. 771–858.

26   Quinn, in *ELH,* XXVII, pp. 284–85.

27   For circles, see VI, No. 11, ll. 169–71; X, No. 2, ll. 537–42; II, No. 9, ll. 107–9; IV, No. 2, ll. 175–81. For a long discussion of water by Donne, with citation of his sources, see IX, No. 14, ll. 557–632. As indication of the prevalence of sea symbolism in seventeenth-century Christian literature, see the meanings assigned to the word by Thomas Wilson, in *A Complete Christian Dictionary,* 7th ed. (London, 1661), pp. 562–63; or its emblematic use, as in Michael Hoyer, *Flammulae Amoris S. P. Augustini* (Antwerp, 1608), p. 35.

28   Donne, *Devotions upon Emergent Occasions,* pp. 40–41.

29   *Poems of John Donne,* ed. H. J. C. Grierson, (Oxford, 1912), I, 157.

30   See, for the first point, C. S. Lewis, *The Allegory of Love* (London, 1936), pp. 45–47, and William York Tindall, *The Literary Symbol* (Bloomington, 1955), p. 19; for the second, Wallerstein, "Studies in Donne."

VI. THE MODEL OF THE WHOLE

1   Richard Bernard, *The Faithfull Shepheard* (London, 1607), p. 79; Bartholomew Keckermann, *Rhetoricae Ecclesiasticae Sive Artis Formandi et Habendi Conciones Sacras,* 3rd ed. (Hanau, 1606), p. 118; Andreas Gerardus Hyperius, *The Practice of Preaching* (London, 1577), p. 15^v; Nicolaus Hemming, *Pastor Sive Pastoris Optimus Vivendi Agendique Modus* (Erfurt, 1585), p. 149. For summaries of much of this material, and for extensive bibliographies, see W. Frazer Mitchell, *English Pulpit Oratory from Andrewes to Tillotson;* and Ruth Bozell, "English Preachers of the Seventeenth Century on the Art of Preaching" (Unpublished Ph.D. dissertation, Cornell, 1939).

2   Richard Bernard calls it a preface (*Faithfull Shepheard,* p. 13); so does

Hyperius (*Practice of Preaching*, p. 27ʳ). See also Henry King's, *A Sermon of Deliverance* (London, 1626), p. 1: "I stay not upon unneedfull Preface, to show with what accord the Text suits this Time."

3 Keckermann, *Rhetoricae Ecclesiasticae*, p. 118.

4 Bernard, *Faithfull Shepheard*, p. 58; Erasmus, *Ecclesiastes* in *Opera Omnia* (Leiden, 1703–6), V, col. 955F.

5 Keckermann, *Rhetoricae Ecclesiasticae*, pp. 113–14.

6 *Ibid.*, pp. 67, 113; Hyperius, *Practice of Preaching*, p. 28ᵛ.

7 Keckermann, *Rhetoricae Ecclesiasticae*, p. 43.

8 The rhetoricians make a sharp distinction between scholastic and popular preaching; cf. Hyperius, *Practice of Preaching*, p. 1ʳ: "No man doubteth but that there bee two maner of wayes of interpreting the Scriptures used of skilful divines, the one Scholastical, peculyer to the scholes, ye other popular, pertayning to the people. That one is apt for the assemblies of learned men and young students somedeale profited in good letters. This other is altogether applied to instructe the confused multitude." He goes on to say that scholastic preaching is straightlaced, savoring of philosophical solitariness and severity, and analyzes every word and syllable, while popular preaching is "stretched forth, franck & at lybertie, yea & delightinge in the light." Certainly Donne's method varies with his audience, but he is almost always very concerned to make his preaching clear, troubling his hearers neither with unresolved disputes, nor with excessive complication of theme, nor with obscurity of expression.

9 For discussion of Puritan metaphor and allegory, see William Haller, *The Rise of Puritanism* (New York, 1938), pp. 128–72. The extent to which any Puritan sermon of the time is literary depends both on the specific period of its preaching and on the character of the individual preacher. In general, the Puritan sermon is most literary at its earlier stages, in clergymen like Henry Smith, and least so at the time of the Commonwealth. For specific examples of allegory in Puritan prose, see Richard Bernard, *The Isle of Man* (London, 1635); [Richard Overton], "The Arraignment of Mr. Persecution," in *Tracts on Liberty in the Puritan Revolution*, ed. William Haller (New York, 1934), pp. 203–56. A closely related stylistic trend is the robust Puritan treatment of Bible stories; see, for example, Henry Smith's sermons on Nebuchadnezzar, in *The Works of Henry Smith* (Edinburgh, 1866), I, 167–200. On this point, see Katherine Koller, "The Puritan Preacher's Contribution to Fiction," *Huntington Library Quarterly*, XI (August, 1948), 321–40.

10 For medieval background, see G. R. Owst, *Literature and Pulpit in Medieval England* (Cambridge, 1933), especially pp. 56–109 on "Scrip-

ture and Allegory." See also William York Tindall, *John Bunyan: Mechanick Preacher* (New York, 1934).

11 See Lancelot Andrewes, *Ninety-six Sermons* (Oxford, 1856), III, 198. See also "A Fruitful Exhortation to the Reading of the Holy Scripture," *Certain Sermons or Homilies Appointed to be read in Churches in the Time of Queen Elizabeth,* pp. 7–15.

12 On this point, everyone was agreed. See Ruth Bozell, "English Preachers," pp. 176–77, for a summary, and for general agreement that the literal sense must be considered first. See also Keckermann, *Rhetoricae Ecclesiasticae,* p. 73, for a clear statement taken from Thomas Aquinas: "Atque ex his id etiam intellegi potest, sensum dictorum in sacris literis, primariò ac principaliter tantum unum esse, eum videlicet, quem Spiritus sanctus principaliter intendit, qui quidem literalis dici potest, ex illa definitione Thomae Aquinatis, cum ait: *Sensum literalem esse, quem autor praecipué intendit."*

13 Dennis Quinn, "Donne's Christian Eloquence," *Journal of English Literary History,* XXVII (December, 1960), 281.

14 VI, No. 2, ll. 45–53: "In the figurative exposition of those places of Scripture, which require that way oft to be figuratively expounded, that Expositor is not to be blamed, who not destroying the literall sense, proposes such a figurative sense, as may exalt our devotion, and advance our edification; And as no one of those Expositors did ill, in proposing one such sense, so neither do those Expositors ill, who with those limitations, that it destroy not the literall sense, that it advance devotion, do propose another and another such sense."

15 For example, Richard Bernard cites Jeremy 31:31, "I will make a new convenant," as a text suitable for a sermon proving it lawful for a minister to marry (*Faithfull Shepheard,* p. 45).

16 Millar Maclure, *The Paul's Cross Sermons, 1534–1642* (Toronto, 1958), p. 165.

17 Hyperius, *Practice of Preaching,* p. 24^v.

18 Keckermann, *Rhetoricae Ecclesiasticae,* pp. 106–7.

19 For a striking example, though written at a later time, when the Puritans had gained an uneasy control of the country, see Edmund Calamy, "An Indictment Against England . . . Preached . . . at the late Solemne Fast, December 25, 1644" (London, 1645).

20 Compare, for a different approach, with a similar idea, St. Bernard, *Sermons for the Seasons and Principall Festivals of the Year,* trans. by a Priest of Mount Melleray (Westminster, Md.), I, 381: "Truly great, my dearest brethren, is the festival we keep to-day in honour of the Lord's nativity."

21 Symbolism employing directions had a long tradition. See, for example,

the concept of the world shaped like a cross, in *Legends of the Holy Rood,* ed. Richard Morris (London, 1871), p. xxx; the use of directions in the Bible; and the traditional importance of directions in construction of churches.

22 See also IX, No. 7, ll. 391–94. Of the device of interrogation, Richard Bernard says it forces the conscience to answer, makes the hearers judges, "and so causeth them will they nill they, to goe on with the speaker" (*Faithfull Shepheard,* pp. 66–67).

23 VI, No. 2, ll. 4–13. Compare Henry Smith, *Works,* I, 47–48: "Now, there is no sentence of the Scripture, which the wiser papists alledge boldly for their transubstantiation, but this, that Christ said, 'This is my body,' Matt. 26:26; by which they may prove as well that Christ is a door, because he saith, 'I am the door,' John 10:7,9; or a vine, because he saith, 'I am the vine,' John 15:1; for his sayings are like. Figurative speeches must not be construed literally, but this is heretics fashion." The passages Donne chose had served for polemics as well as for exegesis.

24 II, No. 1. Dennis Quinn's Ph.D. dissertation, entitled "John Donne's Sermons on the Psalms and the Traditions of Biblical Exegesis," (Wisconsin, 1958), was made available to me when I had nearly completed a first draft of this book, and our work inevitably overlaps at some points. In his article, "Donne's Christian Eloquence," (*ELH,* XXVII), published in 1960, he reproduced his comments on this particular sermon, which I had also considered. It has seemed best to me now, however, to retain my own analysis, so that the two, which do differ in content, may be compared. Anyone interested in Donne's other sermons on the psalms may consult Quinn's thesis.

25 Quinn, in *ELH,* XXVII, p. 288.

26 Rosemary Freeman, *The English Emblem Books* (London, 1948), p. 89, cites the use of this emblem in J. A. Comenius, *Orbis Sensualium Pictus,* trans. Charles Hoole (London, 1658) as *Ethica,* personification of one of nine moral virtues; "This Life is a way/ or a place divided into/ two ways, like Pythagoras's letter Y./ broad 1./ on the left-hand track;/ narrow 2./ on the right . . ."

27 Evelyn Simpson comments at length on the style of this sermon and of this passage, in her introduction to III, pp. 21–26.

28 VI, No. 18, ll. 491–93. This is one of the passages which Evelyn Simpson calls morbid (VI, p. 35), but as she herself points out, consolation follows. The pattern is the normal meditational one that we have already observed.

29 Hemming, *Pastor,* p. 149; R. Bernard, *Faithfull Shepheard,* pp. 33–34;

Hyperius, *Practice of Preaching,* p. 36ʳ.

30 William York Tindall, *The Literary Symbol* (Bloomington, 1955), p. 10.

VII. CONTRARY MUSIC

1 Quoted from Gibbons' translation of Vincentius Bruno, in Louis L. Martz, *The Poetry of Meditation* (New Haven, 1954), p. 14. Other books which I have found useful are Helen C. White, *English Devotional Literature—Prose: 1600–1640* (Madison, 1931) and *The Tudor Books of Private Devotion* (Madison, 1951). John Garrett Underhill, *Spanish Literature in the England of the Tudors* (New York, 1899), gives an account of religious translations, including some discussion of style.

2 *The Early Works of Thomas Becon,* ed. John Ayre (Cambridge, 1843), p. 160.

3 Bernard of Clairvaux, *The Steps of Humility,* ed. and trans. George Bosworth Burch (Cambridge, Mass., 1940), pp. 152–54.

4 Antithesis: "It was part of *Adams* punishment, *In the sweat of thy browes thou shalt eate thy bread:* it is multiplied to me, I have earned bread in the sweat of my browes, in the labor of my calling, and I have it; and I sweat againe, and againe, from the browe, to the sole of the foot, but I eat no bread, I tast no sustenance" (*Devotions,* p. 6, l. 24– p. 7, l. 1.).

   Amplification: "Yet we cannot awake the *July-flowers* in *January,* nor retard the *flowers* of the *spring* to *autumne.* We cannot bid the *fruits* come in *May,* nor the *leaves* to sticke on in *December.* A woman that is weake cannot put off her *ninth moneth* to a *tenth,* for her *deliverie,* and say shee will stay till shee bee *stronger;* nor a *Queene* cannot hasten it to a *seventh,* that shee may bee ready for some other pleasure." (p. 111, ll. 12–19).

5 It would be interesting to compare at greater length Donne's discussions of time with the passages in Bk. XI of Augustine's *Confessions,* which he appears to have in mind.

6 Compare "Deaths Duell": "Our blessed *Saviour* suffered *colluctations* with *death,* and a *sadnes even in his soule to death,* and an *agony* even to a *bloody sweate* in his *body,* and *expostulations* with *God,* and *exclamations* upon the crosse" (X, No. 11, ll. 386–89).

7 John Cosin, "A Collection of Private Devotions," in *The Works of the Right Reverend Father in God, John Cosin* (Oxford, 1845), II, 89–91.

8 *The Prayer-Book of Queen Elizabeth,* ed. William Benham, (Edinburgh, 1911), p. 146.

9 Italics in this passage indicate the main outline of the period. Donne's italics have been omitted.

Index

This index is limited to proper names and such stylistic terms as can be listed conveniently. I have not included subjects like sentence structure with which whole chapters are concerned, or subjects for which there is no brief descriptive name.

225